The Best Guide to

American Politics

The Best Guide to American Politics

Tom Waldman

Series Editor Richard F. X. O'Connor

RENAISSANCE BOOKS

Los Angeles

ISBN: 1-58063-084-7

10 9 8 7 6 5 4 3 2 1

Design by Jesus Arellano

Published by Renaissance Books
Distributed by St. Martin's Press
Manufactured in the United States of America
First Edition

To Steve Tamaya, who, in his all-too-brief life, never
stopped loving politics

Acknowledgments

The author thanks Richard F. X. O'Connor and Matt Daley for their patience and guidance in seeing this book to its conclusion. I am grateful to Jim Parish for first alerting me to this project. I also want to acknowledge Peter Sanders and Delia M. Rios for their assistance and suggestions in the history portion. Finally, to my parents, Ted and Nancy, who got me interested in politics and history before I reached the second grade.

Contents

The Best Guide to American Politics and Working the System

*T*his book is for you who care, who want to get involved, but at times feel powerless, alienated, or even disgusted. Yet the system is not as remote as it seems, and in America you are never as powerless as you think.

One advantage of life in the United States is that you are not *forced* to think about politics every day. The U.S. has neither a totalitarian system—where getting on the regime's bad side can be punishable by death—nor one in which the government could collapse at any moment, as is the case with some democracies in Asia or Europe. The United States is a *stable* country where for the most part citizens are left alone. An exception is the dreaded event that occurs every April 15, tax time.

Yet freedom to choose means freedom not to choose. For any number of reasons—work, family, apathy, cynicism, or sheer laziness—there are those who sweep politics from their lives. This too is their right. No one in the U.S. is required to follow the issues, have an opinion, or go to the polls.

The right not to choose is exercised more and more. Since 1964, the percentage of voters participating in presidential elections has steadily declined. The only important exception to this pattern—1992—we know now was an aberration. In 1992, 55.09 percent of the voters went to the polls, a jump of some 5 points over 1988. But the 1996 figures ended any hope that this was a trend. In the last presidential election, only 49.69 percent of the voting-age population cast their ballots. At this rate one shudders to think what the turnout will be in the year 2000.

Some people vote because they believe it is their duty, and others because they have been given a reason by the candidate or party. It's the second group that probably accounts for the anemic numbers in the latest election. Even enthusiasts or political junkies would have to admit the 1996 presidential campaign between Bill Clinton and Bob Dole was lackluster at best. The staged conventions, tepid debates, and politically safe platforms were symptomatic of a race that lacked fire, drama, and intelligence. Never did politics seem so dull.

Dull, perhaps, but not irrelevant. In America, political expression can take many forms—another benefit of freedom. You may cast a ballot every year, or every four years, but in another sense you vote frequently. Maybe you write a letter to the editor, or decide not to travel to a country whose policies you abhor. Maybe you have an impromptu discussion about foreign policy or the balanced-budget amendment with a neighbor. These are all political acts—even if you do not consider yourself an especially political person.

And yet is it possible to truly remain apolitical? Most Americans eventually decide to get more involved. Indeed, the percentage of voters increases with age. As people mature, they become more serious about their lives, and pay closer attention to what goes on in city council, the state legislature, or the halls of Congress.

Those in their twenties and thirties who lived by the credo of "work hard, play hard," could well find by the time they reach forty that their priorities have changed. They start by learning more about the city council and school board, if not for their own sake, for the sake of their children. Their political education continues with county government, the state assembly, and, finally, Congress, the presidency, and the Supreme Court. At the end, they feel they know the system.

Here are some questions you may have asked yourself:

- What is the League of Women Voters?

- Where do I go for a problem with Social Security?

- What is a city committee?

- What's the difference between a centrist, a moderate, and a progressive?

- How do I run for the school board?

> ### WHAT DEMOCRACY MEANS
>
> *In an article on Czechoslovakian president Václav Havel for the* New York Times Magazine, *author Paul Berman described the requirements of a citizen living under democracy. His words should resonate with every American who cares about his community and his country:*
>
> *It [democracy] requires citizens who feel responsible for something more than their own well-feathered little corner; citizens who want to participate in society's affairs, who insist on it; citizens with backbones; citizens who hold their ideas about democracy at the deepest level, at the level that religion is held, where beliefs and identity are the same.*
>
> —Paul Berman, "The Philosopher-King Is Mortal," New York Times Magazine, May 17, 1997

This book is the vehicle for you to take a quick trip through the system to answer those questions and many more. It looks at all levels of government, as well as campaigns, media, ideology, institutions, and legislation. There are also synopses of some key issues and conflicts over the last two hundred–plus years that have brought us to this point.

Don't Just Stand There . . .

*I*f you don't like your leaders in Washington, the legislature, or city hall, you have the right to "turn the rascals out." "They" cannot take that right away. When you have lost faith in the president, Congress, the governor, or the county board of supervisors, you can make a personal choice to throw them out. If enough voters agree, come election day, the bums will be out and the good guys will be in.

Maybe you like the way things are going. Then you can vote to keep the good guys in power. Your ballot can express satisfaction as well as anger. "Stay the course" is a phrase from politics. Thumbs up or thumbs down, you are making a statement about how you view the situation.

Voting is something more as well: your contribution to the success of American democracy. Our political system relies on people voicing their opinions. Without voters, democracy is a sham.

Every election is an historical event. When Ronald Reagan defeated Jimmy Carter in 1980, it made history. When Bill Clinton was reelected in 1996, that made history. And when the three-term councilwoman from your city goes down to defeat, it merits banner headlines in the local paper.

In Part 1, we'll discuss the power of the voter on the local level. This is the place you can see most clearly your potential as a citizen. You can effect meaningful and tangible changes in your local political system and through that, changes in your life. But nothing will happen if you don't take the first step. So learn your rights, discover your your power, and take control!

Your Vote Counts

*T*he right to vote, and to free elections, are the reasons why this country was founded in the first place. It's also why no elected official can turn his back on the public. *Your vote is power. When you sit out an election, you lose that power.* Remember what the colonists said to the Mother Country: *No taxation without representation.* The colonists spilled tea, and later, blood, to be able to choose their own leaders.

Political empowerment starts with voting. But it doesn't end there. You can walk precincts and make phone calls for your candidate, contribute funds to his or her campaign, even decide that you want to run for office yourself. You might file for an open seat on the school board, or challenge a city council incumbent. You go out, raise a little money, and convince your friends and your ideological soulmates to be part of your team. Pretty soon, you've got a full-blown campaign.

This is the political version of the American Dream. It can happen; it has happened; it will continue to happen; and the American political system will be infused with new life and spirit.

IN THIS CHAPTER:

- *The power of voting in America*

- *Voter eligibility*

- *How to register to vote*

- *The Voting Rights Act, with provisions*

- *Motor Voter*

- *Voter fraud*

- *You, the candidate*

WHEN YOU DON'T VOTE

The United States has no kings, nor dictators. And though America can be a violent country, it does not have a tradition of politicians murdering their opponents to stay in power. As any reader of Shakespeare knows, even England cannot make that claim.

The idea of voting is ingrained in American political culture. It would be absurd for a politician to argue that we should get rid of the ballot and find another way of picking our leaders. You would vote such a person out of office at once.

Yet it has become evident in the past twenty-five years that while the vote itself may be popular, voting is not. Using presidential elections as a guide, Americans don't go to the polls in anywhere near the numbers they did in the past. The decline began in 1972 and continued until 1992, when for a variety of reasons, turnout climbed above 55 percent for the first time since the 1972 election. But when it seemed things had finally improved, along came 1996. The turnout for the Clinton-Dole contest was 49.7 percent—one of the lowest of any presidential election in this century.

Why aren't more people voting today? Most have an opinion, but nobody knows for sure. The reasons most often cited? Dull or cynical campaigns; the process of registration is too complex and time-consuming; the voting-age population is getting younger; the feeling that all politicians are crooks; and a greater percentage believing our leaders are indifferent to the needs of the public.

What this suggests, of course, is that contemporary voters insist on a good reason to go to the polls. No one feels guilty anymore about having stayed away from an election or two.

This chapter will not analyze why turnout is so low. That's a job for political scientists. Nor will it give you a *reason* to vote—that responsibility is best left to parents, peers, civics teachers, politicians, and the media. But should you choose to participate in elections, or wish to encourage others, then this

VOTER TURNOUT PATTERNS

	Presidential Election Years			Non-Presidential Election Years		
	Number*	%**			Number*	%**
1992	104,405,155	55.09	1994	75,105,860	38.78
1990	67,859,189	36.52	1988	91,594,691	50.11
1986	64,991,128	36.40	1984	92,652,680	53.11
1982	67,615,576	40.52	1980	86,515,221	52.56
1978	58,917,938	37.20	1976	81,555,789	53.55
1974	55,943,834	38.23	1972	77,718,554	55.21
1970	58,014,338	46.78	1968	73,213,371	60.84
1966	56,188,046	48.38	1964	70,644,592	61.92
1962	53,141,227	47.27	1960	68,838,204	63.06
1958	47,202,950	45.36	1956	62,026,648	60.70
1954	43,854,454	44.00	1952	61,551,543	63.34
1950	41,983,798	43.69	1948	48,261,189	51.65
ALL YEARS PERCENT		56.01	ALL YEARS PERCENT		40.98

* Total national number of persons voting for the highest office.
** Percentage of the total national voting age population who voted for the highest office.

Source: Congressional Research Service, Library of Congress, Washington, D.C.

is a good place to start. Registering to vote need not be confusing or intimidating. And, once registered, the rest is easy.

WHO CAN VOTE?

When deciding to register, the first thing you should do is check your eligibility. It was once the case that only white males were permitted to vote in this country, but Congress and the states ended that with a series of constitutional amendments.

The Fifteenth Amendment, ratified in 1870, guaranteed the vote regardless of "race, color, or previous condition of servitude." In the aftermath of the Civil War, former slaves and free black males were granted the same constitutional rights as everyone else, including the right to vote. The Nineteenth Amendment, ratified in 1920, extended the vote to women. Finally, the Twenty-Sixth Amendment, ratified in 1971, lowered the voting age from twenty-one to eighteen.

Anyone living in America who is at least eighteen years old meets the *constitutional* requirement of voter eligibility.

VOTER REGISTRATION

"... [V]irtually all of the states have chosen to require United States citizenship as a prerequisite for voter registration. Some states, but not all of them, implement this prerequisite through voter registration forms that clearly alert prospective registrants of the citizenship requirement and require registrants to affirmatively asset their citizenship. In such states, non-citizens who illegally register and vote may be prosecuted federally. ..."

—Federal Election Commission

Doesn't the Constitution Require Citizenship as a Condition of Voting?

Technically not. Outside the constitutional amendments covering race, sex, and age, voter eligibility—even in federal elections—is left to the states.

Though states appreciate their autonomy, it seems highly unlikely that any legislature would give non-citizens the right to vote. Should that happen, a court challenge would certainly follow, as well as a call for a constitutional amendment establishing citizenship as a condition for voting.

REGISTRATION REQUIREMENTS

You need to keep track of registration deadlines. There must have been at least one election season in your past when you decided too late that you wanted to register. This can be very frustrating, especially if you have a strong interest in the upcoming race or races.

Most states require that you register at least thirty days before an election. However, in 1997, six states—Idaho, Maine, Minnesota, New Hampshire, Wisconsin, and Wyoming—allowed election-day voter registration. North Dakota does not require any voter registration.

Data from the 1988 presidential election indicate that *election-day registration increases voter turnout*. In that year the four states that permitted voters to register on the day of the election, or had no registration requirement (Maine, Minnesota, Wisconsin, and North Dakota), had a 62.8 percent voter turnout. The states that did not allow election-day registration had a turnout of 49.52 percent.

In the 1992 election, the comparative figures were 70.3 percent and 54.3 percent.

The Rules

The Voting Rights Act of 1965, and its subsequent amendments, plus the National Voter Registration Act of 1993, established certain federal guidelines that apply to elections in the United States. You should know the key points of each of these measures.

The Voting Rights Act of 1965 and Amendments

The Voting Rights Act, signed by President Johnson on August 6, 1965, was originally designed to prevent states from using homegrown election laws to discriminate on the basis of race. The rise of black political power in the South can be traced directly to passage of the Voting Rights Act. The act is one of the greatest accomplishments of the Johnson presidency and the Civil Rights movement.

LBJ and civil rights will be discussed further in chapter 15 (see page 225).

Language Minority Groups

Today, all states are prohibited from applying election laws that discriminate on account of race, color, or language. This includes a ban on literacy tests, a device once used to keep African-Americans from voting in the South, and which today might be used against new citizens not yet fluent in English or familiar with American ways.

RESIDENCY REQUIREMENTS AND ABSENTEE BALLOTS

These requirements apply only to general elections for U.S. president and vice president.

If you want to file an absentee ballot, there are some rules you need to know:

- *Residents of a state who may be absent on election day can vote absentee if they apply for an absentee ballot no later than seven days before an election and have returned the ballot to the appropriate election official no later than the close of polls.*
- *If you move to a different state prior to thirty days before an election, and therefore miss the registration deadlines, you can vote absentee in your former state.*
- *The Voter Assistance Provisions amendment applies in all elections held everywhere.*

This amendment states: "Any voter who requires assistance to vote by reason of blindness, disability, or inability to read or write may be given assistance by a person of the voter's choice, other than the voter's employer or agent of that employer or office or agent of the voter's union."

This means that people with physical or learning disabilities can legally seek help in marking their ballot without being penalized. Their votes still count.

Bilingual Election Requirement

Are you a recent citizen who is not yet comfortable with English? The bilingual election requirement recognizes your predicament.

Under this amendment, language minority groups include Latinos, Asian-Americans, American Indians, and Alaskan Natives. The amendment applies to all elections, but not to all jurisdictions. States in which few members of these groups reside are not required to provide bilingual ballots.

On the other hand, Los Angeles County, which has a huge Asian and Latino population, provides bilingual materials in Spanish, Chinese, Japanese, Vietnamese, and Tagalog, one of the native languages of Filipinos.

The National Voter Registration Act of 1993

The best-known component of this legislation, commonly known as Motor Voter, does not apply to the six states that already allow election-day registration: Idaho, Maine, Minnesota, New Hampshire, Wisconsin, and Wyoming.

The bill makes registration more accessible to the general public. It says individuals must:

- be given the opportunity to register when applying at any office in the state for public service or assistance (these include the Food Stamps program, the Medicaid program, the Special Supplemental Food Program for Women, Infants and Children [WIC], and the Aid to Families with Dependent Children program);

- be provided the opportunity to vote at any office in the state that provides state-funded programs mostly engaged in offering services to people with disabilities; and

- be given the opportunity to vote at armed-forces recruitment offices.

QUESTIONS ABOUT THE VOTING RIGHTS ACT CAN BE ADDRESSED TO

*The Voting Section
Civil Rights Division
U.S. Department of Justice
P.O. Box 66128
Washington, D.C. 20035*

TEL: *(202) 307-3266*

FAX: *(202) 307-3691*

Motor Voter

A national voter registration system has been discussed and debated in Congress since the early 1970s, when dwindling turnout was first recognized as a national problem. And it is a problem. Remember the title of this chapter: "Your Vote Counts". The phrase is meaningless if you don't make it to the polls.

A steady, significant drop in voting is nothing less than a failure of democracy. A voter turnout of 25 percent for a local election, or 50 percent for a national election, is an embarrassment to all Americans.

Motor Voter is based on the theory that many non-voters are not cynical or apathetic, but simply too busy to register. If you lead an especially hectic life, you can understand this reasoning. To get more people to go the polls, Congress devised a convenient, less time-consuming method of registration. The bill made it possible for eligible citizens to register:

- when applying for a driver's license,

- by mail, and

- at selected state and local offices that serve the public.

The idea was to make registration as easy as getting a driver's license. And everybody (or certainly most of us) obtains a driver's license. (Motor Voter also specifies that any change of address for a license serves as a change of address for voter registration purposes—unless otherwise indicated by the applicant.)

The results of this system are mixed. According to a survey conducted by the National Association for Secretaries of State in early 1997, of the forty-three states covered by the National Voter Registration Act of 1993, registration had increased in each. For the month of August 1997, California reported that 121,023 used Motor Voter registration. "The number of people who have registered and otherwise would not have not done so is impressive," Conny McCormack, Los Angeles County's registrar-recorder, told the *Los Angeles Times* on November 2, 1997. "But voter turnout continues to go down."

Clearly registering to vote, and voting, are not the same. *An understanding of the importance of voting* is the only thing that consistently gets people to the polls. You must make a personal commitment to vote even if you are not wild about the candidates, or are being forced to endure a nasty, negative race. The Founding Fathers guaranteed the right to vote, but not quality campaigns.

During election season, the political parties intensify their effort to attract new voters. This is the time you are likely to see voter registration tables at shopping malls, near restaurants, at supermarkets, and in other public places.

Voter Fraud

You don't hear much about "stolen" elections in this country. The actual voting process is seldom tainted. Still, there are laws on the books to ensure that free and fair elections are the rule rather than the exception. Few things are more destructive of democracy than widespread voter fraud.

Acts specifically prohibited by federal election statute include:

- intentionally preventing a qualified voter from casting a ballot

- ballot-box stuffing

- forging or altering ballots

- impersonating qualified voters

- illegally registering voters and casting absentee ballots in their name

It is also illegal to give false information to an election official for the purpose of establishing voter eligibility. This statute has received considerable attention in recent years due to the large numbers of immigrants coming to this country. In many states, proof of citizenship—or even proof of residency—is not required when registering to vote. The registrant has only to affirm that he is telling the truth on the application.

Some politicians have expressed concern that non-citizens—with the active encouragement of political parties or immigrants'-rights groups—are registering to vote. But as yet there is no federal legislation proposed that would require an applicant to provide proof of citizenship.

ELECTIONS

The following facts illustrate both the nature and the scope of voting in America:

- Precincts are established by city or county authorities within each state. As of 1992 there were more than 150,000 precincts across the nation.

- Federal law encourages but does not require that the flag be flown at polling places.

- Certain federal employees are allowed time off to vote, but otherwise no federal statute requires employers to provide this service.

- If you live in Hawaii, Indiana, or Kentucky, don't forget the polls close at 6 P.M., the earliest of any state. In New Hampshire the polls open at 11 A.M., the latest of any state in the union. In New York the polls are open fifteen hours, from 6 A.M. to 9 P.M. Only in parts of Rhode Island do the polls remain open as long.

- Just as Thanksgiving always falls on the last Thursday in November, every presidential election and off-year election falls on the first Tuesday in November. This is not an accident.

You would think that picking an election day would be simple. No way. The torment Congress went through to finally agree on the first Tuesday in November makes current budget negotiations seem simple. See if you can follow this:

In 1845, Congress chose the date because it came after harvest, meaning farmers were more likely to vote. Congress considered every day of the week before choosing between two finalists, Tuesday and Wednesday. Before 1845, elections had been held in the first week in December.

Running for Office

Running for elected office is the final step in your evolution as a political animal. You've come to the conclusion that voting and working on campaigns is important, but not enough.

Your decision to run is a way of saying that you can do better than the people in power. Without that commitment, there's no good reason for your candidacy. The voters might as well go with what they've got.

Chapter 18 will go into detail on how to qualify for the ballot, with twenty-five steps the candidate should make in preparing a run for office. You should study this information carefully if you are at all serious about launching a campaign at any level.

The rules for getting on the ballot differ from campaign to campaign and from state to state. The Federal Election Commission puts out a book called *Ballot Access for Congressional Candidates* that cites the rules in every state for qualifying to run for the U.S. Senate or House of Representatives. (Alaska charges a $100 filing fee for Senate and House races; Kansas requires that a House candidate from one of the major parties obtain signatures from no less than 2 percent of the registered voters from his party that reside in the district; in North Carolina, a write-in candidate for Senate needs 500 qualified voters to sign his petition in order to stand for election).

The rules are complicated in any one state, let alone fifty. If you want to know more, write the Federal Election Commission at 999 E Street, NW, Washington,

D.C., 20463, and request *Ballot Access 2*, which is for congressional candidates. The FEC has a toll-free number: (800) 424-9530.

If you're thinking about running for president you can request *Ballot Access 3*, that tells how to qualify for the presidential primary in each of the fifty states.

You don't have to make your campaign debut with a run for Congress or the presidency. You can try for anything from the state assembly to city council to school board. Many successful political careers began with victory in a local election.

What you must do as soon as you make up your mind to run is find out how legally to get on the ballot. You don't want to line up support only to learn that you are ineligible, which would not only be embarrassing for you, but a possibly fatal blow to your credibility in the future.

Ask your local school district or city clerk about the rules governing a run for board of education or city council. For a state office, inquire with the secretary of state.

RUNNING FOR THE LOS ANGELES BOARD OF EDUCATION

Here is what one city—a very big one—requires of candidates running for the board of education:

- *You must be a registered voter in the district you wish to represent;*
- *you must submit the signatures of 500 registered voters within the district and a $300 filing fee to the Los Angeles City Clerk; or*
- *you may submit the signatures of 1000 registered voters and waive the fee.*

The signatures and fee, or signatures alone, must be submitted by a designated date prior to the election.

CHAPTER RECAP

- Never forget the importance and significance of casting your ballot.

- Political empowerment starts with voting.

- All Americans 18 or older meet the constitutional requirement for voting.

- You must be aware of registration deadlines.

- Assistance is provided to voters who are not fluent in English, or who are disabled.

- You can now register to vote when you renew your driver's license, or apply for various forms of government assistance.

- Federal election law specifies many different forms of voter fraud.

- You could become so intrigued by politics and government that you will file for elected office.

"Power to the People"

You don't remember the 1960s? Surely you've *heard* of them. It's the decade you can't escape. This book even has a chapter devoted to the sixties.

The phrase "Power to the People" is as much part of that time as the free-speech movement, the Civil Rights movement, and the war in Vietnam. The words suggest street demonstrations and other forms of social protest. John Lennon had a hit record with that title in May 1971.

"Power to the People" has made a comeback. The idea, not the phrase. While George Bush would have never considered shouting, "Power to the People!"—Republican presidents don't say that sort of thing—his well-known "Points of Light" initiative from 1989 was in a similar vein. Here is a synopsis of what Bush proposed:

- the call to claim society's problems as your own

- to identify, enlarge, and multiply what community service projects and initiatives are working

- to discover, encourage, and develop leaders

Political participation and civic involvement can take a number of forms. The most common of these is voting, which was discussed at length in the last chapter.

Free and fair elections are the essence of American democracy. But free and fair elections don't mean much if a large portion of the voting public doesn't go to the polls. That's why it's essential that you and your friends cast ballots for every race, for local school board, and for president. If they are reluctant or skeptical, get them to change their minds.

VOLUNTEERISM AND NON-PROFITS

However, you (and your friends) can do more than vote to make your voices heard, and to keep our system strong. For example, you can join one or more of the many non-profit organizations and associations in the U.S. committed to making this a better world. The American Civil Liberties Union, the Sierra Club, the Christian Coalition, and others play a vital part in the political process by taking public positions on important issues. They get the attention of politicians and the media.

Imagine American democracy as a university, then think of voting as a requirement and volunteerism as an elective. While you must vote in order to "graduate," you can slide by without volunteering, but should you choose to volunteer, you will graduate with extra credit.

Volunteering does not only mean joining political organizations such as those mentioned above, it involves responsibility for your community. Habitat for Humanity, which builds homes in low-income areas, rarely injects itself into political issues, but it's dedicated to making this a better world, a faultless goal.

You needn't be a cynic to look for political motives in political acts. The Points of Light initiative was not only a strike against lethargy, but a response to a change in the relationship between the American public and the federal government.

Beginning with Ronald Reagan in the early 1980s and continuing through Bill Clinton in the 1990s, both political parties argued that the United States has too much government, especially at the federal level. Consensus breaks down over where to cut, or what to eliminate, but the idea has triumphed.

Implicit in the call for increased civic involvement is the thought that Washington can no longer be expected to tackle every problem that comes along. If government is expected to do less, then the citizenry must do more. Fewer programs mean fewer services.

This is where volunteerism picks up the slack. You can start, logically enough, with your own community. Take care of the homefront first. An example is Neighborhood Watch groups, which formed in response to the rise in crime and the decreased number of officers on the streets, especially in southern California.

If you have time and energy left after taking care of your own area, maybe you can help in the poorer sections of town that have received less and less support from government in the 1980s and 1990s.

Bush and Clinton, opponents in the 1992 race, could share the fictional title of "The Volunteerism President." In 1997 Bush, Clinton, and General Colin Powell jointly sponsored "The Presidents' Summit for America's Future," a three-day session promoting volunteerism. It is probably no accident that the highest levels of volunteerism in several years occurred during the Bush and Clinton administrations.

A THOUSAND POINTS OF LIGHT

According to an April 23, 1997, story in the *Wall Street Journal,* the number of volunteers in America peaked at nearly 100 million in 1989. The reasons for this are not clear, although it may have something to do with the emphasis placed on volunteerism by President Bush. It could also have something to do with efforts by churches, schools, and businesses to get people to volunteer.

The next five years saw a decline in people becoming volunteers. By 1993, the number was closer to 75 million. But that trend was reversed as well; in 1996, the figure was nearing 80 million.

What do the numbers mean? Well, I don't know about you, but I think a lot of us would prefer to live in a society where volunteerism is on the rise. Even though people may choose to become volunteers due to "selfish" motives—to make new friends, find a mate, receive extra credit in a class—the end result is that *their actions help the community and help build a sense of community.* In a world of cell phones, faxes, supermoms, and overachieving dads, there is nothing more important than a sense of community. It reminds us of who we are, and why we are here.

Perhaps you think you might want to become a volunteer, but are not sure you have what it takes. Before you make a commitment you can't keep, examine some of the main reasons for involvement. A chapter in the second edition of *The Nonprofit Organization Handbook* describes volunteering in the 1990s. The author, Eva Schindler-Raiman, discovered several trends that characterize the motives of volunteers.

A consistent theme is that volunteering is a way to keep in touch with the world. The global economy, the exorbitant cost of political campaigns, the disjunction between government policies and the public, make the political process seem increasingly remote. No doubt you have felt this more than once. Volunteering gets you close.

Volunteering is good for the soul, but it's hard work and involves long hours. You can always find excuses for declining opportunities to volunteer. You have to make the commitment. A cause is serious business, but volunteering can also be fun. Indeed, having fun is one of the reasons people volunteer in the first place. Enjoying yourself and doing good is an unbeatable combination.

Political Volunteerism

You already know that political campaigns have a constant need for volunteers. Strapped for cash, but in desperate need of bodies, campaigns love volunteers. Merely showing up at headquarters and offering to help is all it takes. Only a stupid operation would turn down an eager volunteer.

You will probably be put to work walking precincts, phoning potential voters, stuffing envelopes, compiling lists, running errands, or any combination of the above. There are few better ways to become familiar with the political process than working on a campaign. You meet those who have careers in the "political industry"—consultants, pollsters, press secretaries—and speak daily with people to whom politics and elections matter.

If you volunteer in a political office, you can learn the arts of answering mail, taking constituent opinions, working on special projects, and putting together community events. You will gain invaluable experience should you someday want to work in public affairs.

The Thousand Points of Light initiative and Clinton's call for volunteerism were non-partisan by design. The point was to be inclusive, not exclusive. Who, after all, would be against Americans taking responsibility for their own communities? It was the proverbial no-brainer.

This is an example of neutral volunteerism, or volunteerism without an obvious political motive. However, there is another kind of volunteerism where the goal is just the opposite.

As you get further into politics, you might like to join an organization dedicated to advancing its agenda through Congress or the state legislature.

Here is a sampling of some of these organizations, plus information on how they started and what they believe. This is the stuff you will need to know when you are thinking of becoming involved at this level.

The Christian Coalition

Though Christians have been around for two thousand years, the Christian Coalition has been in existence only since late 1989, making it one of the newer players in American politics. Make that one of the newer *major* players in American politics. In 1997 the Coalition had a budget of $27 million and 1.9 million members, as opposed to merely $200,000 just eight years earlier. Even secular journalists flock to the Christian Coalition's conventions to file stories on who the membership prefers for president (in an election year) and issues the group hopes to see emphasized in the campaign.

Since Ronald Reagan's 1980 presidential race, people identifying themselves as fundamentalist Christians have become an ever more potent political force, especially within Republican ranks. Like the female vote, the African-American vote, and so on, the Christian vote is now considered pivotal in both state and national elections.

Ralph Reed was executive director of the Christian Coalition from 1990 until 1997. His book, *Active Faith: How Christians Are Changing the Soul of American Politics*, is explicit about the Coalition's "raison d'être": "The real battle for the soul of our nation is not fought primarily over the gross national product and prime interest rate, but over virtues, values and the culture" (page 7).

You can assume that most who join the Christian Coalition believe in Jesus Christ and that politics can influence morals, both for good and evil. To increase education and awareness the Coalition holds training seminars for state and local candidates and distributes voter guides. According to Reed, the Christian Coalition increased the number of local chapters from under one hundred in 1990 to over two thousand in 1996.

The Christian Coalition has become the most visible symbol of the connection between religion and politics in the 1980s and 1990s. The legal protection of abortion, gay rights, and pornography are bitterly opposed by the Christian Coalition and like-minded groups, who have in turn been demonized by their political foes.

American Civil Liberties Union

According to its mission statement, the ACLU "does not defend people as much as it defends the right to equal justice under the law. The ACLU protects everyone's rights in order to prevent discrimination against anyone."

The ACLU was founded by Roger Baldwin in 1920, partly as a consequence of restrictions of civil liberties after America's entry into World War I, and the terrifying examples of repression seen in the Russian Revolution. The war led to what some viewed as unjustified attacks on civil liberties (spying and keeping files on people because of their background, for instance) while the Russian Revolution of 1917 played a big part in the Red scare that gripped the United States in 1918–20.

Over the last eighty years the ACLU has been involved in many of the major issues the country has faced. Indeed, one way to tell the story of America from the end of World War I to the end of the Cold War is through the history of the ACLU. In his book, *In Defense of American Liberties: A History of the ACLU,* author Samuel Walker takes that approach. Walker has chapters on McCarthyism, Vietnam, Watergate, and civil liberties during the Reagan era.

Today the ACLU claims 300,000 members across the country and 53 professional affiliates. The ACLU's mission statement describes the organization as "non-partisan and politically independent." Defending a neo-Nazi in Chicago and blacks in the segregationist South certainly meets the definition of "politically independent."

You might find it hard to believe, but the Christian Coalition and the American Civil Liberties Union have actually worked closely together on an issue. In 1994 the two groups and others combined to defeat a bill in the Senate that would have restricted the activities of lobbyists. The Christian Coalition felt the legislation unfairly limited its activities; the ACLU believed it unfairly restricted the First Amendment's right to free expression.

Stranger still was the time in 1977 when the ACLU went to court to defend the right of an American Nazi, Frank Collin, to demonstrate in Skokie, Illinois. As a result of its representation of Collin, the organization was lambasted by many supporters and lost thousands of dollars in contributions. Yet defending Collin and working with the Christian Coalition seems consistent with the ACLU's stated goals.

And yet the ACLU is most often identified with the left. George Bush successfully pinned the charge, "a card-carrying member of the ACLU," on his Democratic opponent Michael Dukakis in the 1988 presidential election. It is true that most—but certainly not all—cases where constitutional rights were allegedly violated, involve the downtrodden or politically weak members of society. A vast majority of this group are either aligned with, sympathetic to, or embraced by the left.

Non-profit, non-partisan, and private, the ACLU has its national headquarters in New York City. The organization's funding comes from private donations, foundation grants, court-awarded legal fees, and membership fees. The ACLU never charges clients for legal representation.

The Sierra Club

There are few more popular positions in America than supporting a pristine coastline or a beautiful forest, as the Republicans who took control of Congress in 1995–96 could tell you. The GOP members swept into office determined to either roll back or overturn certain environmental regulations. Yet they soon discovered there is a pro-environment consensus that cuts across both parties. Many of their ambitious plans for changing environmental laws in this country were downplayed or shelved.

The Sierra Club is probably the best-known environmental organization in the U.S. Founded one hundred years ago by naturalist John Muir, it is one of the few environmental organizations that predates the environmental movement. The Sierra Club's own timeline shows a quickening of activity after 1969, when the movement exploded into the public arena.

The time line lists ten major accomplishments in the 1970s, as opposed to five between 1901 and 1910, the next-busiest decade. The Club's '70s highlights include helping to secure passage of the Water Pollution Control Act (1972), joining in the successful effort to strengthen the Clean Air Act (1977), and leading a campaign to add 48,000 acres to Redwood Park (1978).

Today the Sierra Club has 550,000 members, 65 chapters, and 396 groups. Membership is $35 per year, and the organization's annual budget is $45 million. The Sierra Club Political Committee, founded in 1976, promotes environmental candidates for public office and educates the public about environmental positions and votes of various candidates.

The League of Women Voters

Founded in the same year as the ACLU (1920) the League of Women Voters was formed because of a new constitutional right, not the denial of existing ones. This was also the year the Nineteenth Amendment to the Constitution was ratified, which gave women the vote.

The League of Women Voters "promotes political responsibility through informed and active participation of citizens in government. The League of Women Voters is non-partisan in that it does not support or oppose any political party or candidate. . . ." The organization does, however, take positions on government issues.

The League of Women Voters is neither overtly partisan nor really neutral. It takes positions on issues, but most of all it educates voters about the political process. You may know that the League has sponsored the presidential debates during the past several elections. These debates are often the most exciting things about the campaign.

The League, which today claims 140,000 members, operates at the local, county, state, and national levels of government. Membership is open to all citizens, men and women, who are of voting age. The League requires dues to join (the Burbank-Glendale chapter in California charged a $45 annual fee in 1997), which are non-taxable.

The LWV is an all-purpose guide to the political scene. Compared with the Christian Coalition, whose core concerns are moral issues, or the ACLU, which emphasizes civil liberties, the League of Women Voters has a wider agenda.

HELP FROM THE LEAGUE OF WOMEN VOTERS

One of the League's most valuable services is providing a non-partisan account of legislation pending before all levels of government. Don't feel bad if you are unaware of the specifics of major legislation; bills are complicated, they are constantly being amended, and the media are spending less and less time covering the nitty-gritty of Congress and state legislatures.

The League can help clarify matters. Local branches regularly give an assessment of key measures soon to be put to a vote. For instance, the April 1997 pamphlet of the League's Burbank-Glendale chapter included a discussion of two state bills on tax expenditure and an education bond measure, and an endorsement of county fire and county library ballot propositions.

The League distributes election guides, provides speakers on ballot-measure issues, and promotes voter registration. Its many activities and publications help simplify an often complex political process.

It is impossible to divorce politics in the 1990s from organizations such as the Christian Coalition, the ACLU, the League of Women Voters, and the Sierra Club. These, and others, exert a profound influence on what politicians say and how politicians act. To some voters this is an example of how politicians are manipulated by special interests, but it contradicts the notion that the American public has no voice or influence. It is the contemporary form of "Power to the People."

CHAPTER RECAP

- Volunteerism, plus voting, guarantees that you will make an impact.

- A volunteer must be dedicated to a cause.

- You can certainly have fun while doing good deeds.

- You must ask yourself several questions before deciding to volunteer.

- The Christian Coalition, the ACLU, the Sierra Club, and the League of Women Voters are four non-profit organizations, among many, that have made an obvious difference in American politics. They are always looking for you or your friends— people who care.

All Politics Is Local

*A*day will come when you and your neighbors will join together to oppose a decision—actual or proposed—by the city council, school board, planning commission, or parks-and-recreation department. Your rallying cry? "Enough is enough!"

Maybe you're upset about the construction of a high-rise office building too close to your home, maybe you're trying to prevent a rowdy nightclub from locating down the street, or maybe you have strong disagreements with the curriculum designed for your nine-year-old.

COMMUNITY ACTIVISM AND POLITICAL ACTION

In the beginning, there may be no one to argue your side but you and your small band of allies. Elected officials, city bureaucrats, and political appointees will either be supporting what you oppose, keeping quiet, or deliberately keeping themselves in the dark. Either they know, or they don't want to know. This presents you with a big problem:

How to fight city hall? To be even more blunt, *can* you fight city hall?

You have no choice: If you don't stand up for yourselves, who will? You must first organize, and then get *noticed*. It sounds crass, but you have to have an angle.

The "angle" is crucial to generating media interest, which is a major goal in community activism. Without media interest, you will go nowhere, especially in a big city. To get papers, radio, and TV to pay attention, you must issue press releases, organize events/press conferences, and introduce yourselves to reporters.

A few sympathetic stories about your cause can make a big difference. You will feel the balance of power shift. Now your phone calls will be returned.

Politicians hate being embarrassed in public, and they hate looking like the bad guy. Like everyone else, they want to be loved. And like anyone else, they want to keep their jobs, which means getting reelected. One of the main reasons a politician will change his or her position(s) is because he or she has been turned by public opinion. Politicians will not go down with the ship, or fight to the last man. They survive by knowing when to fold.

Your task is to put them in that position. Getting there takes hard work, and perhaps a bit of luck as well, such as one of your antagonists making an ill-advised remark in the press. But you can't count on the other side committing errors. They are professionals. You and your group must plot strategy, cultivate influential friends, and keep on top of the latest developments regarding your issue. You don't want to open your paper one morning to discover that what you bitterly oppose was quietly approved last night by the city council.

Knowledge of the system is critical here. You cannot expect to triumph in the political arena without having some political smarts. It's essential, for example, to be aware of the difference in the various levels of government.

Is your issue handled by the city, the county, the state, or Washington, D.C.? Or are all of these entities involved? Chapter 6 will go into more detail on what defines city, county, state, and federal government in the United States (see page 87).

It's also a good idea for you to be familiar with the politicians—pro and con—relevant to your cause. This means not only how they feel about this one issue, but their overall political philosophy. Are they liberal or conservative? Do they believe in local control, or tend to prefer big-government solutions? Do they always play it safe and vote with the majority, or are they willing to take a chance? Finally, and most important: Do they listen to people like you? Do your research. Read the paper, study voting records, talk to people. And be sure to get copies of agendas and schedules, which by law are made available to the public.

NOT IN MY BACKYARD!

Don't be surprised if the phrase "not in my backyard" or NIMBY for short, is applied to any homeowners' organization you might happen to join. "NIMBY" is a recent addition to the American political lexicon. It describes groups who come together to oppose new projects in their neighborhood; NIMBY folks have been known to object to apartment complexes, strip malls, or multiscreen theaters. In poorer areas, citizens have mobilized to fight proposed prisons or trash incinerators.

Neighborhood Watch

You have no doubt heard about Neighborhood Watch groups in the past decade. Neighborhood Watch groups are officially recognized by local police departments, who enlist their help in reporting crimes in progress, or to keep an eye on suspicious persons hanging around your area.

The members of Neighborhood Watch regularly meet with the local police captain.

- Neighborhood Watch is not vigilantism. No one is encouraged to take the law into his or her own hands; quite the contrary. During the late 1980s and early 1990s, when the crime rate was up and the number of officers in many cities was down, Neighborhood Watch served as a way for you and your neighbor to unobtrusively join the fight against crime.

THE POLITICS OF ACTIVISM

Like voting or giving money, joining a neighborhood group is a political act. When you make that choice, you surrender your innocence. Nothing wrong with that. The alternative is standing on the sidelines while decisions are made that adversely affect you and your family.

You may find you like being in the spotlight. You won't be the first with those feelings. It's not unusual for the leader or second-in-command of a neighborhood organization to eventually run for office. If this person worked successfully on a highly publicized issue, then he or she has gained name identification and a base of support from which to launch a campaign.

- Neighborhood Watch is a form of empowerment, a way for you to avoid that awful feeling of helplessness as you hear stories about criminal activity throughout society. The police will tell you that working with Neighborhood Watch makes it easier for them to catch crooks.

- As society has become more affluent, and its citizens more savvy, it is clear that neighborhood movements can and do succeed. The print and electronic media often run stories of a project halted because of local opposition.

- You should never think that challenging business and political interests is a futile exercise. By now you know what you have to do to win, or at least compete. But you also know you can't make it happen alone. This is not a job for Clint Eastwood, the lone cowboy who cleans up the town. Community

activism is more in line with the 1960s tactics of
"Power to the People."

- But you have an advantage over sixties activists:
  technology. Local-access cable, fax machines, the
  Internet, and computers are all weapons in your
  arsenal.

The Studio City Residents' Association

An example of a NIMBY group is the Studio City
Residents' Association, located in the community of Studio
City in Los Angeles.
The Studio City
Residents' Association,
which was founded in
1962, is run by a board
of directors. The board
consists of officers,
chairpersons of stand-
ing committees, and
the retiring president. Officers are elected annually for
one-year terms. Elections are held each January; nominations are accepted from the floor in December.

> ### AN ACTIVIST'S CREDO
>
> *The Studio City Residents' Association's mission, goals, and objectives include developing programs to increase property values, promoting a sense of neighborhood, and "enhancing the physical environment, while recognizing that change is inevitable." The Association also actively encourages communication between board members and local police in an effort to reduce crime.*

Standing committees of the Studio City Residents'
Association:

- Airport

- Beautification

- Crime and Safety

- Development

- Environment

- Parking

- Membership

> **PTA PRINCIPLES**
>
> *One of the objects of the PTA is to secure adequate laws for the care and protection of children and youth. It is by educating its members— and through them, the general public—on the impact of issues affecting children and youth, that PTAs can best influence the course of action of those who make policy decisions, thereby achieving the objects of PTA . . .*
>
> *The National PTA Board of Directors has stated that all PTAs have certain organizational rights, which are to function as an independent, non-partisan child advocacy group; seek enactment of policies and practices that protect children and youth; participate in making decisions affecting policies, rules and regulations; and meet with appropriate school officials to discuss matters of mutual concern affecting children.*
>
> *—from The Guidebook of the California State PTA*

- Special Traffic Problems

- Transportation/ Traffic

The Studio City Residents' Association mails a monthly newsletter to all its members. The Association charges basic annual dues of $15 per household; $10 for seniors. The Association's slogan is, "Alone, you have one vote. Together, we've got clout."

THE PTA

Probably the most venerable citizens' action group in America is the PTA, which celebrated its one-hundredth birthday in 1997. You may well be a member. The PTA currently claims a membership of more than 6 million across the country. If you haven't joined, here is a brief overview of perhaps the most successful and best-known organization of its type in the United States.

The PTA fights for children at all levels of government, from the local school board to Congress. It also provides child-care programs, medical/dental clinics, emergency food and clothing, leadership training and workshops on parenting, and citizenship and English as a Second Language classes.

The PTA's Statement of Principles endorses human values, spiritual faith (in the home), good homes, sound health, safety, educational opportunity, vocational technological competence, conservation of natural resources, constructive leisure, human relations, civic responsibility, and international understanding. That covers about all aspects of our lives. To the left are some of the PTA's core principles.

THE GOOD FIGHT—
A 16-POINT CHECKLIST

Throughout this chapter you have been given some suggestions and ideas about fighting the political fight. You have to know this stuff. But there is a mental process you must undergo when deciding to get involved. You cannot have any doubts about what you are about to do. In that way community activism is like running for office: a half-hearted effort is bound to fail. You will end up disappointing yourself, and those who believed in you.

The book *Organize!—Organizing for Social Change: A Manual for Activists in the 1990s* includes a sixteen-point checklist for choosing an issue; this is a good guide for activists everywhere. When thinking about joining an activist group, you may want to consider whether your cause will:

- result in a real improvement in people's lives

- give people a sense of their own power

- alter the relations of power

- be worthwhile

- be winnable

- be widely felt

- be deeply felt

- be easy to understand

- have a clear target

- have a clear time frame

- be non-divisive (avoiding such conflicts as neighbor against neighbor, black against white, Asian against Latino)

- build leadership

- set up an organization for the next campaign

- have a pocketbook angle ("Issues that get people money or save people money are widely felt.")

- raise money (Where will funding come from?)

- be consistent with the organization's values and visions

Thus far, the discussion of activism has centered around you and your neighborhood. If all politics is local (to paraphrase late Speaker of the House Tip O'Neill), then it makes sense to start with protecting home and hearth. This is where you learn the trade.

ADVOCACY GROUPS—ADDRESSES

There is a whole other world of nationally known advocacy groups in Washington, D.C., and many of these groups have the clout to take on the president. Rather than a complete breakdown of each one, following is a list of many of these groups, including phone and fax numbers and Web sites where applicable. You can pick your issue.

Key Washington, D.C.–based interest groups.

Accuracy in Media
4455 Connecticut Avenue NW, #330
Washington, D.C. 20008
TEL: (202) 364-4401
FAX: (202) 364-4098
http://www.aim.org

American Association of Retired Persons
610 E Street NW
Washington, D.C. 20049
TEL: (202) 434-2277
FAX: (202) 434-2320

American Civil Liberties Union
122 Maryland Avenue NE
Washington, D.C. 20002
TEL: (202) 544-1681
FAX: (202) 546-0738
http://www.aclu.org

American Heart Association
5335 Wisconsin Avenue NW, #940
Washington, D.C. 20015
TEL: (202) 686-6888
FAX: (202) 686-6162
E-MAIL: amhrt@erols.cim

American Israel Public Affairs Committee
440 First Street NW, #600
Washington, D.C. 20001
TEL: (202) 639-5200
FAX: (202) 638-0680
http://www.aipac.org/

American Legion
1608 K Street NW
Washington, D.C. 20006
TEL: (202) 861-2711
FAX: (202) 861-2786

American-Arab Anti-Discrimination Committee
4201 Connecticut Avenue NW, #300
Washington, D.C. 20008
TEL: (202) 244-2990
FAX: (202) 244-3196
E-MAIL: adc@adc.org

Center on Budget and Policy Priorities
820 First Street NW, #510
Washington, D.C. 20002
TEL: (202) 408-1080
FAX: (202) 408-1056
E-MAIL: cbpp@clark.net

Children's Defense Fund
25 E Street NW
Washington, D.C. 20001
TEL: (202) 628-8787
FAX: (202) 662-3510
http://www.childrensdefense.org

Christian Coalition
227 Massachusetts Avenue NE, #101
Washington, D.C. 20002
TEL: (202) 547-3600
FAX: (202) 543-2978
http://www.cc.org

Citizens Against Government Waste
1301 Connecticut Avenue NW, #400
Washington, D.C. 20036
TEL: (202) 467-5300
FAX: (202) 467-4253
http://www.cagw.org

Citizens for Tax Justice
1311 L Street #400 NW
Washington, D.C. 20005
TEL: (202) 626-3780
FAX: (202) 638-3486
http://www.ctj.org

Coalition to Stop Gun Violence
1000 Sixteenth Street NW, #603
Washington, D.C. 20036
TEL: (202) 530-0340
FAX: (202) 530-0331
http://www.gunfree.org

Common Cause
1250 Connecticut Avenue NW, #600
Washington, D.C. 20036
TEL: (202) 833-1200
FAX: (202) 659-3716
http://www.commoncause.org

Family Research Council
801 G Street NW
Washington, D.C. 20001
TEL: (202) 393-2100
FAX: (202) 393-2134
http://www.frc.org

Friends of the Earth
1025 Vermont Avenue NW, #300
Washington, D.C. 20005
TEL: (202) 783-7400
FAX: (202) 783-0444
E-MAIL: foedc@igc.apc.org

Gray Panthers
2025 Pennsylvania Avenue NW, #821
Washington, D.C. 20006
TEL: (202) 466-3132
FAX: (202) 466-3133

Mexican American Legal Defense
    and Education Fund
1518 K Street NW, #410
Washington, D.C. 20005
TEL: (202) 628-4074
FAX: (202) 393-4206

National Abortion and Reproductive Rights
    Action League
1156 Fifteenth Street NW, #700
Washington, D.C. 20005
TEL: (202) 973-3000
FAX: (202) 973-3096
http://www.naral.org

National Council of La Raza
1111 Nineteenth Street NW, #1000
Washington, D.C. 20036
TEL: (202) 785-1670
FAX: (202) 776-1792

National Gay and Lesbian Task Force
2320 Seventeenth Street NW
Washington, D.C. 20009
TEL: (202) 332-6483
FAX: (202) 332-0207
E-MAIL: ngltf@ngltf.org

National Urban League
1111 Fourteenth Street NW, #1001
Washington, D.C. 20005
TEL: (202) 898-1604
FAX: (202) 408-1965
http://www.nul.org

National Women's Political Caucus
1211 Connecticut Avenue NW, #425
Washington, D.C. 20036
TEL: (202) 785-1100
FAX: (202) 785-3605
E-MAIL: mailNWPC@aol.com

Points of Light Foundation
1737 H Street NW
Washington, D.C. 20006
TEL: (202) 223-9186
FAX: (202) 223-9256
E-MAIL: robertplof@aol.com

Public Citizen
1600 Twentieth Street NW
Washington, D.C. 20009
TEL: (202) 588-1000
FAX: (202) 588-7799
http:www.citizen.org

Rainbow/Push Coalition
1700 K Street NW, #800
Washington, D.C. 20006
TEL: (202) 728-1180
FAX: (202) 728-1192
http://www.rainbow.org

U.S. Chamber of Commerce
1615 H Street NW
Washington, D.C. 20062
TEL: (202) 659-6000
FAX: (202) 463-5836

Veterans of Foreign Wars of the U.S.
200 Maryland Avenue NE
Washington, D.C. 20002
TEL: (202) 543-2239
FAX: (202) 543-6719

Zero Population Growth
1400 16th Street NW, #320
Washington, D.C. 20036
TEL: (202) 332-2200
FAX: (202) 332-2302
E-MAIL: zpg@igc.apc.org

CHAPTER RECAP

- You can force government to change a decision through social activism.

- You must organize, and then use various means to rally public opinion; this can include press conferences, events, and public speeches.

- You must be intimately familiar with local politics, including the dates and times of meetings and who the key players are.

- Groups such as the PTA and homeowners' associations have been successful in changing unpopular policies and implementing important ones. You might want to inquire about these organizations in your area.

- There are sixteen valuable points that go with effective social activism.

- Washington is filled with organizations that might be perfect for your own political needs.

What Is Citizenship?

Do you remember your elementary school report card? In the left-hand column were your letter grades, A–D, representing your academic prowess in a particular subject. In the right-hand column was your citizenship grade, which was either "outstanding, " "satisfactory," or "poor."

"Citizenship" considered several factors, including attendance, the ability to get along with fellow students, and willingness to help the teacher when asked. The implication was that a well-behaved pupil and a model citizen were one and the same: courteous, friendly with others in the "community," and respectful of the rules.

In this chapter you will not be graded on your citizenship skills. That effectively ended when you left sixth grade, but the question of what makes a good citizen is one that you should ponder well into your adult life. It's central to any discussion about the meaning of political participation.

An example is your decision to vote. It's possible that you will register to vote and then cast your ballot solely because you are excited about a particular candidate. Once

IN THIS CHAPTER:

- *The responsibilities of U.S. citizenship*

- *Immigration*

- *The meaning of citizenship*

- *How to apply to become a U.S. citizen*

- *The naturalization process*

the election is over, however, you've had enough; only another extraordinary candidate will bring you back.

On the other hand, you might register to vote and go to the polls because you believe it is your duty as an American. Even a choice between the lesser of two evils will not keep you away. You vote because you believe it is one of the fundamental requirements of being a good citizen.

AMERICANS BY CHOICE

In chapter 1 the question "Why vote?" was answered by saying that voting is an act of empowerment, the best way of making your voice heard and your opinions count under this system. In this chapter you are given another reason: To be a good citizen. Your vote validates democracy. Without voters, elections are a sham. By voting you are doing your part in keeping America true to its ideals.

You have just read how the concept of citizenship applies to Americans. The goal is not to become a citizen, but to become a *better* citizen. For foreigners living and working in this country, however, citizenship is the difference between being an American and remaining an outsider.

If you have been following the debate over immigration, then you know some politicians want to make citizenship harder to obtain. This is in response to constituents' demands on what, if anything, their elected officials are going to do about the increase in immigration.

Members of Congress have proposed a constitutional amendment denying citizenship to children born in the United States to parents who are not legal residents. This amendment would repeal Section One of the Fourteenth Amendment.

> ### SECTION ONE OF THE FOURTEENTH AMENDMENT
>
> *All persons born or naturalized in the United States, and subject to the jurisdiction thereof, are citizens of the United States and the state wherein they reside.*
>
> —*U.S. Constitution*

The proposed repeal of the Fourteenth Amendment has support among conservatives in states where there are many illegal immigrants, but has not yet been approved and sent to the states for ratification.

IMMIGRATION

A comprehensive discussion of citizenship will eventually get around to immigration. The two are closely related, especially in the political arena.

The Illegal Immigration and Immigrant Reform Act of 1996 doubled the border patrol to 10,000 officers by the year 2000 and increased penalties for document fraud. It also restricted public benefits to aliens, set new rules for readmissibility, and limited voluntary departures to 120 days.

At the same time a record number of legal immigrants are making the decision to become American citizens. In 1996, the number of immigrants naturalized was nearly 1.1 million. This total was higher than the number of immigrants admitted to the country—916,000. The main reason offered for the increase is the recent anti-immigrant mood of many in Congress. Immigrants were fearful of being targeted by new, punitive legislation. Citizenship offers them protection against these measures.

Many people have emigrated to America to escape the wrath of their own governments, and then chosen to become U.S. citizens to avoid policies of the U.S. government. With immigration at its highest levels since the 1930s, the impact of new citizens will be felt for several years. In 1997 the foreign-born population of the United States was 9.3 percent; up from 4.8 percent in 1970, although this is still well below the peak of 15 percent during the early part of this century.

Immigration is often a long, slow process. It requires an intellectual commitment by the prospective citizen.

Along with demonstrating an understanding of English, applicants for citizenship must take a written test culled from one hundred questions about the American system of government and American history. It makes sense that one must know something about America to be an American.

The native-born, of course, don't have to pass a test to become citizens. Still, it might not be a bad idea to administer the test to everybody. You would like to think your fellow voter has at least some knowledge of the country. A way to find out is by taking the questionnaire (for fun, of course) compiled by the Immigration and Naturalization Service and administered to all prospective citizens. People eager to become Americans must answer correctly 7 of 10, or 12 of 20, of these randomly selected questions. How well can you do?

1. What are the colors of our flag?

2. How many stars are there on our flag?

3. What color are the stars on our flag?

4. What do the stars on the flag mean?

5. How many stripes are there on the flag?

6. What color are the stripes?

7. What do the stripes on the flag mean?

8. How many states are there in the Union?

9. Why do we celebrate the Fourth of July?

10. What is the date of Independence Day?

11. Independence from whom?

12. What country did we fight during the Revolutionary War?

13. Who was the first President?

14. Who is President today?

15. Who is Vice President today?

16. Who elects the President of the United States?

17. Who becomes our President if the President should die?

18. For how long do we elect the President?

19. What is the Constitution?

20. Can the Constitution be changed?

21. What do we call a change to the Constitution?

22. How many changes or amendments are there to the Constitution?

23. How many branches are there in our government?

24. What are the three branches of our government?

25. What is the Legislative branch of our government?

26. Who makes Federal laws?

27. What is Congress?

28. What are the duties of Congress?

29. Who elects Congress?

30. How many Senators are there in Congress?

31. Can you name the Senators from your state?

32. For how long do we elect each Senator?

33. How many voting members are in the House of Representatives?

34. For how long do we elect the Representatives?

35. What is the Executive branch of our government?

36. What is the Judiciary branch of our government?

37. What are the duties of the Supreme Court?

38. What is the supreme law of the United States?

39. What is the Bill of Rights?

40. What is the capital of your state?

41. Who is the governor of your state?

42. Who becomes President if both the President and the Vice President die?

43. Who is Chief Justice of the Supreme Court?

44. Can you name the thirteen original states?

45. Who said, "Give me liberty or give me death"?

46. Which countries were our allies during World War II?

47. What is the forty-ninth state added to our Union?

48. How many full terms can a President serve?

49. Who was Martin Luther King Jr.?

50. Who is the head of your local government?

51. According to the Constitution, a person must meet certain requirements in order to be eligible to become President. Name one.

52. Why are there one hundred Senators in the United States Senate?

53. Who nominates judges of the Supreme Court?

54. How many Supreme Court Justices are there?

55. Why did the Pilgrims come to America?

56. What is the head executive of a state government called?

57. What is the head executive of a city government called?

58. What holiday did the American colonists celebrate for the first time?

59. Who was the main writer of the Declaration of Independence?

60. When was the Declaration of Independence adopted?

61. What is the basic belief of the Declaration of Independence?

62. What is our national anthem?

63. Who wrote "The Star-Spangled Banner"?

64. Where does freedom of speech come from?

65. What is the minimum voting age?

66. Who signs bills into law?

67. What is the highest court in the United States?

68. Who was President during the Civil War?

69. What did the Emancipation Proclamation do?

70. What special group advises the President?

71. Which President is called the "Father of Our Country"?

72. What is the fiftieth state of the Union?

73. Who helped the Pilgrims in America?

74. What is the name of the ship that brought the Pilgrims to America?

75. What were the thirteen original states of the United States called?

76. Name three rights or freedoms guaranteed by the Bill of Rights.

77. Who has the power to declare war?

78. Name one amendment that guarantees or addresses voting rights.

79. Which President freed the slaves?

80. In what year was the Constitution written?

81. What are the first ten amendments to the Constitution called?

82. Name one purpose of the United Nations.

83. Where does Congress meet?

84. Whose rights are guaranteed by the Constitution and the Bill of Rights?

85. What is the introduction to the Constitution called?

86. Name one benefit of being a citizen of the United States.

87. What is the most important right granted to United States citizens?

88. What is the United States Capitol?

89. What is the White House?

90. Where is the White House located?

91. What is the President's official home?

92. Name one right guaranteed by the First Amendment.

93. Who is the Commander in Chief of the United States Army and Navy?

94. Which President was the first Commander in Chief of the United States Army and Navy?

95. In what month do we vote for President?

96. In what month is the new President inaugurated?

97. How many times may a Senator be reelected?

98. How many times may a Congressman be reelected?

99. What are the two major political parties in the United States today?

100. How many states are there?

Answers can be found in appendix D, page 389.

THE MEANING OF CITIZENSHIP

You may feel that voting is sufficient to make you a good citizen. You don't need to do more, and you don't particularly want to do more. Fine. But you may consider voting just one step in the process of becoming a good citizen. So you volunteer for a campaign, join a neighborhood organization, or work with the disadvantaged. This is also part of the meaning of citizenship.

Over the last two hundred–plus years many people have written about the duties and requirements of citizenship in the United States. America is a nation in which the individual is essentially free to choose his or her own way. You can become the kind of citizen you want.

You may find it helpful to read what others have said on the subject. Below are two definitions of good citizenship, each of them expressed many decades ago. But the relevance is clear. The meaning of citizenship has been debated and discussed since the time of the ancient Greeks.

> A self-governing people must either participate actively in the making of the decisions which determine its destiny, or its destiny will not be determined.
> —*Archibald MacLeish, librarian, Congressional Library, Washington, D.C., in a commencement address at Sarah Lawrence College, Bronxville, New York, May 28, 1943*

> Aggressive citizenship implies the presence of freedoms. And in the presence of freedoms, there can be no communism or any other form of total state. In the absence of freedoms, there can be no democracy. The atom bomb could never destroy communism. But I think that freedoms eventually will.
>
> For our freedoms to flourish, we must exercise in fuller measure our responsibilities as individuals. We in America talk so much about our Bill of Rights. But I never thought it meant we could rest on our oars and be rowed by the other fellow.
> —*Eric Johnston, president, Motion Picture Association of America, in a speech to the annual convention of Kiwanis International, Convention Hall, Atlantic City, New Jersey, June 23, 1949*

You have seen in this chapter that citizenship is two things: an idea and a set of rules. For those of you who are not yet citizens, you must learn the rules. For those of you who are citizens, you should know them all the same. It will help you put the issue of immigration in perspective.

The four ways to qualify for citizenship are:

- being born in the United States;

- being born to parents who are American citizens;

- your parent's becoming U.S. citizens while you are still a child (age restrictions apply, so it's a good idea to check with an immigration expert); or

- naturalization.

Following are the requirements for naturalization.

- You must be 18 or older.

- You must be a lawful permanent resident of the United States.

- You must have a green card.

- You must have been a permanent resident of the United States for five years (with a green card). People who have obtained a green card through marriage have to wait only three years.

- You must have been physically present in the United States for at least one-half of the required residency period. (There are exceptions to this rule.)

- You must reside in the state in which you apply for at least three months.

- You must be a person of good moral character.

- You must have the ability to speak, read, and write English.

- You must have a basic knowledge of the history and government of the United States.

You will have to supply the following documents:

- form N-400—Application for Naturalization
- fingerprints
- photographs
- a copy of the front and back of your green card
- a filing fee
- a stamped, self-addressed envelope for filing of return receipt

The citizenship examination can be taken as part of a course of study on U.S. citizenship offered through an independent organization approved by the Immigration and Naturalization Service, or at the INS naturalization interview.

CHAPTER RECAP

- A good citizen goes to the polls.
- The increase in new arrivals in the 1990s has made immigration a hot political issue.
- Immigration can be a slow and lengthy process, involving interviews and passing a test on American politics and political history.
- The meaning of citizenship includes caring about the community and meeting one's obligations to society.
- You must be able to provide a series of documents when applying for U.S. citizenship.

To become a naturalized citizen, you must fulfill several requirements, including being able to speak, read, and write English.

Making the Federal Government Your Ally

*T*he time might come in your life when you have no choice but to seek the assistance of government. When your Social Security check doesn't arrive, or you're getting short-changed on your veterans' benefits, or the Immigration and Naturalization Service delays processing your papers, you have no other recourse. Even people who truly hate government would concede the point.

WORKING THE SYSTEM

Have you heard the things that are said about the federal government?

- It's big, impersonal, and inefficient.

- You should forget trying to get any help from Washington.

- The bureaucrats up there couldn't care less about your troubles.

- Bureaucrats are only interested in keeping their jobs.

- Bureaucrats derive satisfaction and power from saying no to people.

- Government will oppose you until you're too tired to fight.

In other words, don't bother asking for government help. You may have noticed it's often politicians or aspiring politicians who peddle this line. Assailing Washington has become a popular campaign theme of candidates for federal office. But you have to be more realistic.

Government is not your enemy. It may make you angry, it may do things you don't like, but its purpose is not ruining the lives of its citizenry. If that were true, we would have had a second American Revolution by now. The American people have proven they are not passive in the face of tyranny.

However, government is not automatically your friend, either. Like any relationship, this one takes work. You have to make the first move.

Any U.S. House or Senate office has staff members who spend their days doing nothing but trying to make life easier for constituents who have a problem. If you have a legitimate case, these men and women will work hard to get you a favorable resolution.

You may not realize it, but you have considerable leverage with your representative or senator. There is no more important purpose of a local political office than keeping the customer—you, the voter—satisfied. Remember the lesson of chapter 1: your vote is power. If you get bad service at a restaurant, you will urge your friends not to eat there. If you get bad service from a political office, you will urge your friends to vote for the other guy in the next election.

Politicians know this. The smart ones assemble a staff that is eager to help the public. A friendly disposition is essential. Few things make an elected official angrier than learning that his or her staff has upset a constituent.

As much as they want to help, House or Senate staff do not take just any case that comes along. It helps you to know ahead of time what does or does not make you qualified to receive federal help. You should never stroll unprepared into the office of your local congressman.

APPROACHING A CONGRESSIONAL OFFICE

The first step—Before you even decide to go, you need to be certain that the member you intend to visit is *your* congressional representative (U.S. House of Representatives). Otherwise you will be wasting your time, as well as that of the staff. If you go to the wrong place, you will be redirected to the office of your local congressman or -woman. Congressional courtesy requires each member's office to handle the cases in his or her particular district.

A voter should have no difficulty recalling the name of his or her representative; it was on the ballot. If you haven't voted for a while, however, this could be a problem. If you don't know who your representative is, the best thing for you to do is call the office of any nearby representative (it's in the phone book) and tell the person on the other end of the line your street address. Most congressional offices have maps of the various districts in the area.

You will have no such difficulty with your two U.S. Senators; they represent the entire state. Just be sure you know their names.

On to step number two—Before you call or visit a congressional office you should know whether your particular issue is under the jurisdiction of federal, state, or local authorities. The next chapter goes into greater detail about the differences between these levels of government. Suffice it to say for now, that questions or disputes having to do with Social Security, Medicare, Veterans' Affairs, or Immigration—to name some of the most important—are handled at the federal level. A noisy neighbor, a deadbeat dad, or a hassle with the Department of Motor Vehicles are not federal issues. If you call a congressional office to get help in these areas you will be referred to your local or state representative.

The final step: Have your papers in order. The fewer questions a caseworker has to ask you, the quicker he or she can get to work on your behalf. Requests for assistance can be faxed from the congressional office to the proper federal agency that same day. Now you're in the system.

Don't try to argue the facts of your case with congressional staff, who are only go-betweens. Final decisions are made by the various agencies involved. Staff members can apply pressure to get you an answer, but they don't have the power to overrule bureaucrats.

BRINGING CONGRESS TO YOU

There are no guarantees in federal casework. You could do everything right, and still receive a thumbs-down. But enlisting the active support of a political office significantly increases your chances of the final decision going your way. When congressional staff call an agency, they get an ear. That's a good start.

Our system of government is a two-way street. In order to make government your ally you need to tell government what you want. The most basic way to do this is to vote. But it is not the only option. If you have a telephone, fax machine, computer, typewriter, or a thirty-three-cent stamp, you can let your representative know why you feel the way you do about a particular issue.

CONTACTING A MEMBER OF CONGRESS

The word "ally" in the title of this chapter has two meanings: congressional staff, giving help when asked; and an active dialogue between you and your elected representative.

The dialogue can take two forms. Every six months or so, members of Congress hold town-hall meetings at various locations in their district. If you are a registered voter, you will receive a notice in the mail from the member's office, alerting you to the meeting in your area. Often the notice will list the subjects that the congressman/woman or senator wishes to discuss. These meetings are a great opportunity to have a dialogue with your representative.

Don't make a speech; the audience will get upset. Town-hall meetings can draw as many as several hundred people—so your question should be brief and to the point.

Perhaps you don't want to wait for one of these meetings, or are more comfortable writing than speaking. In that case, send your representative a letter, either to his or her district office, or the Washington address, giving your views on an issue or on a bill before Congress. Once again, make sure you are sending your letter to *your* congressman or senator; with few exceptions, members answer mail from constituents only.

Be assured: you *will* receive a response. It may take a few weeks, but it will come. This doesn't mean that you should dash off anything that pops into your head. Here are some points to remember when writing your congress-man or -woman;

- Always include a return address. You won't get an answer if the office has no idea who you are or where you live.

- One issue per letter. More than one issue means more than one letter in return, which slows down the process for everybody. A member wants to be able to give a thoughtful and thorough answer to each letter.

- Provide as much information as you can. The number of the bill, and a concise description of what it is supposed to do, are helpful, along with your opinion, of course.

- Make your letter legible.

- If you are concerned about a bill that is being voted on in Congress today or tomorrow, send a fax. At least your representative will know how you feel prior to casting his or her vote.

- In addressing a government official it's always best to use the proper form of address. A list of these appears in appendix E, page 397.

Special Services of a Congressional Office

Not everything that comes to you from Washington is "serious." Your congressional office can make it possible for you, your family, or friends to receive special greetings from the President of the United States. The designated categories are wedding anniver-saries, births, birthdays (particular years), condolences, Eagle Scout Award and Girl Scout Gold Award, and graduation, both individual and class. For more, check chapter 9, page 155.

STATE YOUR VIEW!

You can always call a congressional office and express your opinion over the phone. Give your name, address, phone number, and point of view. You can be assured that you will get a response.

The White House also issues presidential greetings to individuals who are being honored for volunteer activities, or for significant contributions to the arts, education, or community help. You need to contact your representative's office to find out about getting one of these messages or letters of congratulation.

A congressional office can help arrange tours for these Washington landmarks:

- Capitol Building (usually a limited number of House and Senate gallery passes are available)

- Federal Bureau of Investigation

- Library of Congress

- Pentagon

- State Department

- Supreme Court

- Treasury Department

- White House

- Federal Reserve Board

- Bureau of Engraving and Printing

Useful Telephone Numbers

A House or Senate office can always provide you with key federal government phone numbers. You may want to place a direct call yourself. Below is a list of some important numbers:

- Tax Information (IRS): (800) 829-1040

- Tax Forms and Publications (IRS): (800) 829-3676

- Social Security and Medicare Queries: (800) 722-1213

- The President: (202) 456-1414

- The Vice President: (202) 456-2326

- The First Lady: (202) 456-6266

- Department of Agriculture: (202) 720-8732

- Department of Commerce: (202) 482-2000

- Department of Defense: (703) 545-6700

- Department of Education: (202) 401-2000

- Department of Energy: (202) 586-5000

- Department of Health and Human Services: (202) 619-0257

- Department of Housing and Urban Development: (202) 708-1112

- Department of the Interior: (202) 208-3100

- Department of Justice: (202) 514-2000

- Department of Labor: (202) 219-6666

- Department of State: (202) 647-4000

- Department of Transportation: (202) 366-4000

- Department of the Treasury: (202) 622-2000

- Department of Veterans' Affairs: (202) 273-5717

Useful Web Sites

- Department of Agriculture: http://www.usda.gov

- Department of Commerce: http://www.doc.gov

- Department of Defense: http://www.defenselink.mil

- Department of Education: http://www.ed.gov

- Department of Energy: http://www.doe.gov

- Department of Health and Human Services: http://www.os.dhhs.gov

- Department of Housing and Urban Development: http://www.hud.gov

- Department of the Interior: http://www.doi.gov

- Department of Justice: http://www.usdoj.gov

- Department of Labor: http://www.dol.gov

- Department of State: http://www.state.gov

- Department of Transportation: http://www.dot.gov

- Department of the Treasury: http://www.ustreas.gov

- Department of Veterans' Affairs: http://www.va.gov
- Executive Office of the President: http://www.whitehouse.gov

Many of the cabinet departments have regional offices near your home. For that information consult your local congressional office.

THE FREEDOM OF INFORMATION ACT

The Freedom of Information Act, enacted in 1966, gives the public the right to acquire information about federal agencies and departments. The law allows you to access existing agency records without having to provide a reason or demonstrate a need for your request. The burden of proof for withholding documents lies with the government.

To request records under the Freedom of Information Act, write the relevant agency, stating both what is being sought and that you are using the Act. The lower left-hand corner of the envelope should be marked "FOIA Request."

EXPRESS YOURSELF

The theme of this chapter could be stated as follows: If you want something from government, you are going to have to ask for it. Being passive doesn't work in the American system. The country is too big. You have to make yourself visible.

This doesn't mean resorting to desperate measures. You can do just fine by going to the office of your congressman or senator, and explaining in clear and measured language the problem you are having with the federal government. This is American democracy in action. You have asked one

CONTACTING YOUR REPRESENTATIVE

NOTE: Your local representative's office should have the Washington addresses of every member of Congress and U.S. senator.

The members of the House have their D.C. offices in one of these locations:

- *Cannon House Office Building—First Street & Independence Avenue, SE; 20515*
- *Longworth House Office Building—Independence & New Jersey Avenues, SE; 20515*
- *Rayburn House Office Building—Independence Avenue & S. Capitol Street, SW; 20515*
- *O'Neill House Office Building—New Jersey Avenue & C Street, SE; 20515*
- *Ford House Office Building—Second & D Streets, SW; 20515*
- *House Office Building Annex No. 3—501 First Street, SE; 20515*

The members of the U.S. Senate have their D.C. offices in one of three locations:

- *Russell Senate Office Building—Delaware & Constitution Avenues, NE; 20510*
- *Dirksen Senate Office Building—First Street & Constitution Avenue, NE; 20510*
- *Hart Senate Office Building—Second Street & Constitution Avenue, NE; 20510*

When you're in Washington, drop by the office of your representative or senator. Chances are you won't meet the congressman/woman or senator (D.C. is a busy place), but you can certainly chat with staff.

branch of government—the legislative—to work on your behalf with another branch of government—the executive—which includes the Social Security Administration, the Department of Veterans' Affairs, the Immigration and Naturalization Service, and so on. Did I mention that the budgets of these departments are set by Congress? That alone will get bureaucrats' attention when a representative's office is calling.

But nothing happens unless you take the first step. When you feel the government has done you wrong, or when you have a strong opinion on a particular bill, get out there and say so. You can do so without fear of reprisal. This is what it means to live in a free country.

CHAPTER RECAP

- You should expect help from a congressional or senate office. A politician whose staff ignores your request, or who does a poor job on your behalf, should not expect your support in the next election.

- When approaching a congressional office, make sure you know if the person is in fact your representative, and if your problem actually is with the federal government.

- Feel free to write or fax your congressman/woman or senator on issues of importance. In your letter, stick to the point, and include a return address.

- If you're traveling to Washington, D.C., and have time to see some sites, call the office of your local representative to inquire about tours.

Government from Bottom to Top

You are a busy person. You also like to leave a little time for relaxation. And as much as possible, you want to keep your schedule.

You hate to waste time. You especially hate to waste time being shuffled from one agency to another, or being bounced between political offices. So when you want someone to fix a busted streetlight on your block, need to learn the hours of your local DMV, or have to know whether the neighborhood park is ever going to add basketball courts, you want an answer fast. You haven't the patience nor inclination to make several calls to find the person with the relevant information.

THE RUNNING OF AMERICA

You can make your life easier. Before you pick up the phone, you should be clear in your own mind who does what in government. What are the responsibilities of the city council? Where does the state's jurisdiction end and the federal government's jurisdiction begin? In which county do you reside?

IN THIS CHAPTER:

- *Learning the different levels of government can save you time*

- *Distinguishing between the duties and responsibilities of city, county, and state government*

- *A guide to the different systems under which city, county, and state government operate*

- *Understanding the relationship between federal and state government*

Not every question can be answered for every American in a single chapter. The system in Idaho is different from the system in Ohio, and so on across the United States. Some states have townships, others have counties. A bit of research on your own is needed.

"WHO'S IN CHARGE?" QUIZ

Here are some questions you may have asked yourself.

1. What is a city committee?
2. Which level of government oversees the Department of Motor Vehicles?
3. Which level of government handles trash removal?
4. Where do I go for help on a zoning matter?
5. Which government entity oversees jails?—prisons?
6. Are welfare checks distributed by the federal government?
7. What is a county commission?
8. To whom do I complain about a stoplight that has stopped working?
9. To whom can I speak about noise from aircraft?
10. Where can I get funding for an arts project?
11. Who keeps the neighborhood nice?

For answers see appendix D, page 394.

But there are general points that can be made about the separate levels of government from bottom to top. City governments have common characteristics, as do county governments and state governments. This information will not only be useful to help you cut through the bureaucratic jungle, it is also essential background for anyone else who wants to be involved with politics.

You must have a firm grasp, from the start, on what distinguishes city government from county government, or county government from state government. This will help you make informed decisions, and help you understand the whole picture—the American political system.

HELPFUL HINTS

Imagine government as an inverted pyramid. The pyramid consists of four sections, each representing a level of government. It is arranged from least powerful at the bottom to most powerful on top. From bottom to top, the order of the pyramid is city, county, state, and federal.

This is not an arbitrary designation. City government represents the least number of constituents, the federal government represents the most. Thus, the federal government governs more people and is more powerful than your city government. This is the case wherever you may live.

This distinction is largely because of the power of the purse. The feds have the biggest share of dollars to spend, some of which inevitably gets funneled to the cities. Washington also establishes rules that cities, or counties, or states, must follow in order to qualify for these funds.

If money is the sole criterion, then the federal government wins the prize. No argument there. But as far as direct impact on your life, city government is more of a force, or presence, than federal government. For one thing, you may talk to your council representative on a regular basis. You may have friends and acquaintances on a number of commissions. Unlike lobbying your member of Congress or representative in the state assembly, you don't have to wade through staffers to discuss an issue with a key political player.

You see on a daily basis the impact of city government. This is true if you live in a desert ghost town or in New York City. Where and when you can legally park your car, how to dispose of your Christmas tree, what to do about a noisy neighbor, and where to go to get a new stoplight installed are examples of ordinances, services, and decisions that originate with the city.

According to the U.S. Bureau of the Census, as of 1993 Americans received service from 3,043 counties, 19,296 municipalities, 16,666 townships, 14,556 independent school districts, and 33,131 special districts.

Your political education is not complete without working knowledge of the various levels of government. Consider the next few sections.

CITY GOVERNMENT

The National League of Cities is a Washington, D.C., advocate for cities. The League currently represents more than 1,400 cities directly, and more than 17,000 through various leagues.

You might find interesting the four roles developed by the NLC's Advisory Council for local officials in connecting citizens and their government. Do your council members meet the test?

THE ANCIENT CITY

"... polis—the Greek city-state, the small self-governing community was the characteristic political unit of the Greek world.... The citizens lived in city or country, but the government of the state was entirely concentrated in the city, and in the hands of those citizens empowered by the constitution to exercise it."

—M.C. Howatson, editor, The Oxford Companion to Classical Literature

---

- *As a model*—By maintaining a spirit of civility and cooperation both within the municipal government and among local governments, local officials can help set the tone for civil discourse and productive problem-solving.

- *As a messenger*—Local officials can take advantage of their "bully pulpit" to encourage citizens, business, the media, community organizations, and others to play an active role in community-building initiatives. Critical tasks are identifying and defining the problem of civic disengagement, and encouraging people in the community to think and talk about it.

- *As a shaper of processes that connect citizens and government*—There is no one way to get citizens involved in government. Local officials can structure various processes, programs, and interventions to engage citizens in community problem-solving and to identify different players' roles in different situations.

• *As leaders with the necessary skills to bring people together and build trust*—Energizing and engaging citizens is a job that calls for an array of skills, from facilitating community discussions to resolving conflicts. By enhancing their skills in these and other areas, local officials can ensure they're ready to make the most of new opportunities for engagement.

BEST AND WORST PLACES TO LIVE IN THE UNITED STATES, 1997

	Best Places			*Worst Places*	
1.	Nashua, NH	(42)*	291.	Youngstown, OH	(224)
2.	Rochester, MN	(03)	292.	Waterloo, IA	(274)
3.	Monmouth/Ocean Counties, NJ	(38)	293.	Topeka, KS	(121)
4.	Punta Gorda, FL	(38)	294.	Billings, MT	(272)
5.	Portsmouth, NH	(44)	295.	Decatur, IL	(287)
6.	Manchester, NH	(50)	296.	Sioux City, IA	(288)
7.	Madison, WI	(01)	297.	Lima, OH	(296)
8.	San Jose, CA	(19)	298.	Anniston, AL	(226)
9.	Jacksonville, FL	(20)	299.	Rockford, IL	(300)
10.	Fort Walton Beach, FL	(18)	300.	Davenport, IA	(297)

* Last year's ranking in parentheses.
Source: Associated Press

Some Facts about City Government

(From *State Laws Governing Local Government and Administration*, a March 1993 pamphlet issued by the U.S. Advisory Commission on Intergovernmental Relations.)

Note: You don't have to quote these responses verbatim to show you know about city government. But they do provide some much-needed clarification about what goes on at this level.

- Municipal governments provide public services "for a specific concentration of population in a defined area." This is in addition to those services provided by counties and special districts.

- All fifty states have units of municipal government. Hawaii has the least (1); Illinois has the most (1,282).

- Generally an area must have a minimum population or density before it is eligible for incorporation (cityhood). The requirements are established by the states. For example, Alabama sets a 300-person population minimum. Florida requires an average of 1.5 persons per acre before a community can incorporate. Georgia requires that any new community seeking incorporation must be at least three miles from an existing municipality.

FUNDING THE CITY

In 1990, municipal revenues came from the following sources; property taxes, 50.9 percent; general and selective sales and gross receipts taxes, 27.9 percent; and individual and corporation taxes, 13.13 percent.

The three basic forms of municipal government are mayor-council, council-manager, and commission. Under the mayor-council system, the council is the legislative body. Councils usually have five to seven members, who may be elected at large or by district. In most cities, serving on the council is a part-time job. Some cities have direct election of mayors, while in others the mayoral position is rotated, usually for one year, among members of the council.

In larger cities, mayors tend to have considerable power, including the right to appoint commission members, the right to vote council actions, and budget authority. The mayors of New York, Chicago, and Los Angeles are nationally known political figures.

- The council-manager form, conceived in 1908, consists of an elected council and a professional city manager hired by the council. The council establishes tax rates, decides on the budget, and sets policy, which the manager implements. Approximately 2,500 municipalities operate under this style of government.

YOUR CITY GOVERNMENT

Los Angeles has 15 council members, or one for every 200,000–250,000 residents. Chicago has 50 aldermen, or one per every 55,000 residents.

- The commission form involves a nonpartisan elected commission of three to five members who perform legislative and executive duties. It is used in less than 5 percent of all municipalities.

The 1997 All-American Communities Selected by the National Civic League

1. Fremont, California

2. Aberdeen, Maryland

3. St. Joseph, Missouri

4. Asheville, North Carolina

5. Hillside Neighborhood (Colorado Springs), Colorado

6. Bronx County, New York

7. Aiken, South Carolina

8. Texas City, Texas

9. Bismarck, North Dakota

10. Statesville, North Carolina

COUNTY/TOWNSHIP GOVERNMENT

The next tier in the pyramid is reserved for county government. If you live in an unincorporated area, then county government plays a big role in your life, providing police and fire, trash collection, and other essential services. But if you live in a city, as most of us do, then you probably think of county government as somewhat obscure. It's out there doing something, but you're not quite sure what. Unlike city, state, and federal jurisdictions, it's difficult to know the precise boundaries of your county, which adds to the confusion.

You should be familiar with the county in which you live, and have some idea of the officials who constitute county government. You never know when you will be involved in a county issue. You need to be prepared.

"Traditionally, counties performed state mandated duties, which included assessment of property, record keeping (e.g., property and vital statistics), maintenance of rural roads, administration of election and judicial functions, and poverty relief."

—*from the National Association of Counties,* The Many Hats of County Government

Forms of County Government

Note: The Research Division of the National Association of Counties has a breakdown of the three basic forms of county government. Do you recognize your own county in any of these descriptions?

- *Commission*—Legislative authority and executive powers are exercised jointly by an elected commission of a board of supervisors. The legislative authority includes enacting ordinances and adopting budgets, while executive powers involve administering policies and appointing county employees.

- *Commission-Administrator*—The county board of commissioners appoints an administrator who serves at its pleasure. That person may be vested with a broad range of powers, including the authority to hire and fire department heads, and put together a budget.

- *Council-Executive*—A county executive is the chief administrative officer of this jurisdiction.

He/she typically has the authority to veto ordinances enacted by the county board and hire and fire department heads.

COUNTING COUNTIES

County government exists in 48 states (Connecticut and Rhode Island abolished counties as governmental units). Parts of Alaska, Montana, and South Dakota are not contained within counties. The county designation includes boroughs in Alaska and parishes in Louisiana.

—from the pamphlet State Laws Governing Local Government Structure and Administration, *March 1993, published by the U.S. Advisory Commission on Intergovernmental Relations*

President Clinton declared that "the era of big government is over." Nowhere is this more apparent than in the expanding duties of counties. Both the federal and state governments are turning more responsibilities over to county government. This is known as "devolution." However, counties are finding it hard to make devolution succeed.

History of County Government

Counties trace their roots to the English shire of a thousand years ago. Serving a dual function, the shire acted as the administrative arm of the national government as well as the citizen's local government. The structural form of the shire was adopted along the eastern seaboard of North America by the colonists and adapted to suit the diverse economic and geographic needs of each of the colonies.

When our national government was formed, the framers of the Constitution did not provide for local governments. Rather, they left the matter to the states. Subsequently, early state constitutions "generally conceptualized county government as an arm of the state. . . ."

Devolution works only if local government is up to the task, and counties in many states lack the funds, freedom and finesse to get the job done.

—Dana Milbank, Wall Street Journal, *June 5, 1997*

(Tanis Salant, "County Governments: An Overview," *Intergovernmental Perspective 17,* Winter 1991: 6.)

After World War I, population growth, suburban development, and the government reform movement strengthened the role of local governments. Those developments set the stage for post World War II urbanization. Changes in structure, greater autonomy from the states, rising revenues, and stronger political accountability ushered in a new era for county government. The counties began providing an ever widening range of services. These trends continue apace today.

> STATEHOUSE TO WHITE HOUSE
>
> In the past few decades, state governors have emerged as genuine presidential material. Three out of the past four presidents—Jimmy Carter, Ronald Reagan, and Bill Clinton—once served as governors.

"Today counties rapidly are moving into other areas, undertaking programs relating to child welfare, consumer protection, economic development, employment training, planning and zoning, and water quality, to name just a few."

—from the National Association of Counties, The Many Hats of County Government

County Characteristics

Forty-eight of the fifty states have operational county governments. Connecticut and Rhode Island are divided into geographic regions called counties, but they do not have functioning governments, as defined by the Census Bureau. Alaska and Louisiana call their county type governments boroughs and parishes, respectively.

STATE GOVERNMENT

We have already discussed the first two levels of government. Now we will look at the third level of the inverted pyramid, the first level with real muscle: state government. This level of government has notable control over your life. However, it does not have anywhere near as much power as the federal government has. Your state does not have the power to send troops to war, but it can levy taxes. Which means that the state government determines what you pay in state income tax, property tax, and even in sales tax. This power is necessary because the state funds many programs and institutions that affect you and your family. Public education, welfare, roads, and medical care are only a small percentage of vital programs provided by the states. When your state is broke, you will feel the pinch in many areas.

You can reach out and touch city government, but you are more dependent on state government.

STATES RANKED BY POPULATION, HIGHEST TO LOWEST

1. California	18. Wisconsin	35. West Virginia
2. Texas	19. Maryland	36. New Mexico
3. New York	20. Minnesota	37. Nebraska
4. Florida	21. Louisiana	38. Nevada
5. Pennsylvania	22. Alabama	39. Maine
6. Illinois	23. Arizona	40. Hawaii
7. Ohio	24. Kentucky	41. Idaho
8. Michigan	25. Colorado	42. New Hampshire
9. New Jersey	26. South Carolina	43. Rhode Island
10. Georgia	27. Oklahoma	44. Montana
11. North Carolina	28. Connecticut	45. South Dakota
12. Virginia	29. Oregon	46. Delaware
13. Massachusetts	30. Iowa	47. North Dakota
14. Indiana	31. Mississippi	48. Alaska
15. Washington	32. Kansas	49. Vermont
16. Missouri	33. Arkansas	50. District of Columbia
17. Tennessee	34. Utah	51. Wyoming

Source: The World Almanac of U.S. Politics

Some Differences Among States

- California is the only state that requires a super-majority in the Assembly and Senate—two-thirds approval—to pass a budget under any circumstance.

- Nebraska is the only state with a unicameral (one chamber) legislature. Nebraska has only a state senate.

- In most states the lower house is called the House of Representatives. But in California, Nevada, New York, and Wisconsin, it's called the Assembly; and in New Jersey it's called the General Assembly.

- California, Washington, and Wyoming have the lowest minimum age to be eligible to run for governor—eighteen. In most states, the age of eligibility is thirty; Oklahoma has the highest, thirty-one years old.

- At $130,000, the governor of New York has the highest annual salary of any governor in the nation. The lowest annual compensation is $55,310 for the governor of Montana.

- The Book of the States handed out awards for sixteen innovative programs selected by regional panels of state officials in 1994 and 1995. The programs covered were in health care, welfare, economic development, the environment, criminal justice, and government operations, including tax and child-support payment collection.

- "Operation Immunize." Kansas immunized more than 35,000 children during several days in April 1993, October 1993, and April 1994. This was the first mass immunization in the United States since the 1960s.

• New York's Partnership for Long-Term Care Program encourages middle-income, elderly people to secure nursing-home insurance. The cost of a policy for a sixty-five-year-old is approximately $1,400 per year. The intention was to prevent recipients from depleting or transferring their financial assets to qualify for New York's Medicaid long-term care program. The state's long-term Medicaid costs had reached $7 billion annually.

• A program in Washington called "Marketplace" consists of a database containing 35,000 businesses that are assigned eight-digit codes to identify their products and services. Marketplace software electronically matches the codes of trade leads to those of companies in the database. The volume of trade leads—2,000 per week—makes the information an important resource for companies of all sizes.

• Ohio's "Operation Crackdown" was responsible for the boarding-up of about one hundred houses in Cleveland and other areas around the state where drugs were being sold. Operation Crackdown assists local police departments in closing houses and apartment buildings used for drug sales. Its legitimacy is based on a seventy-seven-year-old law that allows law enforcement officials to close for one year houses creating a public nuisance.

The above information is taken from *The Book of the States,* volume 31, 1996–97 edition (Lexington, Kentucky: The Council of State Governments).

Unfunded Mandates

In the next part you'll read more about the history of federal-state conflicts. The struggles continue today. You may have heard about these; they've been in the news lately. The Republicans in the House, who came to power in 1995, made eliminating unfunded mandates one of their priorities. They felt states should not have to pay for programs imposed from Washington. (From time to time the federal government directs states to adopt a program—Motor Voter would be an example—but does not provide the dollars for implementation.)

Some Key Events in State Government–Federal Government Relations

See also chapter 8.

- McCullough v. Maryland—Supreme Court decision in 1819 that established federal law as the supreme law of the United States. The decision reinforced Article 6 of the Constitution.

- Doctrine of Nullification—In 1828 Vice President John C. Calhoun, from South Carolina, argued for the theory of nullification. This would have allowed a state to declare federal law null and void within that state unless three-quarters of the states ratified an amendment that granted Congress the power to enact the law.

- The Civil War

- The Interstate Commerce Commission Act (1887) and the Sherman Anti-Trust Act (1890)—Both acts gave the national government a greater role in the economy. The first strengthened Congress's role in the regulation of commerce among states, while the second allowed Congress to control the formation of business monopolies.

- Brown v. Board of Education, see chapter 17.

- New Federalism—In the 1970s President Nixon attempted to shift responsibility and authority for managing grants to states and local governments. Federal aid programs were consolidated into six special revenue-sharing programs.

Information in this section comes from the Congressional Research Service report American Federalism, 1776 to 1997: Significant Events. CRS is a branch of the Library of Congress.

One of the first bills passed and signed into law by the 104th Congress (1995–96) was called the Unfunded Mandates Reform Act. The Act was one of the provisions of the Republicans' Contract with America.

Under the legislation, committees considering bills with mandates must identify the mandates and submit them to the Congressional Budget Office for cost estimates. In addition, the bill requires the U.S. Advisory Commission on Intergovernmental Relations to study the role and impact of existing federal unfunded mandates, and of unfunded state mandates imposed on local governments.

The legislation is supposed to make Congress more aware of the burdens placed on states through unfunded mandates. In a few years we should have a good idea whether the law is having the desired effect.

CHAPTER RECAP

- Familiarity with the different levels of government saves you time and aggravation.

- Learn what agencies and powers are administered by each.

- County government usually consists of a board of supervisor or commissioners; city government is run by a council. The size of the governing bodies can vary.

- All states except Nebraska have a bicameral legislature.

- Federalism is the proper term for relations between Washington and the states.

- The Supreme Court case *McCullough v. Maryland*, the Doctrine of Nullification, and the Civil War established parameters of federal-state relations.

- The 104th Congress (1995–96) modified the rules covering unfunded mandates, federal programs in which states were required to put up the money.

The Feds

The average citizen may feel more in touch with local government than federal government (except perhaps at tax time). But the history of the republic shows a general tendency for federal government to take power from state government. You will read about the powers and duties of the federal government in detail in the chapters on the presidency, the Senate, the House of Representatives, federal legislation, and the Supreme Court.

The Presidency

So maybe you don't know *all* the presidents in the Twentieth century, but you can name those who served from Franklin Roosevelt to Bill Clinton. Not enough to run the "Presidents" category on *Jeopardy*, but a good start nevertheless.

THE CHIEF EXECUTIVE

The president is the closest thing we have in America to a political celebrity. He is a star. Have you ever been to a presidential rally, or seen the president speak before a large group? When he enters the room, or the arena, even veteran politicos get excited. The only ones remaining impassive at that moment are Secret Service agents.

You know something about the president, his family life, his rise to power, his political philosophy. This is the standard stuff of campaign biographies, newspaper articles, and Sunday talk shows. But you are less certain of what a president actually does. Not just the current president, but any president.

IN THIS CHAPTER:

- *The risks and rewards of being president*

- *The order of presidential succession*

- *Our system of primaries, conventions, and the electoral college*

- *The power of the presidency*

- *The president and the media*

- *A little bit of presidential history*

- *The vice presidency*

What are a president's specific powers? You are not alone in asking the question. Even some in the White House inner circle may not be entirely clear on all the president's duties and responsibilities. You will have a better understanding by the end of this chapter.

There is also the confusing process of electing a president; our system of caucuses, primaries, and nominating conventions is not easy to comprehend. You may have turned off the TV in frustration while trying to follow the week-by-week delegate count. This chapter will try to make sense of it all.

And finally the chapter will provide some offbeat facts and a few memorable scenes from the history of the presidency. These will impress your friends, or maybe get you that spot on *Jeopardy*.

If power equals money, then the presidency is not the most powerful job in the country. Not even close. At an annual salary of $200,000, one could argue that the U.S. president is underpaid, especially when compared with the money *corporate* presidents take home in the 1990s. When you also consider that no chief executive has had a raise since 1969, it could be said that he's underappreciated as well.

As is clear from table 2, (which can be found in appendix C, page 376) no man pursues the job to get rich. But certainly George Washington's $25,000 per year bought a lot a more in 1789 than Bill Clinton's $200,000 annual salary does now, two hundred years later.

You know very well that being president is not the safest occupation (table 3, appendix C, page 378). The record documents thirteen assassinations or attempted assassinations of presidents and presidential candidates since 1835. Though there were six incidents in the eighteen years between the killing of President Kennedy on November 22, 1963, and the wounding of President Reagan, three presidents were *assassinated* in the thirty-six years between 1865 and 1901.

For all the risks, disappointments, and humiliations there are still plenty of men, and an increasing number of women, who want to be president. Some of them have had this dream since high school. Take Bill Clinton. He was already running for president when, as a sixteen-year-old in 1963 he shook hands with John F. Kennedy at the White House. You've probably seen the famous photo of this handshake several times since Clinton was elected. Others such as Ronald Reagan only decided late in life that they wanted to be president.

> **ORDER OF PRESIDENTIAL SUCCESSION**
> 1. The Vice President
> 2. Speaker of the House
> 3. President pro tempore of the Senate
> 4. Secretary of State
> 5. Secretary of the Treasury
> 6. Continues through Cabinet to sixteenth—the Secretary of Education

Gerald Ford (1974–76) was the only man in history who served as chief executive but was never elected president or vice president. He had the good fortune to follow Spiro Agnew and Richard Nixon, both of whom resigned in disgrace. When Ford ran for president in 1976, he was defeated by Jimmy Carter.

You've probably heard the adage that, in America, anyone can grow up to become president. While that is technically true, a lot depends on preparation. Each of the forty-two presidents through Clinton either served in the military or in government prior to getting elected.

Your chances also increase if you happen to have been vice president. In the twentieth century, seven vice presidents (Theodore Roosevelt, Calvin Coolidge, Harry Truman, Lyndon Johnson, Gerald Ford, Richard Nixon, and George Bush) reached the top spot.

ELECTING A PRESIDENT

You have decided to run for president. You've talked it over with family and friends, and everyone agrees now is the time. After going to all that trouble, wouldn't it be embarrassing to discover that you don't meet the constitutionally mandated qualifications? Here is what you need to know before making a final decision.

A candidate for president has to be born in the U.S., can be no younger than 35, and must have resided in America for at least fourteen years. The same requirements apply for vice president. If these apply to you, you're ready to roll.

The Primaries

Having met the qualifications, you're prepared to enter the primaries, an exhausting process that, for all practical purposes, determines who will be a party's nominee. The official start of the primary season does not actually begin with a primary at all, but with the Iowa Caucus. The Iowa Caucus usually occurs during the second week of February in an election year. The New Hampshire Primary, which used to be the traditional opening of the campaign, is held about a week later.

In caucuses, party members or party leaders elect delegates to the national convention. By contrast, primaries are state-run elections open to all eligible voters.

THE FIRST PRIMARY

In 1904 Florida became the first state to use primaries as a way of selecting presidential delegates. Twelve years later, twenty state Democratic and Republican Parties had adopted this system.

As you race around the country seeking votes ("If it's Tuesday, it must be California"), you need to keep in mind that primaries serve two important functions. For both Democrats and Republicans, primaries have become the prime tool for assigning delegates to the nominating convention. This is their reason for being.

However, equally important is the part played by the national media during the primary season. Reporters love to keep a running tab on who's up and who's down. They are merely filling a need; voters enjoy keeping score in their living rooms. Primary elections can be as much fun as going to a baseball game.

You may have laughed out loud watching journalists change their minds from week to week. In 1996, for example, Pat Buchanan, Steve Forbes, and finally, Bob Dole, were all "awarded" the Republican nomination by the media during the early part of the primary season.

If you've survived the primaries, it's on to the nominating conventions. Conventions are a blast for political junkies. Where else can you experience four solid days of the leading politicians, journalists, and consultants gathered in one place at one time to discuss politics? This may well be the only reason to watch conventions anymore. The countdown to the nomination is anticlimactic.

The Conventions

Since 1952 conventions have always occurred in the July or August preceding the presidential election. Since 1932, the party out of power has held its convention first. The day-to-day schedule has remained consistent for both parties over several decades.

- Day one—The keynote address is delivered.

- Day two—Adoption of the rules and party platform.

- Day three—The names of the candidates for president are placed in nomination, and the delegates vote for their choice.

- Day four—The vice president is nominated, and he or she and the presidential candidate deliver their acceptance speeches.

What has changed from convention to convention is the total number of delegates.

The Most Powerful Job in the World

Now you've been elected president. As was noted earlier, the salary will not make you rich. The real money comes later, after you have left the White House: speaking fees, advances for memoirs, membership on prestigious corporate boards. Since a president is limited by the Constitution to two four-year terms in office (the Twenty-Second Amendment, ratified by the states in 1951), you will not have to wait long to embark on your second career.

In the meantime console yourself with the thought that you have the most powerful job in the world. *Why?* you ask. As leader of the strongest nation—militarily and economically—in the world, you have a lot at your disposal. In your role as Commander in Chief of the Army, Navy (including the U.S. Marine Corps), and Air Force, you are not only in charge of a well-armed fighting force, but you have final say on the use of nuclear weapons. But no president can govern successfully without the cooperation of Congress.

Presidential Election Process

Now that you're the nominee, you and your vice presidential running mate will automatically appear on the ballot in all fifty states. This assumes, of course, that you're either a Democrat or a Republican. Minor-party candidates must satisfy different requirements per state, such as collecting signatures on a petition or having received a sufficient number of votes in the most recent statewide election. Some states allow for write-in votes for president.

Presidents Who Were Not Inaugurated

- *John Tyler*—Vice President John Tyler became president upon William Henry Harrison's death one month after his inauguration. U.S. Circuit Court Judge William Cranch administered the oath to Mr. Tyler at his residence in the Indian Queen Hotel on April 6, 1841.

- *Millard Fillmore*—Judge William Cranch administered the executive oath of office to Vice President Millard Fillmore on July 10, 1850, in the Hall of the House of Representatives. President Zachary Taylor had died the day before.

> **ELECTING A PRESIDENT**
>
> *The popular vote awards electors to the candidate who receives the higher percentage. The number of electors in each state is determined by the number of congressional districts plus the two senators. In California, for example, there are 54 electors: 52 congressional districts plus 2. The electoral college, which consists of all fifty states and the District of Columbia, currently has 538 members when constituted.*
>
> *Pay close attention to this next bit.*
>
> *On the first Monday after the second Wednesday in the December after the November election (that's how it's designated!) the electors vote separately for president and vice president. The electoral college meets in fifty-one electoral colleges, usually in the state capital, to make its selection. In the unlikely event that no candidate for president or vice president has received a majority, the House of Representatives, voting by states, elects the president, and the Senate, voting as individuals, elects the vice president. A few weeks later, on January 20, the president is inaugurated.*
>
> *Five men in American history have served as president without experiencing that special event.*

- *Andrew Johnson*—On April 15, 1865, after visiting the wounded and dying President Lincoln in a house across the street from Ford's Theatre, the vice president returned to his rooms at Kirkwood House. A few hours later he received the cabinet and Chief Justice Salmon Chase in his rooms to take the executive oath of office.

- *Chester A. Arthur*—On September 20, 1881, upon the death of President Garfield, Vice President Arthur received a group at his home in New York City to take the oath of office, administered by New York Supreme Court Judge John R. Brady. The next day he again took the oath of office, administered by Chief Justice Morrison Waite, in the Vice President's Office in the Capitol in Washington, D.C.

- *Gerald R. Ford*—The Minority Leader of the House of Representatives became vice president upon the resignation of Spiro Agnew, under the process of the Twenty-Fifth Amendment to the Constitution. When President Nixon resigned on August 9, 1974, Vice President Ford took the executive oath of office, administered by Chief Justice Warren Burger, in the East Room of the White House.

WARTS AND ALL

You should not expect a free ride from the press. Other presidents have made that mistake.

Since the assassination of President Kennedy, many events and images have made presidents seem confused, clumsy, or weak. The American public has witnessed Johnson agonizing over Vietnam, Nixon agonizing over Watergate and lashing out at the press, Ford tripping and falling in public, Carter hesitant and uncertain during the Iran hostage crisis, Reagan straining to hear questions and getting his facts wrong, Bush getting sick in the lap of Japanese dignitaries, and Clinton changing his mind on policy questions and confessing embarrassing details of his personal life. In an age when the President's every step—and misstep—is recorded by the media, the job itself becomes almost secondary. We know, or think we know, a lot about our presidents. But do we?

ASSEMBLING A CABINET

The closest you'll get to a honeymoon with the press is the period between being elected (first Tuesday in November) and the inauguration on January 20. The media will be so busy trying to figure out whom you will pick to serve in your administration that they won't have much time to cover the unpleasant stuff. You'll have a little breathing room here— enjoy it because it won't last. Once you've picked your administration the press will begin shifting around again.

There are few things you do as president that will attract more public attention than picking the members of the cabinet. Journalists have a great time with the process, floating names and investigating backgrounds. A reporter with well-placed administration sources can scoop his colleagues and reveal the name of the person selected for a particular position.

You will probably enjoy the process as well, as long as it does not drag on too long. You get to interview a cross-section of the more ambitious and/or intelligent men and women in America, all of whom are dying to work for you in the White House.

Here's some history:

The first Congress created the Departments of State, Treasury and War, and established the Office of the Attorney General. In the subsequent two hundred–plus years of the presidency the cabinet has grown to fourteen departments, the newest being Veterans' Affairs. The backlash against big government probably means that few, if any, departments will be added to the cabinet over the next several years.

The cabinet currently consists of these departments:

- Agriculture

- Commerce

- Defense

- Education
- Energy
- Health and Human Services
- Housing and Urban Development
- Interior
- Justice
- Labor
- State
- Transportation
- Treasury
- Veterans' Affairs

The Clinton administration has accorded cabinet-level rank to the Chief of Staff to the President, the Chairman of the Council of Economic Advisors, the U.S. Representative to the United Nations, the U.S. Trade Representative, the Administrator of the Environmental Protection Agency, and the Director of the Office of Management and Budget.

Other Assistants to the President

These are a lot of titles to remember. And more are being added all the time, in 1939, the White House and Executive Office of the President was formally established, which includes a number of the posts that have attained cabinet rank.

In the spring your nominees for cabinet positions will undergo the confirmation process. These hearings can be either deferential, hostile, or matter-of-fact. Article II, Section 2 of the Constitution gives the Senate the power

WHITE HOUSE AND EXECUTIVE OFFICE OF THE PRESIDENT

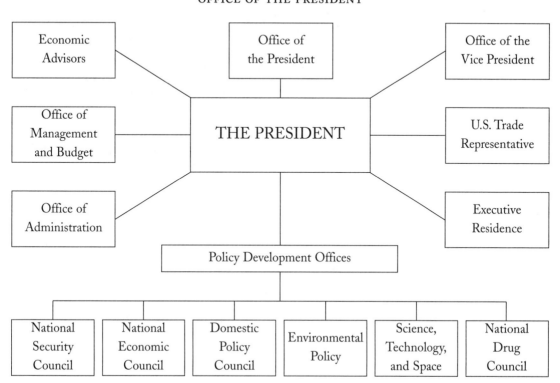

Source: Our American Government, *pamphlet, 1993*

to confirm the nomination of public officials and consent to the ratification of treaties.

Most confirmation hearings go well; the appointee is confirmed and the process attracts little attention. Those that don't often provide the leader of the opposition with national exposure. A recent example is Republican senator Richard Shelby of Alabama, who became widely known in early 1997 when he led the attack against Anthony Lake, President Clinton's nominee for director of the Central Intelligence Agency. Lake, to avoid unpleasantness, subsequently withdrew his name from consideration.

The Presidency and Foreign Affairs

As the head of state, a president naturally meets other heads of state. Given America's global reach, this means that a great deal of his or her week is spent talking with foreign leaders who have made their way to Washington.

This part of the job is ceremonial and political. Here and abroad the president simultaneously represents the United States and represents the interests of the United States. It must be an exhilarating feeling.

You might be surprised at the few constitutional duties required of a president. Much of what he or she does is either ceremonial or political in nature.

Article II, Section 2 of the Constitution defines the powers of the president. It's a short list:

1. The President is Commander-in-Chief of the Military.

2. The President has the power to make treaties, which must be confirmed by a two-thirds vote of the Senate.

3. The President appoints ambassadors, other public ministers and counsuls, judges of the Supreme Court, and all other officers of the United States. These appointees are subject to Senate confirmation by a simple majority vote.

4. The President shall give Congress information on the State of the Union. (The State of the Union Address is delivered annually by the President to the Congress.)

5. On extraordinary occasions, the President may convene both houses of Congress.

Article I, Section 7 of the Constitution specifies that no bill passed by Congress becomes law until it's signed by the president. If the president chooses to veto the bill,

Congress can override by a two-thirds vote in the House of Representatives and the Senate. (See the United States Constitution in appendix B, page 343.)

Key Moments in Presidential History

One way to study the history of America is to study the history of the American presidency. You will discover that the role of the president has changed according to trends, events, or threats of the time. Here are some key moments in presidential history to illustrate the point:

- *The establishment of the Monroe Doctrine.* In 1823 James Monroe, the fifth president of the United States, inserted in his State of the Union Message to Congress the idea that "the American continents, by the free and independent condition which they have assumed and maintained, are henceforth not to be considered as subjects for future colonization by any European powers." This constituted the Monroe Doctrine, which at one time every child in America was required to learn in school. In case you've forgotten, the Monroe Doctrine was a response to reports that European powers might have designs on Latin America.

  Though the Monroe Doctrine was never confirmed by Congress nor enforced by its author, it represented a major development in the growth of the presidency.

- *The Civil War and its aftermath.* Abraham Lincoln is generally regarded as the best president in American history. Lincoln's leadership during the greatest crisis in American history—the Civil War—is the primary reason for his status.

  Andrew Johnson, who assumed the office following Abraham Lincoln's assassination on April 14, 1865, was a much less popular leader than Lincoln.

His career gives us an excellent example of what can happen when a president is overwhelmed by Congress. In 1866 Johnson vetoed the Civil Rights Act, which declared blacks to be citizens under the law. An angry Senate and an equally angry House of Representatives both voted to override Johnson's veto, marking the first time in American history such action had been taken on an issue of importance.

But this was a minor skirmish compared to what happened two years later, when the House of Representatives voted 126–47 to impeach President Johnson. Many members of the House from Northern states were engaged in a running battle with Andrew Johnson over civil rights and the direction of the country after the Civil War. The main issue in the impeachment proceedings was Johnson's unilateral firing of Secretary of War Edwin M. Stanton. In so doing, he disregarded the requirement for Senate authorization.

A total of eleven articles of impeachment were brought against Johnson in the House. After a six-week trial, the Senate voted not to impeach. The Johnson episode has served as a warning of what can happen when the relationship between Congress and the presidency is consumed by hate, mistrust, and a desire for vengeance.

In 1998, President Clinton became the second chief executive in history to be impeached. After a lengthy Senate trial he was acquitted. The Clinton trial was also filled with acrimony. If you become president, be careful!

Facts about the Presidents

Who is the youngest man to ever assume the presidency? You would probably guess John F. Kennedy. But Kennedy, forty-three when he took over in January 1961, is the country's youngest *elected* president. Vice President Teddy Roosevelt was 42 when President William McKinley died from an assassin's bullet on September 14, 1901.

TR and JFK are linked in another way that is important to the history of the presidency. Both men were masters at wooing—some might say manipulating—the press. TR took advantage of the introduction of large-circulation newspapers and popular magazines, while JFK arrived just in time for the television age. Though his predecessor, Dwight Eisenhower, held taped press conferences, Kennedy was the first president to answer reporters' questions live on TV.

Since then, televised presidential press conferences have become a standard feature of American political life. Press conferences rarely make history, although you may recall Richard Nixon's declaration, "I am not a crook," during the height of the Watergate scandal.

As great as were the communication skills of Teddy Roosevelt and John Kennedy, it could be argued that Ronald Reagan's were even better. Of course, Reagan was a movie actor, which gave him a distinct advantage—especially in front of the camera.

In the mid-1960s, long before he became president, Reagan began delivering what would come to be known within his circle as "The Speech." Though the theme of The Speech is accepted wisdom today, it was not so in 1964, when Lyndon Johnson's activist government was immensely popular

WHAT TO CALL THE PRESIDENT

You are going to love this.

In the early days of the United States, a Senate committee recommended that the president be addressed as "His Highness, the President of the United States of America, and Protector of the Rights of the Same." That regal-sounding title lasted only until George Washington's first inaugural speech, when the House in formal reply called him "the President of the United States." Today the proper form of address has been shortened to "Mr. President," although many people have referred to the man who won in 1992 with a simple "Bill." Once you get elected, you can decide how formal, or informal, you would like to be.

When writing the president, you should address the letter to "The President, The White House. . ." (see also appendix E, page 397).

around the county. But Reagan kept at it, and by the late 1970s his ideas had gained wide support. In 1980 Reagan was elected president in a landslide over Jimmy Carter.

THE VICE PRESIDENCY

Let's return to your dream of being nominated for president. Now the time has arrived to pick the number two person on the ticket. One thing's for sure: your vice president better have a sense of humor. Though they are technically "a heartbeat away" from the presidency, vice presidents are often viewed as mere appendages to the White House. Like children, they are supposed to be seen and not heard.

Even Al Gore, widely viewed as one of the more involved, intelligent, and influential vice presidents in U.S. history, frequently cracked jokes at his own expense. Gore made fun of his job as much as he did his stiff public image. If he were to be elected president Gore would probably be much less inclined toward self-deprecating humor.

The vice president's most important constitutional duty is to cast tiebreaking votes in the Senate. Unless, of course, something happens to the president.

The Twenty-Fifth Amendment to the Constitution, ratified in 1967, explicitly states, "In the case of the removal of the President from office or of his death or resignation, the Vice President shall become President." The amendment also established procedures to be followed in the case of presidential disability.

CHAPTER RECAP

- A president is more—much more—than a political celebrity.

- Being president has its good points, but the salary is not one of them.

- Our method of electing a president can be a confusing maze of caucuses, primaries, conventions, and electoral votes. Learning the system can help you understand American politics.

- One of the most important tasks of a president takes place soon after the election: picking the cabinet.

- Presidential powers are very succinctly defined in Article II of the Constitution.

- The Twenty-Fifth Amendment, ratified in 1967, specifies when the vice president assumes the presidency.

The Senate

Had you lived and died in the nineteenth century, you would not have had the opportunity to vote in United States Senate elections. From the time the country was founded until 1912 senators were elected by their home state legislature. At the turn of the century, however, reformers successfully argued that this method of selection was inherently corrupt. On May 13, 1912, Congress offered the Seventeenth Amendment to the Constitution, which among other things specified that senators would be elected by a vote of the people. The amendment was ratified by the necessary three-fourths of the states in 1913.

IN THIS CHAPTER:

• *The power and prestige of the Senate*

• *The function, duties, and responsibilities of the Senate*

• *Confirmation hearings and treaty ratification*

• *Use of the filibuster*

• *Four famous senators*

DIRECT ELECTION

The title of chapter 1 is "Your Vote Counts." Prior to adoption of the Seventeenth Amendment your vote didn't count, at least in the case of electing United States senators. Yet the creators of the Constitution had a specific reason for keeping Senate elections out of the hands of what we would today call "the masses."

Since the senators were elected by the state legislatures for six-year terms, since the president was chosen by an electoral college, and since the judges were appointed, no part of the government was exposed to direct public pressure except the lower house of Congress.

—*Henry Steele Commager and Allan Nevins,*
A Pocket History of the United States

WHAT IS CONGRESS?

You may have been misled by the phrase "member of Congress," which is frequently used in newspapers and on television. In that case, "member of Congress," along with the titles "Congressman" and "Congresswoman," means a person serving in the House of Representatives. That title is never applied to senators, although both the Senate and the House of Representatives make up the U.S. Congress. The title for a senator is, simply, "Senator." A member of the House can either be referred to as "Representative X" or "Congressman/woman X."

Clearly the architects of the Constitution believed that having the legislature pick a state's two senators was the lesser of evils. Today most of us would argue the opposite, so ingrained is the idea of voting as a true expression of the popular will.

You've no doubt noticed that nothing on the above list has changed except the election of senators. And even in that instance, the six-year term still applies.

THE STYLE OF THE SENATE

The U.S. Senate has traditionally been the more "deliberative" of the two chambers in Congress. This is consistent with the Founders' intent. From the beginning each state in the Union was allowed two senators, which was intended as a way to spread power and influence evenly throughout the country. In the Senate, Rhode Island has the same voting clout as California.

This is different from the House of Representatives, where seats are apportioned on the basis of each state's population. In the House, California has many more members than Rhode Island; New York dwarfs Wyoming.

> **FROM SENATE TO HOUSE**
>
> *In the last fifty or so years, only the Florida Democrat Claude Pepper began his career in the Senate and ended it in the House. Pepper was a senator from 1936 through 1951, and a member of the House from 1963 until his death in 1989.*

However, this does not mean California or New York always gets its way in the House. Division between Republicans and Democrats, the actions of powerful committee chairs whom may not come from the big states, and other factors, can "level the playing field." (This is an expression people in politics use all the time.)

So if you live in one of the smaller states, don't despair, if you live in one of the bigger states, don't gloat. You will find more in the chapter on the House of Representatives.

As you follow the political scene, you'll notice that the natural progression for a politician in Congress is from the House to the Senate. Ambitious representatives run for Senate; ambitious senators run for president or, maybe, governor. The reasons are clear. A representative represents a district, a senator represents a state. A senator is part of a club with 100 members; a representative is one of 435. It's all about acquiring more power and more fame.

Other than the president, the Speaker of the House is the only political figure whose stature equals that of powerful senators like Jesse Helms of North Carolina or Daniel Patrick Moynihan of New York.

> **VICE PRESIDENT AND PRESIDENT**
>
> *The vice president of the United States is also president of the Senate. This is one of his official duties. On rare occasions you will see the VP cast the deciding vote to break a 50–50 tie. Beyond that, he is not much of a factor in Senate proceedings.*

There is no speaker of the Senate. The Senate has a majority and a minority leader, reflecting which of the two parties is on top. The majority leader is the most influential figure in the Senate because, in theory, he (there never has been a she) controls the most votes. I say "in theory" because neither Democratic nor Republican members are united on every issue.

Despite the fact that senators serve six-year terms, as opposed to the two-year terms for their colleagues in the House, they run as hard for reelection. While the Senate may be more sedate than the House during the congressional session, Senate campaigns can be as vicious as campaigns at any level. At the same time, they are more expensive than any other campaign except the presidential race.

You may recall that in 1994 a one-term Republican congressman from California named Michael Huffington spent $28 million of his own money in an effort to defeat the incumbent, Dianne Feinstein. Feinstein was forced to raise several thousand dollars a day to keep pace. In the end she was barely reelected.

The nasty tone of modern Senate campaigns runs counter to an 1834 appraisal (see below) of that body by the famous student of American democracy, Alexis de Tocqueville:

> The Senate is composed of eloquent advocates, distinguished generals, wise magistrates, and statesmen of note, whose arguments would do honor to the most remarkable parliamentary debates of Europe.

But who could have predicted how campaigns have evolved?

You should know what your senator does. Not on a daily basis—you can find that out from the newspaper, or by checking voting records on the Internet. But what does the Constitution say?

Constitutional Responsibilities
and Powers of a U.S. Senator

Articles I and II of the Constitution define the role of senator:

- To serve in the United States Senate a person must be at least thirty years old, be a United States citizen for at least nine years, and be a resident of the state where the election occurred.

- The first impeachment trial in American history involved the first President Johnson—Andrew Johnson—and was discussed in chapter 7 (see page 117).

> ### THE LAWMAKERS
>
> *The Senate and the House are most involved in making legislation. When a bill goes to the president for his signature, it has been passed by both houses of Congress. In chapter 10 you will learn much more about the legislative process in Washington.*

- The second impeachment trial of an American president took place in the winter of 1999. On February 12, 1999, President Clinton was acquitted by the Senate on charges of obstruction of justice and perjury. As all of America learned during the trial, it takes a vote of two-thirds of the Senate to convict a president. The final tally in the Clinton trial came nowhere close on either charge.

- The Senate has the power to approve or deny treaties made by the president with foreign countries. Treaties require a two-thirds vote of the senators for approval.

- The Senate has the power to confirm or deny all presidential appointments. This includes ambassadors, judges, and members of the cabinet. Confirmations require a majority vote of the full

Senate for approval. The Senate's role in nominations is called the power to advise and consent.

Treaties

Politics and politicians are relevant to your life. One of the purposes of this book is to provide you with several proofs of that. With that in mind, consider one of the most famous events in the history of the United States Senate, indeed in the history of the United States of America. It occurred on March 19, 1920. On that day the Senate voted 49–35 to reject the Treaty of Versailles, the peace negotiated between the victors and Germany after World War I.

A consequence was that the U.S. would not become a member of the League of Nations, the institution proposed by President Woodrow Wilson to prevent a second world war. You may have heard your college history professor argue that America's refusal to join the League was one of the factors that convinced Adolf Hitler to launch a series of provocative acts in the 1930s that culminated in World War II.

Setting aside the historical issues, the rejection of Versailles illustrates the crucial role the Senate plays in American foreign policy. The Constitution requires that the Senate advise and consent to treaties and presidential nominations.

The fate of the Treaty of Versailles was not unique, as shown by table 1 (appendix C, page 375).

In 1997, President Clinton had to work extremely hard to convince the Senate to approve the Chemical Weapons Treaty. It was ironic that former senator Bob Dole, Clinton's opponent in the 1996 presidential campaign, intervened at the last minute to save the day for the administration.

The Drama of the Senate

Do the names Robert Bork, Anthony Lake, John Tower, or Clarence Thomas mean anything to you?

What these men share is the bitterness of their confirmation hearings. Only Thomas was confirmed—and the vote was extremely close. The consideration of a controversial nominee may be the best window on the workings and personalities of the United States Senate. These events are often carried on cable; in the case of Thomas, the major networks provided coverage as well.

Maybe you remember the 1987 hearings on the nomination of Robert Bork to the United States Supreme Court. Bork was defeated because of his views on abortion and race. He offended the liberal members of the Senate, especially Ted Kennedy.

After Bork came Tower, who in 1989 was denied the post of Secretary of Defense in the Bush administration because he was said to be overly fond of liquor and women.

Two years later it was the famous, or infamous, Thomas hearings. President Bush nominated Thomas to the Supreme Court. The hearings were getting the usual amount of press attention until Anita Hill was called to testify before the Senate Judiciary Committee. Then all hell broke loose. You probably remember when Hill accused Thomas of lewd and crude behavior. In the end, Thomas launched a skillful counterattack that barely saved his nomination.

In 1997, President Clinton nominated Anthony Lake to be director of the Central Intelligence Agency. For a variety of reasons, Lake was not a popular figure. After days of hostile questioning from the Senate Select Committee on Intelligence, he asked that his name be removed from consideration.

It is possible, however, to go through the confirmation process, live to tell about it, and even have a laugh at its expense. Robert Reich, the witty and diminutive ex–Secretary of Labor during Bill Clinton's first term, saw humor in having to face his Senate inquisitors:

The ability to extend debate at will, to "filibuster," enables a senator to delay the final vote on a measure, or even to prevent it altogether. Filibusters can be broken only by negotiation or through the use of a formal procedure known as "cloture."A successful cloture motion requires at least a three-fifths vote—or sixty senators.

—Our American
Government, *1993 edition,
published by the U.S.
Government Printing
Office*

> . . . The Senate confirmation hearing is not about answering questions, it's about showing respect; the respect of the executive branch for the legislative branch, the respect of any new government official who has to be confirmed; [you] must genuflect, salute, bow, scrape, tell them you respect them.
>
> —The Hill, *May 5, 1997*

You won't hear as much about the Senate confirming or rejecting presidential appointments to the federal bench—district and appellate. Yet during the Clinton years this became a highly contentious political process. The Republican-controlled Senate deferred votes on many of Clinton's appointees.

With divisive issues such as affirmative action and immigrants' rights being decided in federal courts, politicians from both parties are on guard for the "wrong kind" of judicial activism. (Liberals don't want right-wing judges, conservatives don't want left-wing judges.)

A senator who votes to confirm a controversial judge could get punished by the voters in the next election. Thus the reason for caution.

The House of Filibusters

In the film *Mr. Smith Goes to Washington*, you might remember the scene in which a senator (Jimmy Stewart) collapses in front of his colleagues after an exhausting speech. This is the dramatic end to a filibuster.

You see now why the Senate has the reputation for being the more deliberative body in Congress. In the House filibusters are not permitted. Debate within that chamber is by comparison snappy and to the point.

In 1957 South Carolina senator Strom Thurmond talked consecutively for *24 hours and 18 minutes*—a still-standing record—against a civil-rights bill.

Something else about Thurmond. If his name sounds familiar to you, it should; Thurmond was reelected to the Senate in 1996 at the age of *ninety-three.* On May 25, 1997, Thurmond

AVERAGE NUMBER OF FILIBUSTERS BY YEAR

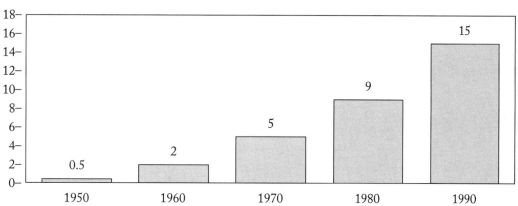

Source: House Democratic Study Group Special Report, "A Look at the Senate Filibuster," June 13, 1994

became the longest-serving senator in the nation's history, according to the Senate Historical Office. Thurmond has said he hopes to still be in the Senate when he reaches the age of one hundred. If he makes it, he would set another record: the first politician to hit the century mark while in office.

You don't hear much about filibusters these days, though they are of greater frequency but shorter duration than in the past. They don't make senators like Thurmond anymore.

You have no doubt read or heard about the tremendous increase in the cost of running for president. Commentators seem as fixated on dollars as they are on the policy positions of the candidates. Even business executives must at times be envious of the ability of top contenders to solicit funds at a moment's notice.

What's not given much publicity is the increase in the number of participants in the Republican and Democratic

National Conventions. (A comic might say that the rise in campaign contributions is merely keeping pace with inflation—you now have to buy more delegates in order to get the nomination. Please understand that's only a joke.

NUMBER OF DELEGATES FROM 1984 TO 1996

	Democrats	*Republicans*
1984	3933	2235
1988	4164	2277
1992	4287	2207
1996	4329	1984

Source: The Republican and Democratic National Committees provided figures for 1984 and 1988; figures for 1992 and 1996 came from final roll-call votes. Thanks to the Congressional Research Service for the comparison.

You can see that from 1988 to 1996 the Republican delegate count showed an apparent decline but the number of alternates increased.

FOUR FAMOUS SENATORS

Famous presidents are better known than famous senators, and famous senators are better known than famous members of the House. Several senators have made an indelible mark on the institution and the country. Here are four:

John C. Calhoun

John C. Calhoun of South Carolina went from vice president to senator, which some might consider a promotion. Calhoun resigned from the vice presidency in 1832, largely because he and President Andrew Jackson disagreed over the question of states' rights. Calhoun was a vocal supporter of the Doctrine of Nullification, which maintained that states had the right to annul federal laws they considered illegal.

As a senator, Calhoun argued the question of states' rights with formidable counterpart Senator Daniel Webster of Massachusetts. The Calhoun-Webster debates are among the most dramatic in American history. While the issue of states' rights—though not the Doctrine of Nullification—is still with us today, our current crop of senators would be hard pressed to match the coruscating oratory of Calhoun and Webster.

In the 1840s, Calhoun was a strong proponent of slavery—he fought efforts to prohibit slavery in new states and territories. Beside a brief stint (1844–45) as Secretary of State under President John C. Tyler, Calhoun remained in the Senate until his death in 1850. During his final weeks in the chamber, he was arguing for the South's secession from the Union over the slavery question. Had he lived ten more years, he would have seen his dream come true.

Robert Taft

A Republican senator from Ohio, Robert Taft is sometimes confused with his father, William Howard Taft, who was president of the United States from 1909 to 1913. The younger Taft entered the Senate in 1939, the year World War II began in Europe. He became an isolationist, arguing in essence that European problems were not America's. He spoke against the Lend-Lease Act, through which the United States provided arms to its allies during the early stages of the war.

After 1945, when the Soviet Union replaced Nazi Germany as America's principal antagonist, Taft remained true to his Weltanshauung worldview. He was critical of the North Atlantic Treaty Organization (NATO), which was created as a Western buffer against Soviet expansion.

He argued that Europe should provide more arms and soldiers for its own defense, a view that was clearly ahead of its time (by the 1970s this idea had become popular with politicians and the general public in the U.S.).

Taft ran for the Republican nomination for president in 1940, 1948, and 1952. He fell short each time, the last to Dwight D. Eisenhower. A year later Taft died at the age of sixty-four.

Lyndon Johnson

At the end of his presidency (1963–69) Lyndon Johnson was a weak, beaten man consumed by the war in Vietnam. This LBJ in no way resembles the strong, confident, and remarkably successful Senate majority leader in the 1950s.

In the Senate, Johnson charmed, bullied, and cajoled elected officials into accepting his position. He explained it like this:

> The only power available to the [Senate] leader is the power of persuasion. There is no patronage; no power to discipline; no authority to fire senators like a president can fire members of his cabinet.
> —Congress A to Z, *Second Edition*

Johnson's greatest triumph was passage in 1957 of the first civil-rights bill since Reconstruction. His success was the more remarkable considering the Southern part of the Democratic Party was controlled by segregationists. Seven years later, President Johnson delivered another political miracle when he convinced Congress to approve the Voting Rights Act and the Civil Rights Act.

Robert C. Byrd

First elected in 1958, Robert C. Byrd, Democrat of West Virginia, may well be the best friend the United States

Senate ever had. Byrd is a constant advocate on behalf of the institution. In 1997 he led a legal challenge against the line-item veto. He believed it would increase the power of the presidency at the expense of the Senate.

Byrd's affection for the Senate is also expressed in other ways. He was author of *The Senate, 1789–1989* (Washington: Government Printing Office, 1989–94), a four volume series that includes *Addresses on the History of the United States Senate* (Volumes 1 and 2); *Classic Speeches, 1830–1993* (Volume 3); and *Historical Statistics, 1789–1992* (Volume 4). From 1959–85 he compiled an extraordinary 98.13 percent voting attendance record, although it should be pointed out it's much easier to get to D.C. from West Virginia than from most other states in the nation.

Byrd is refreshingly candid about what it means to serve in Congress. During the 1980s, when politicians from both parties were assailing Washington and big government, Byrd's campaign issued a booklet that listed at least fifty projects in West Virginia for which he had procured funding.

THE ORIGIN OF THE SENATE

"Senate" comes from the Latin *senatus*. According to the Oxford Companion to Classical Literature, during the Roman Empire "the senate" was the council of kings that survived the abolition of the monarchy. The first Roman senate had 300 members; Julius Caesar increased that number to 900.

Owing to its functions and permanence, the senate was the real head of the state. It prepared legislative proposals to be brought before the people, and its resolutions, called *decreta*, or more commonly, *senatus consulta*, had some measure of effective if not legal authority. . . .

It exercised judicial powers through its right of appointing special courts of inquiry. It administered the finances, assigned magistrates to provinces, and dealt with foreign relations. It also supervised the practice of the state religion.

—M. C. Howatson, editor, Oxford Companion to Classical Literature, new edition, New York: Oxford University Press, 1898, page 515

You can see that other than the last part, the Roman senate was not that different in its responsibilities from the United States Senate.

And you thought we took all our ideas from the English.

President pro tempore from 1989 to 1994, and majority leader from 1977 to 1980 and 1987–88, Byrd is one of only three men in the history of the United States to have been elected to seven 6-year terms in the Senate.

A Few Senate Web Sites

- http://www.senate.gov (official Senate site)

- http://www.senate.gov/~dpc (Senate Democratic Policy Committee)

- http://www.senate.gov/~rpc (Senate Republican Policy Committee)

- http://www.senate.gov/committee/judiciary.html (Senate Judiciary Committee)

- http://www.senate.gov/committee/appropriations html (Senate Appropriations Committee)

- http://www.senate.gov/committee/foreign.html (Senate Foreign Relations Committee)

CHAPTER RECAP

- Until 1912, senators were elected by the state Legislatures.

- Direct election of senators was mandated by the Seventeenth Amendment to the Constitution.

- In recent years, Senate campaigns have become extremely expensive and extremely nasty.

- The responsibilities and powers of the Senate are defined in Articles I and II of the Constitution.

- Senate confirmation hearings have become a political spectacle since Robert Bork's in 1987.

- Calhoun, Taft, LBJ, and Byrd are four of the most famous and powerful senators in American history.

The House of Representatives

*W*hen you watch the proceedings of the House of Representatives on C-SPAN, then switch to coverage of the Senate on C-SPAN 2, you will notice a difference in tone and pace. The men and women of the House tend to speak more quickly and loudly than their colleagues in the Senate.

THE LIVELY HOUSE

From the inception of the United States, the House of Representatives was conceived as the "rowdier" of the two branches of Congress. You will recall from the previous chapter that for 130 years senators were selected by members of the legislature. This was supposed to be the gentleman's way (women did not yet have the vote) of transferring power.

Members of the House, however, have always been chosen by a vote of the people. You can imagine what the electorate was like in the eighteenth and nineteenth centuries: all-male, many of whom were cowboys, farmers, military veterans, and pioneers. These were the men who fought the Indians, served in the Civil War, and would die at the Alamo. In other words, tough. And the men then—like men and women today—voted for representatives who would fight for their interests in Washington. The House in the early days of this country must have been quite a collection of characters.

HOUSE OF REPRESENTATIVES

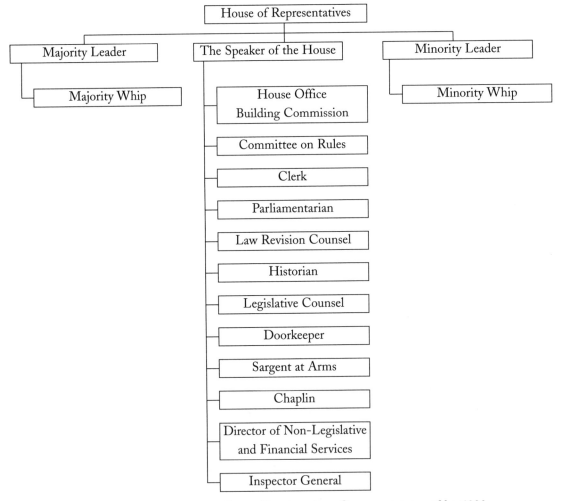

Source: Our American Government, *pamphlet, 1993*

• House members serve two-year terms, as opposed to the six-year terms for Senators. This is another reason the House is the more intense of the two chambers. Our representatives have to make their mark fast, because another election looms just around the corner.

• With 435 members, a total fixed by law, the House comes closer than the Senate or the executive branch of government to representing the diversity of America. You have the Black Caucus, the Hispanic Caucus, and the Women's Caucus, and these are just the best-known. There are members who congregate on the basis of geographic interests, such as those from farm states, or those representing urban America. Indeed, you can listen to an hour of floor coverage on C-SPAN and hear accents from every region of the United States.

> ### DELEGATION SIZE
>
> *Here's an oddity: in sparsely populated states such as Delaware and Wyoming, there are more senators (two) than members of the House (one). On the other hand, California currently has 52 members in the House, more than any other state. You will get a rough estimate of California's population by multiplying 52 x 570,000.*

The House is the branch of the federal government nearest the people. You can reach out and touch your congressman or congresswoman, something not as easy to do with a senator. Chances are you have attended an event where your representative was the featured speaker. Perhaps a Chamber of Commerce breakfast, a supermarket opening, or a July Fourth picnic. The popular phrase, "Call your congressman," implies that he or she is accessible, ready to help whenever needed.

Of course, being a member of the House is not the same as being mayor of a small town. Currently each member represents approximately 570,000 people.

REAPPORTIONMENT

Every ten years the federal government counts heads. You know this process as the U.S. Census. The census tells us many things about America, including the number of congressional districts for each state. Congress determines the number of House members allocated to each state after the national census every ten years. California has 52 members in the 1990s, a state with a small population might have only one, and so forth, but state legislatures draw the boundaries of each congressional district.

According to the U.S. Census Bureau, the year 2000 count will differ from others in several ways;

- The questionnaire will be "friendlier"—easier to complete.

- The Census Bureau is sending an early letter, the questionnaire, and a reminder card in the event the questionnaire has not been returned near the deadline.

- People who have difficulty reading and understanding English will, under certain circumstances, receive questionnaires in English and in their native language.

- People can pick up the questionnaire at specified public locations. In the past, the Census Bureau was concerned this would mean the same person might return more than one form, skewing the results. Now the Bureau believes it has the proper safeguards in place to detect multiple submissions.

- Local officials will be allowed to check the census list against their own records to determine if the Bureau missed any addresses.

- The Census Bureau plans to buy advertising in the year 2000. In the past, all ads were done pro bono.

- The Census Bureau has a contract to do presentations in the schools.

Qualifications

A member of the House of Representatives must be at least twenty-five years old when entering office, be a U.S. citizen for at least seven years, and be a resident of the *state* in which the election occurred.

> **CHANGING THE LINES**
>
> Reapportionment is a politically charged process. If Democrats are in control of the legislature, they will want to draw the lines in such a way as to give their party maximum advantage in the next elections. Ditto for the Republicans. You will often hear politicians "cry foul" during reapportionment.
>
> You will also hear use of the term gerrymandering. In case you've forgotten from school days, "gerrymandering" is the drawing of lines to favor one party over another.

This last point is intriguing. You may have assumed, as do many people, that a member of Congress must live in the *district* in which he is on the ballot. After all, the term *carpetbagger* refers to someone who moves into an area solely to run for political office.

Why move if there's nothing illegal about living in one congressional district while seeking to represent another? Because it looks bad to the voters. Any political consultant can tell you that a man or woman who does not live in the district he hopes to serve will be vulnerable to devastating charges of being out of touch, of not understanding the wants, needs, hopes, and dreams of his or her constituents. It could be a lot of bunk, but try telling that to candidates for the House. They are unwilling to take the chance.

A BRIEF HISTORY OF THE CONGRESS

Every political institution in America has a history. Congress is no exception.

Before America had a president, it had a Congress. It was not exactly the Congress you and I know today, but the Continental Congress, which convened on September 5, 1774. The Continental Congress was an outgrowth of colonial assemblies that had been a vehicle for wresting particular powers from the British crown. When tensions increased between the colonies and the crown in the 1760s and early 1770s

A MOVABLE HOUSE

Until 1913, members of the House had assigned seats on the floor. Since then, they have been allowed to sit wherever they want, Democrats on the Speaker's right, Republicans on the Speaker's left.

(discussed at greater length in chapter 12), a unified body, the Continental Congress, was formed.

You are more likely to know something about the Second Continental Congress than the First. It was this Second Congress that convened after the outbreak of war between the colonies and Great Britain. In June 1775 the Second Continental Congress created the Continental Army and selected George Washington as commander.

The Second Continental Congress did better in times of war than peace. The Articles of Confederation, which were ratified in 1781, have been cited by many as the reason Congress was relatively weak in the 1780s. The main problem, according to historians, was that Congress then lacked the power to prevent disputes between the states over tariffs and trade.

This first Congress (House) had 65 members, each of whom represented a district of approximately 30,000 people. The Senate consisted of 26 members, two from each of the thirteen states.

The operations of Congress have hardly changed in over two hundred years. The Founders knew what they were doing.

Constitutional Duties Assigned to the House of Representatives

You know that your representative is a presence in the district. You may have seen him or her at a number of events over the years, and you have read about frequent local appearances. Ever wonder what they do when they're in Washington?

They may do lots of things. But the Constitution makes very clear the functions of the House: "All bills for raising revenue originate in the House."

That's it.

Sure, the House has internal rules and requirements discussed in the Constitution, but they do not apply here. Regarding legislation, the only specific power assigned to the House is the introduction of bills to raise money.

The only way for government to raise revenue is through taxes or the imposition of so-called users' fees. Cutting spending does not raise revenue—it cuts spending. Members of the House of Representatives are not eager to advertise the fact it's their chamber that initiates revenue-enhancing measures.

Americans don't love taxes. Most of us hate them with a passion. Taxes are tolerated (though not by Libertarians!) as a necessary evil to keep the government running and federal programs operating.

However, you should not get the impression that the only thing a member of the House does is vote up or down on taxes. Representatives are not called "lawmakers" for nothing. They introduce bills, approve bills, and reject bills. In a given session the House might consider legislation regarding congressional term limits, abortion, and national standards for education, among others.

There are also resolutions galore, many of them offering either praise or condemnation for a country or world leader. An atypical, but not extreme, example is the House schedule for Tuesday, September 23, 1997. On that day the members were asked to consider these resolutions:

1. Designating the Carl B. Stokes United States Courthouse

2. Designating the Kiki de la Garza United States Border Station

3. Designating the Ronald H. Brown Federal Building

4. Designating the Robert J. Dole United States Courthouse

5. Fifty States Commemorative Coin Program Act

None of the above specifically involves raising revenues. It's important for you to keep in mind that there is no constitutional requirement that the House take up these matters. But resolutions are also an essential part of House business. Not everything is death and taxes.

(The next chapter is devoted to how laws are made in Washington. You will learn the House and the Senate play a collaborative role in passing bills, which the president can then sign or veto. If he chooses the latter, the decision can be reversed only by a two-thirds vote of both chambers.)

THE SPEAKER OF THE HOUSE

The Speaker of the House is the only member of the chamber who is without question a national political figure. This was never better illustrated than in 1994–95, when Newt Gingrich, the first Republican Speaker in forty years, received as much or more media coverage than President Clinton.

The Speaker of the House is chosen by a caucus of members of the majority party and then formally elected by the entire House at the beginning of each congressional session. A new session begins in January of every odd-numbered year.

The Speaker has a number of duties. He (a woman has not yet held the post) presides over the House, appoints all special or select committees, appoints conference committees, recognizes members to speak on the floor, and makes a number of important rulings and decisions in the House.

The Speaker rarely votes, except in the case of a tie. You could say this allows him to avoid political fallout, but remember that a Speaker leads his party in the House. He is its symbol, good or bad.

The longest consecutive stretch of any Speaker in history was ten years. The legendary Thomas P. "Tip" O'Neill, Democrat of Massachusetts, served as Speaker from 1977 to 1987. Another legend in the House, Sam Rayburn, Democrat from Texas, served off and on as Speaker for seventeen years and two months, more total years than any in history. Rayburn was a member of Congress for more than *forty-eight* years. No wonder they named one of the House office buildings after him.

> ### THE LEGISLATIVE RECORD
>
> *In recent years you may have heard your representative or others blasting Washington. This has become a popular political strategy, a way of exploiting public dissatisfaction with government.*
>
> *But the members cannot have it both ways. When they return to their districts they usually talk about what they have accomplished for their constituents. Americans may be skeptical of government, but they like to think their representatives are getting things done. A do-nothing Congress is no more popular, and may in fact be less popular, than a "do-too-much" Congress.*

HOUSE LEADERS

Each party chooses its own leader at the beginning of the new Congress. The majority leader is chosen by the members of the majority party in Congress, the minority leader is chosen by the members of the minority party. In the 105th

Congress, which began on January 3, 1997, the majority leader was Dick Armey of Texas and the minority leader was Dick Gephardt of Missouri. The same leaders were picked for the 106th Congress, which runs through 2000.

House votes are what make party "whips" important. The whips are the head-counters, the House leaders responsible, in large part, for delivering the troops when a bill comes up for consideration. In the chain of command you saw in the House of Representatives table on page 140, whips are second only to the majority or minority leaders.

Whips track important legislation and have the responsibility of making sure that members are present for key votes. Whips also assist their party's leaders in managing the legislative program on the floor. Whips hold frequent meetings with members and/or their chiefs of staff to coordinate strategy.

The role of House committees will be discussed at greater length in chapter 10 (see page 167). You should note, however, that committee chairs, as well as ranking majority and minority members, are among the most powerful people in the House. You might want to learn their names and their office addresses in Washington—these people can get things done.

An example is Dan Rostenkowski, the Illinois Democrat defeated in the Republican sweep of 1994. For years Rostenkowski was chair of Ways and Means, the only committee in the House permitted to report tax or tariff proposals. He was a legend for getting things done his way.

HOUSE COMMITTEES

While each Congress establishes its own committee structure, these remain generally the same. In the 105th Congress (1997–98) they were as follows:

- Agriculture

- Appropriations

- Banking and Financial Services

- Budget

- Commerce

- Education and the Workforce

- Government Reform and Oversight

- International Relations

- Judiciary

- National Security

- Resources

- Rules

- Science

- Small Business

- Standards of Official Conduct (Ethics)

- Transportation and Infrastructure

- Veterans' Affairs

- Ways and Means

YOUR HOUSE OF REPRESENTATIVES IN ACTION

You don't have to go very far in the past to find an excellent example. In 1994, the Republicans seized control of the House of Representatives, the first time that had happened in *forty* years. Led by Georgia congressman Newt Gingrich, who was elected Speaker of the House by his

Republican colleagues, the new majority took office in 1995, promising action and results.

During the first months of the 104th Congress, many members of the House spent the night in their offices. The pace was astonishing, as a comparison of the last three sessions of Congress demonstrates (see table 5, page 381). From January 3 to March 31, the 104th Congress was in session almost twice as many days as was the case with the 105th Congress, which convened in 1997.

The new Republican class in the House had one overriding goal: pass the Contract with America during the first one hundred days of the session. With the exception of term limits, this was achieved. Still, hard work does not guarantee legislative success. After 486 hours in session, the 104th Congress had not passed a single bill that became law. On the other hand, during 133 hours in session, the 105th Congress had already approved six bills enacted into law.

CONTRACT WITH AMERICA SCORECARD AT 100 DAYS

	Passed by House	Passed by Senate	Signed by President
Congressional reforms	•	•	•
Balanced-budget amendment	•	Defeated	
Line-item veto	•	•	
Anticrime package	•		
Welfare reform	•		
Crime package	•		
Defense package	•		
Unfunded mandates	•	•	•
Regulatory reform	•		
Litigation reform	•		
Tax cuts	•		
Term limits	Defeated		

Source: *Walter J. Oleszek,* Congressional Procedures and Policy Process

You remember, for a bill to become law it must be approved by the House and Senate—which together constitute the Congress of the United States—and signed by the president. You will also recall the House is traditionally a more raucous place than the Senate—things can get a little out of control in the House.

The Republican members of the 104th Congress, front-line troops in what Gingrich and the media called a "revolution," wanted the Senate to get with the program. But the Senate—though it, too, had a Republican majority—was in no hurry to hastily transform American society.

Money and House Campaigns

Candidates who ran for the House of Representatives in 1996 raised $505 million and spent $478 million, according to Federal Election Commission records. This marked a 20 percent increase in receipts and an 18 percent increase in spending over 1994.

SENATE ROLL CALL 4-21-97

	Net Receipts
1. Mark Warner (D–VA)	$11,625,000
2. John Kerry (D–MA)	10,342,000
3. Guy Millner (R–GA)	9,917,000
4. Robert Torricelli (D–NJ)	9,212,000
5. Dick Zimmer (R–NJ)	8,213,000
6. Harvey Gantt (D–NC)	8,129,000
7. Bill Weld (R–MA)	8,074,000
8. Jesse Helms (R–NC)	7,809,000
9. Carl Levin (D–MI)	6,022,000
10. Paul Wellstone (D–MN)	5,991,000

Source: Roll Call

HOUSE ROLL CALL 4-21-97

	House
1. Newt Gingrich (R–GA)	$6,252,000
2. Michael Goles (D–GA)	3,327,000
3. Charles Schumer (D–NY)	3,318,000
4. Dick Gephardt (D–MO)	3,310,000
5. Ellen Tauscher (D–CA)	2,574,000
6. Joseph Kennedy (D–MA)	2,414,000
7. Vic Fazio (D–CA)	2,412,000
8. Greg Ganske (R–IA)	2,338,000
9. John Ensign (R–NE)	1,989,000
10. Martin Frost (D–TX)	1,964,000

Source: Roll Call

The race in Georgia's 6th District was the most expensive in the history of the House of Representatives. The incumbent, the aforementioned Newt Gingrich, raised $6.3 million while his opponent, cookie mogul Michael Coles, came in at $3.3 million. Gingrich won with 57 percent of the vote.

The Local Angle

It's quite possible that one day you will have a problem with the federal government. Not a philosophical problem, but a practical problem. Maybe your Social Security check will get lost in the mail. Maybe the Immigration and Naturalization Service will take a long, long time processing your papers, or those of a relative or friend. Maybe your veterans' benefits will be denied.

When any of the above happens, you call your local member of Congress.

When you have a problem with a federal agency, you will get to know your local congressional office staff very well. And they will get to know you. Though there is no hard and fast rule, local staff usually works the cases referred by a congressional office. Most of these cases involve problems with Social Security, veterans' benefits, immigration, Medicare, Internal Revenue Service, or federal employees who believe they are being discriminated against on the job. A smaller number of cases deal with the U.S. Postal Service. These could include mail not getting delivered to a particular address or a desire to have a zip code changed.

CRISIS INTERVENTION

Perhaps you have firsthand experience of an earthquake, flood, or hurricane. If so, then you know that in a federally declared disaster, congressional offices are all hustle and bustle, helping constituents receive financial assistance through the Federal Emergency Management Agency (FEMA). During the 1994 Northridge earthquake in southern California, the most expensive natural disaster in American history, congressional offices in and around ground zero were handling FEMA cases for two, sometimes three years after the event.

Congressional offices have trained caseworkers who deal directly with the public. When you think you have a problem requiring federal attention, you should contact the local office of your representative to seek help. *Know your congressional district before making the call.* Congressional courtesy requires that each office takes care of its own.

The caseworker who handles the particular agency giving you trouble will ask you to fill out a form specifying the nature of the problem. These forms can be faxed to you, and you can fax them back. Otherwise you can go to the office and fill them out in person.

When he or she has your information, the case will be referred to the relevant federal agency. If the agency seems slow in responding, the caseworker will make inquiries on your behalf. You need patience; it can take months to resolve cases with federal agencies. The federal government is very big, and, often, very slow.

Casework is most—but by no means all—of what the district staff does on behalf of constituents. They also take constituent opinions, write letters for non-profit groups seeking federal support, meet with local groups and arrange White House tours.

Your organization may want recognition. Or the president of your company is retiring, and you are looking for a special way to honor her. Call your congressman or congresswoman. District offices handle many of the honors that a member of Congress chooses to bestow on individuals or groups. These can include a Congressional Insert, which is read into the Congressional Record, a certificate of appreciation, or a congratulatory letter on official congressional stationery.

Are you taking your family to Washington? Or treating yourself to an historical vacation? Call your local congressional office. They can help set you up. For example, gallery passes to proceedings of the House and Senate can be obtained at the Washington office of your representative. You can get information and passes for tours of Capitol Hill, the Bureau of Engraving and Printing (to see how U.S. currency is printed), and the FBI building. Congressional offices can also provide phone numbers and references for tours of the Federal Reserve Board, State Department, National Gallery of the Arts, National Archives, the Supreme Court, and the Pentagon.

You might want to purchase a flag that has been flown over the Capitol Building. These flags, made from either cotton or nylon, come in three sizes: 3x5, 4x6 or 5x8. Prices vary according to the material and size of the flag. If you are interested contact your local congressional office, which can make the necessary arrangements.

TRACKING YOUR MEMBER

E-mail, the Internet, fax machines, and especially C-SPAN, have closed the gap between the House of Representatives and the public. Since 1979 the proceedings of the House have been available for radio and television broadcast, taking some of the mystery out of life on the Hill. But this is still the Washington half of a representative's job. The other half—the District Office—can be as or more important to his or her constituents.

A Congressional Office Can Obtain Presidential Greetings for These Special Occasions

- Wedding anniversaries—50 years, special card; 51–69 years, card; 70 years and above, special letter

- Baby—card addressed to the parents

- Birthdays—13 years, 21 years, and 50 years, special card; 80–99 years, card; 100 years, special card; 101 years and above; special letter

- Condolences—card addressed to the immediate family member

- Eagle Scout Award and Girl Scout Gold Award—card addressed to the awardee

- Graduation—high school or college, card; high school or college, special letter

> **WHITE HOUSE TOURS**
>
> *Your local congressional office can get you tickets to visit the White House. These special guided tours are usually conducted before 10 A.M. Be sure to call for tickets at least a few weeks in advance of your visit, as availability is limited, especially in spring and summer.*

TERM LIMITS

Politics is not immune to trends. You recall, in the mid-1990s, everyone was talking about congressional term limits. It was a legitimate issue, but it was also a trendy issue. Everybody had an opinion about term limits.

Term limits was the only provision of the Contract with America that was defeated in the House of Representatives. At the beginning, GOP members expressed enthusiasm for term limits, an idea backed strongly by Ross Perot and prominent conservatives, including commentator George Will.

Unlike abortion and gay rights, however, term limits quickly became one of those issues on which Republicans could not agree. They argued over the number of terms, the rules governing when a politician required to leave office could run again, or whether to have limits at all. (This is not to imply that Democrats were completely unified on term limits; they weren't. But as the minority party, their lack of consensus was not as important to the end result.)

In 1995 the Supreme Court ruled in an Arkansas case that individual states could not impose term limits on their own congressional delegation. The problem was the lack of a uniform standard: if Oregon's members were limited to *X* number of terms but those in Ohio were not, Ohio would be at an unfair advantage regarding seniority in Congress.

A number of states restrict the amount of time state legislators and city council members can serve, but not congressmen and senators.

The record of Carl T. Hayden of Arizona for longest service in Congress—fifty-seven years—could someday be broken. But don't bet on it.

THE CONGRESSIONAL FRANK

Do you read congressional mail, or throw it away? Other than checking the local newspaper, or catching an occasional story on radio or television, the best way for you to track your local member of Congress is by reading his mail. Not literally *his* mail, of course, but the newsletters, questionnaires, or letters he sends to you and other registered voters in his district.

These pieces—which includes the member's facsimile signature, or "frank," in the upper right-hand corner of the envelope—are paid out of the member's budget. Each piece must now display the following wording: "This mailing was prepared, published, and mailed at taxpayer expense." The notice is required to appear on the face, envelope, or outside cover of the mail being sent.

Every election year there is a brief moratorium on franked mail. Congressional mail can be sent legally up until 90 days before the primary and general election. This restriction is designed to make congressional races more competitive. Later mailings would give incumbents an even greater advantage than they already possess. After all, franked mail is intended to make the member look good. Your tax dollars are not supposed to pay for your congressman's campaign.

With today's computer-generated, laser-print letters, you would think the congressional frank is a recent invention. In fact, the idea predates by about one hundred years the founding of the American republic.

According to the second edition of *Congress A to Z,* published by Congressional Quarterly:

> The first Continental Congress in 1775 adopted the seventeenth-century British practice of giving its members mailing privileges as a way of keeping constituents fully informed." Today members keep their constituents informed on issues of *their* choice.

Congressional mail does provide a picture of what your member of Congress is doing while he or she is in Washington. The pieces are restricted from being blatantly partisan by congressional standards. The congressional franking commission is required to review all franked mail before it gets sent. Pieces that carry an obvious or not-so-obvious political message are sent back to the member for a rewrite.

CHAPTER RECAP

- The House is more diverse and boisterous than the Senate.

- The House consists of 435 members, who are elected to two-year terms. Competitive House races now cost several million dollars.

- Leaders in the House include the Speaker, party whips, majority and minority leaders, and committee chairs.

- There are currently eighteen committees in the House.

- Call your local congressional office to arrange White House tours and other special events in Washington; also, for special presidential greetings.

- Congressional mail is a valuable way for members to communicate with their constituents.

Making Federal Legislation

The transfer of power in America is a simple concept: you register to vote, go to the polls, and cast ballots in free and fair elections. If you're registered, but opt not to vote, you are either bored, perhaps disgusted with all candidates, cynical, lazy, or consumed by despair. But you cannot honestly say you stayed home because you didn't understand the rules of the game.

Voting is the easiest part of being politically engaged. The transfer—or continuation—of power in the United States can be grasped by a novice.

FROM BILL TO LAW

A less simple aspect of American democracy is the process by which a bill becomes law. You have learned in previous chapters how a bill pending in Congress is subject to discussion, debate, compromise, and amendments. This can last for weeks, even months.

When that's done, and the House and Senate vote on the legislation, the president has the option of exercising a veto. If both House and Senate cannot muster the necessary two-thirds majority to override a veto, the legislation is dead until reintroduced in the next Congress. All that work and nothing to show for it.

Getting Your Voice Heard

In order to participate in the system, you have to have faith in the system. Otherwise, why bother? You want your vote to count, and your opinion to matter. It is frustrating to feel politicians don't care what you think.

A good time to raise your voice is when bills are being brought to the floor for a vote. You can do this en masse, by joining like-minded people around the country, or on your own. Your best bet is calling the office of your local congressman and/or U.S. senators and telling a member of the staff how you want his or her boss to vote. Don't be shy—give your opinion, and state your reasons. Politicians do listen; they *must* listen. Our system demands they listen. If they don't vote the way you want, you can remind them on election day.

This is the essence of democracy. If Congress were to pass laws according to arbitrary rules, or the dictates of an oligarchy, then your opinion would be irrelevant. Those in power wouldn't care what you think. The concept of government of, by, and for the people would be but a farce.

The reality, however, is that Congress does pay attention. Sometimes it may seem Congress is *too* concerned with public opinion. Take Social Security. The moment any member proposes cuts, even if it's to save the system from going bankrupt, hordes of seniors write letters and make phones calls in protest. Usually the proposal is abandoned in the face of this onslaught.

For all their public griping, politicians *love* being politicians. They dread being voted out of office. Repudiation at

the polls terrifies them. This is where the voter is in a powerful position. You are the boss. It doesn't mean politicians
will always act according to your instructions, but when
voting on a bill, elected officials cannot be deaf to the
views of their (voting) constituents. That is, not if they like
their jobs.

No system can
guarantee that only
the most virtuous, wise,
and honorable people
get elected. Some
would even argue that
democracy favors
mediocrity. But even

APPROVAL

*The perception of compromise has improved the image Congress has with
voters. An August 1997 Gallup Poll found that Congress' approval rating—
41 percent—was higher than at any time during the 1990s. The poll was
taken a few days after Congress passed a balanced-budget deal that had
overwhelming support from Republicans and Democrats.*

misinformed or lazy politicians must play by the rules of
Congress. And these rules tend to favor compromise and
deliberation—without these things, almost nothing gets
done. It's a process of phone calls, meetings, conces-
sions, and trade-offs. Stubborn politicians might be
heroes to their "true believers," but they don't get much
done in Congress.

The participation of subcommittees, committees,
both houses of Congress, and, finally, the president, is
a safeguard that (most) legislation will reflect a range
of opinion. Key bills pass through many hands on their
way to the floor. Of course, powerful committee chairs
often find ways to play their parliamentary games and
control the debate. But even this is a matter of style,
and not substance.

The press, too, can highlight legislative tricks. Frequently
you read a story about a controversial and/or completely
irrelevant amendment shoved into a bill at the last
minute, when supposedly no one is looking. No one, that
is, but an alert reporter! When the amendment is brought
to the attention of the public, embarrassed members will
tend to vote no.

Casting Key Votes

The sometimes slow pace of the federal government, even gridlock, is a small price to pay for the system of making laws.

You notice I said "*sometimes* slow pace." Despite the anti-government rhetoric common in the 1980s and 1990s, politicians recognize that they must justify their existence. This means casting crucial votes, getting things done.

It was no coincidence that the 104th Congress (1995–96) approved raising the minimum wage, welfare reform, and other legislation in the days just before adjournment. Members could return to their districts, touting their key votes to their constituents.

If they voted. Attendance matters in the House. *You* can't regularly miss work without consequences. Why should members of Congress?

The perception is that a member who misses many key votes doesn't care about decisions affecting *your* life. There's a price to pay: aggressive, well-funded challengers love to run against an incumbent with a shoddy attendance record. Along with poor constituent service, frequent absences can be a major liability for an incumbent.

Voting in the House

Since 1973 the House has had a system of recorded votes; when a representative hits the button, a huge electronic board behind the Speaker's desk flashes green for "yes" or red for "no" next to the member's name. A yellow light on the board indicates "present," if that's the way the congressman or congresswoman chooses to vote.

Recorded votes are taken if demanded by forty-four members—one-fifth of a quorum—the number legally requisite to transact business when the House is meeting in regular session. (A "quorum" is enough people to take official action. In legislative bodies, a quorum is one more than half the total number of members.)

Many newspapers—the *New York Times* is especially good—will publish the votes of the entire House of Representatives and Senate on any measure that has attracted widespread attention, such as partial-birth abortion, welfare reform, or immigration. The state-by-state roll call appears in the paper on the day after a vote is taken. You should look for, and study, this list.

CONGRESS AT WORK

Before discussing how laws are made, you should review the political distinctions between the House of Representatives and the Senate. Though the two bodies combine to approve or reject bills, they do not operate in the same way.

The difference in style may have something to do with their respective constituencies; members of the House are beholden to districts, while Senators are responsible to entire states. Senators answer to a more diverse population than their colleagues in the House, and must consider a wider range of opinions. It is not politically wise for senators to adhere to a rigid creed. They need at least to consider the views of the state as a whole.

Still, ambitious House members aspire to the Senate, not the other way around. The Senate is more prestigious than the House, and Senators have higher name-recognition than all but the top leadership in the House. Dianne Feinstein of California, Daniel Patrick Moynihan and Al D'Amato of New York, Phil Gramm of Texas, Arlen Specter of Pennsylvania, and Bob Kerry of Nebraska are bona fide national political figures in the late 1990s.

The Senate is also a good pad from which to launch a presidential campaign, or lobby to be selected vice president on the national ticket. In the twentieth century five senators—Harding, Truman, Kennedy, Johnson, and Nixon—were elected president. Three of them—Truman, Johnson, and Nixon—also served as vice president.

In the United States Congress, a small percentage of bills actually become law. When someone talks about how Washington controls our lives, inform him it could be a lot worse.

There are several things that can explain the low passage rate. A "political" explanation is that many bills are introduced merely as a way to get favorable press. For example, a congressman may know that his measure has little chance of approval, but he's eager to get his views on the record. Maybe the local paper will write a story when he or she introduces the measure. This is what really matters.

The strategy is especially effective if the legislation is tied to the headlines of the day. The accompanying publicity creates the impression that a politician is doing something, anything, in response to recent events. (A heinous crime, a military blunder, or a natural disaster are frequently the catalysts for this kind of bill. In times of trouble, we want our elected officials to not just sit there, but lead.)

It's up to you to determine whether your congressman's position on an issue is genuine or—here's that word again—"political."

A bill is active for an entire Congress; approximately two years. If the measure is not passed in that time, then it must be reintroduced in the next Congress (unless the sponsor no longer cares).

The accompanying chart points out areas in which the House and Senate vary on parliamentary procedure. You should keep these distinctions in mind when looking at the lawmaking process.

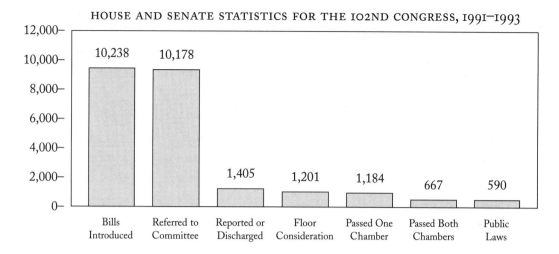

HOUSE AND SENATE STATISTICS FOR THE 102ND CONGRESS, 1991–1993

Bills Introduced	10,238
Referred to Committee	10,178
Reported or Discharged	1,405
Floor Consideration	1,201
Passed One Chamber	1,184
Passed Both Chambers	667
Public Laws	590

Note: Statistics represent only bills and joint resolutions. Simple resolutions, concurrent resolutions, and private bills are excluded.

Source: Ilona B. Nickels, Congressional Research Service, Library of Congress, Washington, D.C.

Below is a description of the steps taken to advance legislation from committee to the House and Senate floors and then on to the president for his signature or veto. When reading this section, keep in mind the House and Senate operate under different systems while working toward a common goal—passing laws.

When you read the following section, think in terms of a controversial bill, such as legislation to reform the welfare system or change immigration laws. The measure has caught the attention of the entire country, not just a handful of lobbyists or a particular industry. As a result, all the instruments of public opinion—talk shows, editorial pages of newspapers big and small, special-interest groups—are making noise. As the vote nears, you will read or hear about the bill almost every day. Congress is going to be watched closely on this one.

Committee chairs or other influential members are usually able to get their bills to the floor. This is a definition of power—and seniority—in Congress.

PATH OF LEGISLATION IN CONGRESS

House	*Senate*
Bills are usually introduced before committee or floor action can proceed.	Bills may originate from the floor.
No effective way to challenge the Speaker's (parliamentarian's) referral decisions.	Referrals are subject to appeals from the floor.
The Speaker is granted authority by House rules to refer bills to more than one committee.	Multiple referrals occur by unanimous consent, although the majority leader and minority leader can jointly offer a motion to that effect.
The Speaker is authorized, subject to House approval, to create ad hoc panels to consider legislation.	Neither the majority leader nor the presiding officer has authority to create ad hoc panels to process legislation.
Difficult to bypass committee consideration of measures.	Bypassing committee consideration of measures occurs more easily.
Floor action is somewhat less important for policy making than committees.	Floor action is as important as committee action in decision making.

Source: Walter J. Oleszek, Congressional Procedures and Policy Process

Offering Legislation

You have seen some examples of how tradition figures in the operations of the House and Senate. Here's another: In the House, members place their bills into the "hopper," a box near the clerk's desk at the front of the chamber. It's been that way for a long as anyone can remember.

Senators can either submit their proposals and accompanying statements to clerks, or they can introduce bills from the floor, but only when the chamber is in session.

Every bill from the House and Senate is printed and made available to the public. If you want a particular bill, call the district office of your representative. Staff members can obtain a copy for you in a matter of days or sooner.

The Committees in Action

Long before television covered sessions of the House and Senate, it covered committee hearings, at least the more controversial and important ones. For example, the Army-McCarthy Hearings (1954) and the Watergate Hearings (1973), both conducted by Senate committees, produced some of the most dramatic moments in American politics.

Committee hearings are in many ways more enlightening, if not more entertaining, than sessions of

> ### PRESIDENTIAL INFLUENCE
>
> *If the president is advocating a particular bill, the chances are quite good it will eventually be put to a vote. Legislation actively promoted by a president tends to get through committee without inordinate hassle. Since neither the president nor any executive official is permitted to introduce legislation in Congress, friendly members—committee chairmen, more often than not—are asked by the White House to introduce "companion" bills in the House and Senate.*

Congress. Committee members are not under restrictive time limits, and are often less interested in scoring political points than eliciting information and reaching a rough consensus. When you go to Washington, you should make a point of attending a committee hearing in the House or Senate. The schedule is usually printed in that morning's edition of the *Washington Post*.

Tracking a Bill

Responsibility for referring legislation formally rests with the Speaker of the House and the presiding officer of the Senate, although the task is usually performed by parliamentarians of the respective chambers. Bills can be sent to one or more committees. For example, legislation in the 105th Congress regarding the Internet and national security was referred to both the Judiciary and International Relations Committees because it had domestic and foreign policy implications. In the case of multiple referrals, the Rules Committee is called upon to reconcile differences between the bills wrought in different committees. This allows for a single measure to be voted on by the full House or Senate.

When you think of a 1,000-page work—*War and Peace*, each of the three volumes of *Remembrance of Things Past*, or various histories—know that committee reports of the House and Senate have been known to *exceed* 1,000 pages. Don't worry. You need not read these reports in order to be an informed citizen. Few people in Washington read them cover to cover.

Reports are written by committee staff at the instruction of the committee chairman, and are compiled whether a bill was reported favorably or not. There is obviously a lot to cover in these reports. The information includes the purpose and scope of the bill, an explanation of committee revisions, the specifics of proposed changes in existing law, and the views of any executive branch agencies consulted.

Committee members opposed to—or supporting—legislation may file minority or supplemental reports. You needn't read these, either, though they are included in the final draft. House and Senate rules require committee reports to include five-year cost estimates, oversight findings, and regulatory impact statements. The reports are the official method of communicating the decision of a committee to the entire chamber.

Both House and Senate set conditions under which a bill is heard by the whole chamber, but these conditions are far from identical.

The House Special Rule and the Senate Unanimous Consent Agreement allow pending bills that require immediate attention to be taken *out of order* and quickly brought up for a vote before the full chamber in the House or Senate. The following chart explains these processes.

MOVING LEGISLATION IN THE HOUSE AND SENATE

House Special Rule	*Senate Unanimous Consent Agreement*
Specifies time for general debate.	Specifies time for debating the bill and amendments offered to the bill.
Permits or prohibits amendments.	Usually restricts the offering of non-germane amendments only.
Formulated by Rules Committee in public session.	Formulated by party leaders informally in private sessions; occasionally on the Senate floor.
Approved by majority vote for the House.	Agreed to by unanimous consent of senators.
Adoption generally results in immediate floor action on the bill.	Adoption geared more to prospective floor action.
Covers many aspects of floor procedure.	Geared primarily to debate restrictions on amendments and final passage.
Does not specify date and exact time for vote on final passage.	May set date and exact time for vote on final passage.
Effect is to waive House rules.	Effect is to waive Senate rules.

Source: Congressional Research Service, Library of Congress, Washington, D.C.

Handling Bills

The Senate, unlike the House, does not impose a five-minute rule for debating amendments. Senators not only have more time to speak, they can offer a number of amendments to a bill unless restricted from doing so by a unanimous consent agreement. In addition, the Senate, again unlike the House, does not require that amendments be germane to the pending legislation.

This last privilege can be a powerful tool in the hands of senators. It is not uncommon for a member of the Senate to add a controversial amendment to an otherwise popular bill, daring his colleagues to vote "aye."

The more controversial a bill, the more likely amended. There are times when amendments can get as much attention as the original legislation.

The Conference Committee

Bills that pass the House and Senate are not always identical. Sometimes the Senate will add amendments to a measure approved by the House. When that happens, the bill goes back to the House. Among several options, the House can request a conference to resolve differences between the bills. If both chambers agree, the Speaker of the House and the presiding officer of the Senate formally appoint the conferees.

Conferees are usually chosen from a list provided by committee leaders. There can be any number of conferees. The largest conference in history involved the 1981 omnibus budget reconciliation bill—258 senators and congressmen—but most conference committees are much smaller.

Conferees haggle. They must by law consider only the points of disagreement between the two measures. After a majority of conferees from each side have reached an agreement, staff aides are instructed to prepare a report explaining the committee's decision. When the report (final bill) is agreed to by the committee, both chambers must vote before it can be sent to the president.

Most of the bills passed by Congress do not go to conference. The convening of a conference committee is a sign that the bill is significant. On major issues, the House and Senate usually have key points of disagreement that need to be resolved.

THE PRESIDENTIAL VETO

You've heard a lot about vetoes—the prime way a president can "check" the Congress in our system of checks and balances. The president's veto power is specifically addressed in the Constitution. A veto is when the president returns legislation to the House without his signature. The veto can be overridden only by a two-thirds vote in each chamber. A "pocket veto" occurs after Congress has adjourned and is therefore unable to vote to override.

Presidents have varied widely in their use of the veto. (see table 4, page 380).

THE BUDGET PROCESS

You cannot follow domestic politics in this country without hearing about the federal budget. Since Ronald Reagan made balancing the budget a major issue in his 1980 presidential campaign, politicians have pointed to huge deficits as a lurid symbol of bloated government. Spending is among the two or three hottest issues of our times.

It is not often easy for politicians to convey why Congress and the president need to reduce the deficit. After all, you may run deficits in your own life—what are credit cards for? Yet you don't think of yourself as irresponsible. Nor are deficits leading you to financial ruin—as long as you stay on top of the situation.

The fact is, politicians and economists don't really know the cumulative effect of large deficits. Some say that a debt of hundreds of billions of dollars is, in essence, stealing from future generations; others argue the impact is minimal. There are experts on both sides.

But there is something else at work here. Deficits don't look good. They have become emblematic of a swollen government that doles out favors in the form of million-, multimillion-, and billion-dollar checks. This argument claims deficits are a national embarrassment. The budget shortfall may not hurt you personally, but it hurts American pride.

Throughout the 1980s and early 1990s, Republicans in Congress, with Presidents Reagan and Bush, made the balanced budget an essential part of the GOP agenda. President Clinton shared their goal; he has always said fiscal responsibility is one of the defining characteristics of a "New Democrat."

There was no consensus, however, on how to reach the promised land of a zero deficit. Republicans, and some Democrats, wanted a balanced-budget amendment; Clinton did not. The proposed amendment, which required a two-thirds vote in both chambers for passage, sailed through the House in 1995 and 1997, but lost narrowly in the Senate. Few doubt that as long as Republicans control Congress, the balanced-budget amendment will keep coming up for a vote. There is no compromising on this one.

The Republican-controlled House and Senate did, however, approve the line-item veto in 1996. This was seen as another needed tool to cut spending. President Clinton eagerly signed that legislation, because it gives the chief executive the authority to cut individual items from spending bills. No president is averse to enhancing his own power, especially with congressional approval.

According to the provisions of the line-item veto, only a two-thirds vote by Congress can restore cuts made by the president.

The 1997 Clinton-Republican rapprochement on the budget is unusual in two respects:

1. it crossed party lines; and

2. it involved two branches of government—Congress and the President are often at odds over the budget.

The President and Congress committed themselves to a balanced budget by 2002, which, if it occurred, would have been the first time in more than thirty years. They reached that goal a few years ahead of schedule. Your children may grow up in a world of fiscal prudence that we only could have imagined. It all depends on what Washington does in the next few years.

The Surplus

In 1997, the federal budget ran a surplus over a twelve-month period for the first time since 1970. Though politicians claimed the credit, several years of strong economic growth was the main reason. If the economy falters, deficits could return. Congress is now trying to find a formula for maintaining a surplus or small deficits even in the event of a slowdown.

Few things in government are more confusing than the congressional budget process. It is not something you need—or would want—to study point by point, but it's important to know the broad outline.

The current method for arriving at a budget was established by the Congressional Budget and Impoundment Control Act of 1974. The act grew out of hostility between Congress and President Nixon. Nixon often refused to spend money for programs approved by Democrats.

According to the 1993 edition of *Our American Government*, the budget act created a blueprint for federal spending in the form of a concurrent resolution. Funds are allocated to congressional committees pursuant to this resolution—the rules of the House and Senate prohibit spending more than these allocations. Any changes in law necessary to reach the targets can be enacted in the form of a reconciliation bill.

The entire budget process can be quite complicated. Perhaps this picture will help.

Getting Your Bill Through Congress

Don't think it's impossible. Don't quit so easily. If you have a good idea for a bill, and you pursue a sensible strategy, you may be pleasantly surprised. Here are some thoughts on achieving a legislative victory:

- Don't be trivial. Leave silly bills to members of Congress. Your issue should have implications for society, not just for you and your friends. Embark on a mission of importance.

- Seek professional help. Not a psychiatrist, but a person or persons in the field in which you have an interest. If you want to change the tax code, talk to a tax lawyer or accountant. If you're interested in criminal justice, find a prosecutor or member of the local police force. Their suggestions can help you organize your thoughts.

- Present your proposal to the person who makes laws for a living—your congressman—or you can try to meet with a member of the committee that would consider your legislation. (The latter may entail a trip to Washington.) Your chances of meeting with either are better if you join a lobbying/advocacy group, such as the Chamber of Commerce. Numbers matter to politicians.

- Don't forget *politics*. A member of Congress will have more interest in a proposed bill that has obvious popular appeal, such as reforming the Internal Revenue Service. Don't tailor your legislation specifically to the market, but always keep the market (voters) in mind.

- Stay current. Use the Internet and your political contacts to monitor your bill's progress through the House and/or Senate. You certainly don't want the final legislation to be loaded with amendments that change the original intent. Keep in touch with the office of the member who agreed to sponsor your bill. Staff should be able to tell you the prospects of your measure being approved by Congress and signed by the president.

CHAPTER RECAP

- The lawmaking process is a cornerstone of democracy.

- Feel free to tell your representative or senator how he or she should vote.

- Political success comes from compromise.

- Thousands of bills are introduced in a given Congress, but relatively few become law.

- Conference committees resolve House/Senate differences in key legislation.

- Both Congress and the president play an important part in the budget-making process.

- Follow some simple steps in trying to get your own bill through Congress.

The Supreme Court

*I*magine the American system of government as a triangle. One side is the president, or the executive branch. A second side is Congress, or the legislative branch. The third is the Supreme Court, or the judicial branch. Each branch compliments and strengthens the others.

Previous chapters have dealt with the roles of President and Congress. This chapter completes the three sides with a discussion of the Supreme Court.

CHECKS AND BALANCES

Before going into detail about the workings of the Court, however, look at this design. This is the famed system of checks and balances. You should have a pretty good sense how the system works in relation to the executive and legislative branches.

Congress passes bills, but the bills do not become law until signed by the president—*check*. But Congress can override the president's veto by a two-thirds majority in both chambers—*checkmate*.

The president nominates cabinet members, judges, and ambassadors, but the nominees cannot assume their posts until confirmed by the Senate—*check*. The president negotiates a treaty with a foreign country or countries, but the treaty does not become the law of the land until approved by two-thirds of the Senate—*check again*. You can almost see the system in motion.

Though this seems a prescription for inefficiency, the system was designed deliberately by the Founding Fathers. They wanted to prevent any one of the three branches from accumulating too much power.

Though the Supreme Court does not make legislation, it plays a vital role in the legislative process. The principle of judicial review lets the Court examine federal laws to determine if they are consistent with the Constitution. Few, if any, political systems in the world incorporate this notion.

You know that the Supreme Court is the final arbiter in cases involving constitutional law. Its rulings tell us what is and is not protected speech, the limits of police powers, the rights of Congress vis-à-vis the President, the power of the presidency, and on and on. *Its role is nothing less than setting the limits of freedom in America.*

You will discover that the Supreme Court is the most remote of the three branches of government. Rarely will you see profiles about the personal lives of Supreme Court justices in newspapers or magazines. The nine justices are known by their work. This is deliberate. Justices do not have to run for reelection, and they must stay distant from public opinion to render decisions without prejudice.

This is not to say that the justices are invisible. On occasion they make speeches, which are often covered by C-SPAN. Sometimes they write articles. But you won't see them appearing on talk shows. That would be inappropriate, even demeaning. The Supreme Court is supposed to decide cases strictly on the basis of constitutional law, not on the particular virtues or failings of the two opposing sides. As much as possible, the justices are swayed by doctrine, not emotion.

Supreme Court justices serve as long as they like. They need not parade themselves before the voters.

There are those in public office who have raised the possibility that Congress initiate impeachment proceedings against judges who advance their own agendas from the bench. (Of course, this would apply only if the agenda of the judge is at odds with the agenda of the offended politician.) This would appear to be a dispute over power. Politicians don't like what they can't easily control.

NO TERM LIMITS FOR JUSTICES

Some politicians are frustrated by the sacrosanct status of the Supreme Court justices. You sometimes hear a politician offer the radical (and probably unconstitutional) proposal that justices be required to stand for election, which is the case with justices in many of the state supreme courts.

But a proposal to make Supreme Court justices stand for election would likely not appeal to a majority of voters. Americans are reluctant to change the Constitution, and even more disinclined to tamper with the independence of the highest court in the land.

The Supreme Court and You

Even if you can't name all nine justices on the Supreme Court, you probably are aware that the Court has a profound effect on your own life. *Roe v. Wade, Bakke*, the Pentagon Papers, the Nixon tapes, are all court decisions with which you should be familiar. Along with the famous ones are dozens of others that influence the direction of our society and politics.

COURT POLITICS

You probably remember the U.S. Senate's confirmation hearings for Supreme Court nominees Robert Bork (1987) and Clarence Thomas (1991)—bitter and mean-spirited affairs that lacked the collegiality and decorum for which the Senate is famous. From the rancor, you could tell how important the Court is in shaping public policy. Each side felt they had to prevail. In fact, the Supreme Court is not now, nor has it ever been, above politics. The confirmation process can get dirty. Judges are appointed by presidents, and presidents have points of view they want represented.

However, the nominee will not always rule the way the president would like. An example is Chief Justice Earl Warren, who was nominated by President Eisenhower in 1953, but who was far more liberal than Ike had presumed.

Don't expect a Democratic president to nominate for justice a person adamantly opposed to abortion; and you would not expect a Republican president to nominate a champion of gay rights. Federal court decisions have profound social and political consequences, which means that politicians have to be very careful about whom they appoint or support. A "mistake" could cost them the next election.

Q AND A ON THE COURT

Why Does the Supreme Court Have Nine Justices?

It hasn't always. From 1789 to 1807 the Court had six justices; from 1807 to 1837 it had seven justices. Since 1837 the Court has had nine justices, although between 1863 and 1869—the years of the Civil War and its immediate aftermath—the total was six. The number of justices is not carved in stone, but authorized by statute. Currently, Congress, which governs the Court's organization by legislation, requires six justices for a quorum, that is, six judges must vote to hand down a ruling.

What Does the Constitution Say about the Supreme Court?

Article III, Section 1 of the Constitution explains the role of the Supreme Court and details its powers and responsibilities: "The judicial power of the United States shall be vested in one Supreme Court, and in such inferior courts as the Congress may from time to time ordain and establish." Article III, Section 2 specifies that "the judicial power shall extend to all cases, in law and equity, arising under this Constitution. . . ."

Article VI of the Constitution proclaims the Constitution the supreme law of the land. The Supreme Court determines how the constitution is interpreted. When the Supreme Court decides a case on constitutional grounds, the ruling serves as a guide for the lower courts and Congress to follow. Now you

> **SUPREME COURT PROCEDURE**
>
> *If at least four Justices agree, a case will be taken by the Court for a decision, with or without oral argument, and the other requests for review will be dismissed. If oral argument is heard, a total of one hour is generally allowed the parties to argue the issues and respond to questions from the Justices.*
>
> —Our American Government, 1993 edition, page 54

can understand why the Supreme Court plays such an important role in this country. Abortion, affirmative action, quotas, pornography, acceptable forms of political protest, and voting rights are among the issues that have been decided by the Supreme Court.

How Does the Supreme Court Decide Which Cases to Hear?

After each justice examines the cases submitted to the Court, the justices meet and evaluate the cases. They decide which cases to schedule for oral argument, which cases to decide without argument, and which cases to dismiss.

The Justices decide a case by simple majority or plurality vote. A tie vote, which can occur if one to three Justices do not take part in a decision, means the decision of the lower court is allowed to stand.

What Is the Tenure of a Supreme Court Judge?

The Supreme Court, along with most federal district courts and courts of appeal, has "good behavior" tenure as specified in the Constitution. This essentially means justices can remain on the bench as long as they want. Justices may be removed from office by impeachment for treason, bribery, or other high crimes and misdemeanors. Some politicians would like to see an expanded definition of "high crimes and misdemeanors."

Most—not all—Supreme Court Justices retire due to advanced age. Below is a list of the current justices and their birthdates. Consider this your Supreme Court scorecard.

1. Chief Justice William H. Rehnquist—born October 1, 1924.

2. Justice John Paul Stevens III—born April 20, 1920.

3. Justice Sandra Day O'Connor—born March 26, 1930.

4. Justice Antonin Scalia—born March 11, 1936.

5. Justice Anthony M. Kennedy—born July 23, 1936.

6. Justice David H. Souter—born September 17, 1939.

7. Justice Clarence Thomas—born June 23, 1948.

8. Justice Ruth Bader Ginsburg—born March 15, 1933.

9. Justice Stephen G. Breyer—born August 15, 1938.

THE LOWER COURTS

Though they lack the ultimate authority of the Supreme Court, the lower federal courts are also important to your understanding of the system.

District Courts

Congress created ninety-four district courts, which are the trial courts in the federal judicial system. Each state has at least one such court, several have two or three; California, New York, and Texas are split into four subdistricts. The district courts are divided into civil and criminal divisions. Each court has from one to twenty-eight judges; trials in these courts are usually heard by a single judge.

Courts of Appeals

Also called circuit courts, courts of appeals are divided geographically into twelve circuits. These courts have jurisdiction over appeals from the district courts and appeals from the actions of government agencies. Cases are generally presented to panels consisting of three judges.

Other Courts

Other federal courts include the U.S. Court of Federal Claims, the U.S. Court of International Trade, the U.S. Tax Court, the U.S. Court of Appeals for the Armed Forces, and the U.S. Court of Veterans' Appeals.

FIVE FAMOUS SUPREME COURT DECISIONS

You cannot properly discuss the Supreme Court without looking at some of its best-known decisions. Here you get a sense of the importance of the Court to history.

Marbury v. Madison (1803)

Writing about Chief Justice John Marshall in the June 6, 1997, *Times Literary Supplement*, Gary L. McDowell, professor of American Studies and director of the Institute of the United States at the University of London, said:

> During his nearly thirty-five years as Chief Justice, Marshall wrote on a largely blank slate, and the decisions he handed down continue to define not just American constitutional law but America itself. . . .
>
> —TLS, *June 6, 1997, page 8*

Marshall was Chief Justice from 1801 to 1835. The decision for which the Marshall Court is probably best known is *Marbury v. Madison*.

The Marbury case involved a statute that Congress had enacted in the belief that it was in harmony with the Constitution. The Court believed the opposite. Marbury, who had been appointed a justice of the peace by President John Adams, asked the Supreme Court to issue a writ of mandamus to compel Secretary of State Madison to give him the commission, entitling him to hold that office. The Judiciary Act of 1789 authorized the Supreme Court to issue writs to remedy wrongs of this kind, but the Constitution did not authorize Congress to pass such an act.

The Court found that Marbury was entitled to his commission, but Marshall also found the Constitution did not give the Supreme Court the power to issue a writ of mandamus. Marshall's ruling established an important principle:

> The decision of the Court that it must obey the Constitution and not the unconstitutional statute entrenched in our constitutional system the practice of judicial review of acts of Congress.
>
> —*Carl Brent Swisher*, Historic Decisions of the Supreme Court, *second edition, New York: Van Nostrand Reinhold Company, 1969*

A recent example of judicial review was the Court's June 1997 decision that struck down the Religious Freedom Restoration Act, passed by Congress in 1993.

This concept harks back to what you read at the beginning of this chapter; the role of the Supreme Court in the system of checks and balances. If legislation passed by Congress is challenged in the Supreme Court, and the justices rule the measure is unconstitutional, then the law is thrown out—*checkmate*.

Plessy v. Ferguson (1896)

The civil-rights marchers who demanded an end to segregation in all its forms were waging war against *Plessy v. Ferguson*. This decision, with only Justice John Harlan dissenting, allowed for the infamous "separate but equal" principle.

The black petitioners in the case challenged a Louisiana statute that required all railroads to provide "equal but separate" accommodations for blacks and whites, and prohibited the two groups from intermingling. The Court ruled against the petitioners, arguing that the Fourteenth Amendment to the Constitution (see chapter 12, page 205) was not intended to abolish distinctions based on color or to enforce social—as opposed to political—equality. Harlan's dissent is worth noting:

> Our Constitution is color-blind, and neither knows nor tolerates classes among citizens. In respect of civil rights, all citizens are equal before the law. . . . In my opinion, the judgement this day rendered will, in time, prove to be quite as pernicious as the decision made by this tribunal in the Dred Scott case.
>
> —*Swisher, page 102*

For more on the Dred Scott case, see chapter 13 on the Civil War, page 207.

Brown v. Board of Education
of Topeka (1954)

In *Brown v. Board of Education,* the Supreme Court took a clear and unequivocal position against the judgement that "separate but equal" was constitutional. This decision reversed the fifty-eight-year-old *Plessy v. Ferguson* ruling. On May 17, 1954, the Supreme Court ruled unanimously that segregation in public schools must end. In a phrase that has become famous, the Court instructed state and local school authorities to end segregation with "all deliberate speed." The Brown decision was the first in a decade of historic rulings and legislation that firmly established the equality of blacks under the law.

The initial *Plessy v. Ferguson* argument had to do with separate accommodations on railroad cars. The fact that the Brown case involved public education and not transportation made a big difference, and gave the Court the opportunity to attack the principle. Here is Chief Justice Warren writing for the majority:

> We conclude that in the field of public education the doctrine of 'separate but equal' has no place. Separate educational facilities are inherently unequal. . . .

Warren adds that the plaintiffs were being denied equal protection under the Fourteenth Amendment.

After the Brown ruling there was a series of efforts to integrate universities and public schools in the South. The most memorable was the admission of nine black students to Central High School in Little Rock, Arkansas, in 1957. Orval Faubus, the governor of Arkansas, intructed the National Guard to prevent the students from entering the school. Segregationists also came to the school to cause trouble. However, President Eisenhower ordered 1,000 paratroopers to Arkansas to ensure that the students were admitted.

Roe v. Wade (1973)

Is this not the most famous case in America today? Even people who know next to nothing about the function of the Supreme Court have heard of *Roe v. Wade*. They know the issue on which the decision was based.

Ever since the Supreme Court voted 7–2 in January 1973 to give women the right to an abortion, this has become the most heated issue in American politics. Abortion has split the Republican Party, and at times has put Democrats on the defensive, such as the vote in the House and Senate in 1997 banning so-called partial-birth abortions.

It also led to the rise of the Christian Coalition, which since the late 1970s has sought to undo Roe by legislative means—including lobbying for the nomination of federal court justices who are opposed to abortion.

Justice Harry Blackmun, writing for the majority in *Roe v. Wade*, said the right to privacy—the constitutional basis for legalizing abortion—was probably based on the Fourteenth Amendment. However, he left open the possibility that states could limit abortion for reasons of health or potential life.

University of California Regents v. Bakke (1978)

Had you followed his career, there are two things you could not have predicted of Richard Nixon when he became president in 1969:

1. His travel to China to meet Mao Tse-tung; and

2. his administration being the first to introduce affirmative-action quotas.

In 1969 Secretary of Labor George Shultz, the man who would later be President Reagan's Secretary of State, issued an administrative order that set hiring quotas for workers in the Philadelphia construction industry. The policy was soon extended to other cities. A number of Democrats—including black Democrats—claimed that Nixon was acting as a partisan politician. They argued that Nixon did not care about civil rights, but wanted to divide the traditional Democratic coalition of labor and blacks.

Regardless, by 1978 there were many white males—and an increasing number of white females—angry about quotas. This was especially true of people applying to college.

An applicant named Alan Bakke challenged quotas after twice being denied admission to the medical school at the Davis campus of the University of California. The Supreme Court ruled 5–4 in Bakke's favor, agreeing with the plaintiff that quotas were a violation of the 1964 Civil Rights Act provision against racial discrimination. But the Court also said that race can be considered as a factor in admissions.

Just as *Brown v. Board of Education* was a catalyst for the Civil Rights movement, the Bakke decision spurred a reaction against affirmative action and quotas. Again the Supreme Court was in the forefront of social and political change.

QUIZ   The Supreme Court Quiz

How much do you know about the third branch of our government? Test your knowledge with this quiz.

(Answers in appendix D, see page 395.)

1. Who was the first Chief Justice of the Supreme Court?

   A. John Marshall
   B. John Jay
   C. Samuel Adams
   D. Oliver Wendell Holmes

2. Which full-term president didn't appoint a Supreme Court justice?

    A. George Bush
    B. Harry Truman
    C. Jimmy Carter
    D. Dwight Eisenhower

3. Which president appointed the most justices?

    A. Ronald Reagan
    B. Franklin Roosevelt
    C. Abraham Lincoln
    D. George Washington

4. Which justice served the longest?

    A. William O. Douglas
    B. Oliver Wendell Holmes
    C. William Brennan
    D. Earl Warren

5. Who was the oldest justice to serve?

    A. Oliver Wendell Holmes
    B. William O. Douglas
    C. John Marshall
    D. Roger Taney

6. Who was the first black justice?

    A. Clarence Thomas
    B. Bayard Rustin
    C. Andrew Young
    D. Thurgood Marshall

7. Who nominated the first woman justice?

    A. Gerald Ford
    B. Richard Nixon
    C. George Bush
    D. Ronald Reagan

8. Which state has produced the most justices?

   A. Texas
   B. Illinois
   C. New York
   D. Ohio

9. Who is the only person who served both as President of the U.S. and as a Supreme Court justice?

   A. Theodore Roosevelt
   B. William Howard Taft
   C. Woodrow Wilson
   D. James Madison

10. Which law school graduated the most justices?

   A. Harvard
   B. Yale
   C. Columbia
   D. Michigan

For the quiz, the *Best Guide* was ably assisted by the 1997–99 edition of *The World Almanac of U.S. Politics*, and, especially, the 1995 edition of *Congressional Quarterly's Desk Reference on American Government*.

CHAPTER RECAP

- Remember the Supreme Court determines the constitutionality of federal legislation.

- Supreme Court justices can remain on the bench for life; they are appointed, not elected. Proposals to make Supreme Court justices accountable to the people do not resonate with most voters.

- In two hundred years of decisions, the Supreme Court has defined the limits of freedom in America, and what it means to be an American.

How We Got Here

*I*t is said with some justification that Americans have no sense of their own history. Pollsters report that a majority of respondents cannot identify the Bill of Rights, are uncertain about the number of Supreme Court justices, or don't realize that the Soviet Union and the United States were allies in World War II. You have probably heard other horror stories along these lines. Somehow we have lost touch with our past.

This is distressing. You cannot be a serious, informed voter without having at least a basic understanding of American history. Politicians often invoke history to justify their policies. That's fine, except when they play loose with the facts, or interpret events contrary to what really happened. If you as a voter do not have sufficient knowledge of U.S. history to recognize and repudiate the mistakes, then the false version of events assumes legitimacy.

That's one reason why it's important to know the past. A second reason is that the right to vote, the Constitution, consumer-protection legislation, Social Security, anti-discrimination laws, and so much more, are part of the history of this country. The rights and freedoms you cherish did not suddenly appear.

The next five chapters show the influence of the past on contemporary politics in the United States. The periods and events selected for this section are the wellspring of today's political system: the Declaration of Independence, the American Revolution, and the Constitution (chapter 12); slavery, the Civil War, and Abraham Lincoln (chapter 13); the Depression, the New Deal, and FDR (chapter 14); the Civil Rights movement and the 1960s (chapter 15); and President Reagan, Newt Gingrich, and the conservative reactionaryism of the 1980s and 1990s (chapter 16).

The historical portion of the *Best Guide* emphasizes the significance of these eras for our time; to cite two examples: the chapter on President Roosevelt covers the New Deal and the buildup to World War II, while the chapter on the 1960s is devoted to the effects of the Civil Rights movement. This is a selective history designed to show how we got "here." A section on each of the historical periods appears in the bibliography at the end of the book.

The American Revolution and the Constitution

*O*ur Revolution succeeded. This statement is not arrogant or self-congratulatory, but factual. The United States has the oldest written constitution of any government in the world. More than 220 years after the Declaration of Independence, nearly 210 years after Congress approved the Bill of Rights, the American system is remarkably similar to its original conception. Seventeen amendments have been added to the Constitution since the adoption of the initial ten, but only one, Prohibition, has been repealed.

Today politicians and the courts may differ over an interpretation of the First Amendment, or the Second, or the Fourteenth, but rarely will they question whether these amendments or any of the others should exist at all.

The Constitution is one of those rare documents popular across the political spectrum. Conservatives, liberals, libertarians, and even militia members swear by the document.

The men who started America are respected and revered today. With the occasional exception of Thomas Jefferson, who has received some rough press in recent years, the Founding Fathers—Jefferson, John Adams, James

Madison, Benjamin Franklin, Alexander Hamilton, and George Washington—still get high marks. Their eloquence and clarity is sorely missed. When you read what the Founders said and wrote, you will probably say to yourself, "They don't make leaders like this anymore."

That's another subject. What follows is a synopsis of the grand first act of the history of the United States of America.

EUROPEAN FORERUNNERS TO AMERICAN DEMOCRACY
Locke and Montesquieu

Two European men—one English, one French—provided the basis for a political philosophy that helped inspire the colonists to cut America's ties to England. The Englishman John Locke (1632–1704) authored many works of philosophy, including *Essay Concerning Human Understanding*. It was Locke's second book, *Two Treatises of Government*, that attracted Thomas Jefferson. Allan Nevins and Henry Steele Commager, two well-known American historians, said this about Locke's influence on the Declaration of Independence:

> Locke maintained that the supreme function of the state is to protect life, liberty, and property, to which every man is entitled. Political authority, he said, is held in trust for the benefit of the people alone. When the natural rights of mankind are violated, the people have the right and duty of abolishing or changing the government.
> —*Commager and Nevins*, A Pocket History of the United States

You cannot read this passage without being reminded of a very famous American document:

> We hold these truths to be self-evident, that all men are created equal, that they are endowed by

their Creator with certain unalienable rights, that among these are life, liberty, and the pursuit of happiness. That to secure these rights, governments are instituted among men, deriving their just powers from the consent of the governed. That whenever any form of government becomes destructive of these ends, it is the right of the people to alter or to abolish it, and to institute new government. . . ."

—an excerpt from the Declaration of Independence

One wonders what Locke would have made of the close approximation of his words—and a literal interpretation of his meaning—that were used to justify the separation from England.

Charles de Secondat, Baron de Montesquieu, was born in 1689 and died in 1755. For our purposes, his most famous work is *The Spirit of the Laws*, which appeared in 1748. Some of the ideas expressed in the work should seem familiar to you.

When the body of the people is possessed of the supreme power, it is called a democracy.

On the subject of what we today call separation of powers, Montesquieu wrote:

. . . [T]here is no liberty if the judiciary power is not separated from the legislative and executive. Were it joined with the legislative, the life and liberty of the subject would be exposed to arbitrary control; for the judge would be then the legislator. Were it joined to the executive power, the judge might behave with violence and oppression.

—Peter Gay, editor, The Enlightenment:
A Comprehensive Anthology

Commager and Nevins on Locke and Montesquieu:

> The eighteenth-century idea of the balancing of power was a Newtonian conception of politics. The principle was naturally derived from colonial experience and strengthened by the writings of Locke and Montesquieu, with which most of the delegates (to the Constitutional Convention) were familiar.
>
> —*Commager and Nevins*, A Pocket History of the United States

The colonists reading these words would think, "That's the system we need in America."

THE COLONIES

You know that United States were originally thirteen colonies, but can you name all thirteen? They are Connecticut, Delaware, Georgia, Massachusetts, Maryland, New Hampshire, New Jersey, New York, North Carolina, Pennsylvania, Rhode Island, South Carolina, and Virginia.

Milestones

Following are a few milestones in the growth and development of the colonies.

- *1607*—Three vessels and 105 colonists from the London Company settle the first permanent English colony in what would become the United States at Jamestown in Virginia.

- *1619*—The first slaves—twenty in all—imported from Africa to the colonies were sold in Jamestown in 1619. For eighty-five years after the American Revolution, slavery was the most contentious issue in the life of the new nation, culminating in the Civil War (1861–65).

- *1692*—In this tragic year, some young girls in Salem, Massachusetts, claimed a group of older women had cast spells over them. The Salem witchcraft trials resulted. Hundreds of people were accused, nineteen people were hanged, and one person was pressed to death under a pile of fieldstone before it was all over. The trials were dramatized in Arthur Miller's play *The Crucible* (Broadway debut, 1953) and the 1996 film of the same name.

- *1756–63*—The French and Indian War resulted in the French losing nearly all their holdings in North America. The war marked the military debut of a young officer—with the British army—named George Washington, who would go on to bigger and better things; and created the need for money to pay to administer territories captured by the victorious British. This resulted in the imposition of taxes which enraged many colonists.

- *1763–65*—George Grenville, who became Prime Minister of England in 1763, made several proposals to acquire needed funds: (1) the Sugar Act (1764), which collected a levy on molasses from non-British sources; (2) the Currency Act (1764), which prohibited further issues of colonial money; and (3) the Stamp Act (1765), which levied an internal revenue tax in the form of stamps to be purchased and affixed to specified documents and publications such as newspapers. In addition, the Quartering Act of 1765 required the colonial legislatures to supply barracks and part of the cost of maintaining 10,000 British troops in the colonies.

   You can imagine how these went over with the colonists!

- *1773*—Many Americans were angered by the Tea Act of 1773, which enabled the East India Company to sell its tea directly to American retailers. This gave the company a distinct advantage over its American competitors. On the night of December 16, a group of fifty men disguised as Indians, and led by Samuel Adams, boarded East India Company ships docked in Boston, opened 343 chests of tea, and dumped them into the harbor. The Boston Tea Party is one of the most famous events in colonial America.

- *1774*—Angered by the Coercive Acts, directed against rebellious Boston by the British Crown, every colony but Georgia convened in the First Continental Congress in Philadelphia. The Congress, symbol of the political unity of the colonies in the face of increasing conflict with the Mother Country, passed three resolutions, including one that declared the Coercive Acts null and void and encouraged forcible resistance.

- *1775*—The Second Continental Congress convened May 10. Paul Revere had already made his famous ride and colonial militiamen and guerilla fighters had fought British troops at Lexington and Concord. The Second Congress laid plans to raise an army, and selected George Washington to be commander-in-chief.

THE DECLARATION OF INDEPENDENCE

Today we call the July holiday Independence Day or simply "the Fourth." On July 4, 1776, the Declaration of Independence was agreed to by Congress and sent to the legislatures of the states. You can find the text of the Declaration of Independence in appendix A, page 337.

In his book *Patriots*, A. J. Langguth sets the scene as Thomas Jefferson sits down to write the words that will change the course of history. (Of how many documents can that be truly said?)

> Jefferson had rented a parlor and bedroom on the second floor of a new brick house on Market Street (in Philadelphia). There he set up a folding writing box that a cabinetmaker had built from his design. He made no claims for its beauty, but the box was plain and neat and took up no more room on the table in his parlor than any moderately sized book.
>
> Jefferson wrote quickly in a small and legible hand, with no attempt at elegance. He made continual changes . . .
>
> —*A. J. Langguth*, Patriots

The Resolution of Independence

On June 7, 1776, one month before the Declaration of Independence, Richard Henry Lee of Virginia introduced a resolution in the Continental Congress, seconded by John Adams, stating that the "colonies are, and of right ought to be, free and independent States." This was the Resolution of Independence, precursor to the Declaration of Independence. On June 10 a committee was appointed to prepare a declaration of independence. Members of the committee included Thomas Jefferson, John Adams, and Benjamin Franklin.

Articles of Confederation

Ratification of the Articles of Confederation took place in 1781. The Articles marked a first attempt at creating a central government in the United States. Among its provisions, the Articles required a yes vote from nine of the thirteen states to pass any important legislation, and a unanimous vote to amend any Article.

The Articles also prohibited the collecting of export and import duties for revenues. This failure of the Articles of Confederation to impose a strong central government in the United States led in part to the convening of the Constitutional Convention in Philadelphia in 1787.

THE CONSTITUTION

The Constitutional Convention met on May 14, 1787. A provision stated that the Constitution would be ratified once it had the approval of nine state conventions. By 1788 it had been ratified by nine states, but not by New York or Virginia, both of which were considered crucial. To get New York's support, Alexander Hamilton, John Jay, and James Madison wrote articles in favor of ratification that were later published as *The Federalist Papers*, one of the most important works of political theory in American history. You may have read part or all of *The Federalist Papers* in an American government class in college. If you did, it might not be a bad idea to read it again; if you didn't, it's highly recommended.

After publication, Virginia ratified; New York quickly followed. The last of the original thirteen states to ratify was Rhode Island (1790).

Some Interesting Facts About the Constitution

- At the time of the Constitutional Convention, the population of Philadelphia was about 40,000.

- Neither Thomas Jefferson nor George Washington signed the Constitution. Washington was an occasional attendee to the Convention, and Jefferson was in France during that time, where he served as the U.S. ambassador.

- Thirty-nine men signed the Constitution.

- The U.S. Constitution has 4,440 words. It is the oldest, and shortest, written constitution of any government in the world.

- The oldest person to sign the Constitution was eighty-one-year-old Benjamin Franklin, the youngest was twenty-six-year-old Jonathan Dayton of New Jersey.

This information is found in The U.S. Constitution and Fascinating Facts About It, *published by Oak Hill Publishing Company.*

What the Constitution Says

You needn't be a superpatriot to acknowledge that the Constitution is a remarkable document. Though it covers only ten or so pages in most books, it is the foundation of the American system. The Constitution is the political and legal Bible of the United States.

In its brevity and simplicity, the Constitution is a wonderful counter to government excess. You can read the entire document in under an hour. Try doing that with an environmental regulation or the defense budget.

Still, it's not easy to recall the precise language or meaning of everything contained in the Constitution. The complete document is included in appendix B, page 343. What follows is a short summary of the articles and amendments.

Articles

- *Article I*—Defines the qualifications to run for Congress, and sets the political limits for representatives, senators, and the states.

- *Article II*—Defines the powers of the president, and specifies the manner in which he is to be elected.

- *Article III*—Defines the judicial powers of the Supreme Court, and indicates the kinds of cases that fall under its jurisdiction.

- *Article IV*—Establishes the basis for relations between the states, and guarantees the federal government will come to the defense of each state in the event of an invasion.

- *Article V*—The "two-thirds and three-fourths rule." The support of two-thirds of each house of Congress is necessary for proposing an amendment to the Constitution. The proposed amendment is then sent to the states, where it must be approved by three-fourths of the legislatures for ratification.

- *Article VI*—Establishes the Constitution as the supreme law of the land, that elected officials at the federal and state level are bound by law to support, and establishes the principle that choice of religion cannot disqualify anyone to hold office or public trust in the United States.

- *Article VII*—The approval of nine of the then existing thirteen states was needed to ratify the Constitution.

Amendments

The first ten amendments to the Constitution are known collectively as the Bill of Rights.

- *First Amendment*—The foundation of what it means to be an American: Congress—the government—cannot make laws restricting

freedom of speech, freedom of religion, or the
right to peaceable assembly.

You can say what you want about the government without fear of prosecution. You can belong to any religion
without fear of discrimination. And you can peaceably congregate with your friends without fear that you and the
group will be harassed by the authorities.

America *is* the First Amendment, and the First
Amendment *is* America.

- *Second Amendment*—Does the right to keep
  and bear arms—as specified in the Second
  Amendment—mean anyone can possess any type
  of handgun or rifle without restriction? This is a
  source of continuing debate between the National
  Rifle Association and proponents of gun control.

Amendment II refers to a "well regulated militia." The
gun enthusiasts think this means *they* have the right to
keep and bear arms, although state militias no longer exist.
(The National Guard is not the same thing.) Many courts
and a sizable portion of Congress agree with this interpretation.

- *Third Amendment*—Protects individual rights
  against infringement by the military. During
  the American Revolution, British soldiers were
  routinely billeted in citizens' homes.

- *Fourth Amendment*—The Fourth Amendment says
  that the authorities need a search or arrest warrant
  from a judge to search a person or home. None of
  that chilling "knock on the door" used by the
  Gestapo and secret police in totalitarian countries.

- *Fifth Amendment*—A person cannot testify against
  himself in a criminal case, be tried for the same
  crime twice, or be denied due process of law.

You might know this one better for the phrases "self-incrimination" and "double jeopardy." The Fifth Amendment is a protection against both.

- *Sixth Amendment*—In criminal prosecutions, the defendant is informed of the charges brought against him, and has the right to an attorney and jury trial. Otherwise, we would live in a Kafkaesque world.

- *Seventh Amendment*—Establishes trial by jury in common lawsuits.

- *Eighth Amendment*—No excessive bail, no excessive fines, no cruel and unusual punishment.

- *Ninth Amendment*—No rights in the Constitution can contradict rights retained by the people. Conservatives like to invoke the Ninth Amendment when they believe the courts have gone too far in interpreting the Constitution.

- *Tenth Amendment*—Protects the states against the assertion of extraconstitutional authority by the federal government. Conservatives like to invoke the Tenth Amendment when they believe the courts have gone too far in interpreting the federal-state relationship.

- *Eleventh Amendment*—Limits the extension of the judicial power of the United States.

- *Twelfth Amendment*—Establishes that candidates for president and vice president must stand for either one office or the other but not for both, and prevents the choice of a president and vice president from opposing parties.

- *Thirteenth Amendment*—The official end of slavery.

- *Fourteenth Amendment*—Anyone born or natural-ized in the United States is a citizen, and the states cannot deny any person life, liberty, or property without due process of law.

- *Fifteenth Amendment*—Race or color cannot be used to deny a person the right to vote. If it is, Congress can pass legislation to enforce the amendment.

- *Sixteenth Amendment*—The Constitution authorizes a tax on income—the Libertarians' nightmare.

- *Seventeenth Amendment*—The public is given the right to vote for senators in a direct election. Senators will not be chosen by state legislatures.

- *Eighteenth Amendment*—Prohibition: no whiskey, no wine, no beer.

- *Nineteenth Amendment*—Women get the right to vote: You've come part of the way, baby.

- *Twentieth Amendment*—The government is put on a new timetable. The terms of the president and vice president end on January 20 at noon, and the terms of senators and representatives on January 3.

- *Twenty-First Amendment*—Start pouring! The Eighteenth Amendment is repealed.

- *Twenty-Second Amendment*—Term limits for presi-dents. No person can be elected president more than twice, and no president can be in office more than ten consecutive years. Republicans thought this amendment was a good idea in the aftermath of FDR, but a bad idea during the Reagan era.

- *Twenty-Third Amendment*—The District of Columbia is admitted to the electoral college.

- *Twenty-Fourth Amendment*—The poll tax—also called a head tax—was collected equally from everyone. The effect, however, was to keep the poor and blacks from voting, primarily in the South. This amendment outlaws the poll tax.

- *Twenty-Fifth Amendment*—When the president dies or resigns, the vice president takes his place. In addition, the vice president succeeds to the presidency if the president become disabled. If the office of vice president is vacant, a majority in *both* houses of Congress is necessary for confirmation of a new VP.

- *Twenty-Sixth Amendment*—Rock the vote: The legal voting age is lowered from twenty-one to eighteen.

- *Twenty-Seventh Amendment*—This amendment prevents Congress from passing immediate salary increases for itself. Salary changes cannot take effect until the next Congress.

Note: The Twenty-Seventh Amendment had no time limit for ratification. It was passed in 1789 and sent to the states for ratification; it became part of the Constitution after Michigan became the thirty-eighth state to ratify, in 1992.

The Civil War

*P*erhaps you are familiar with *The Nation*. It is the principle voice of the American left. But it's also a magazine with a past. You and other serious students of U.S. politics could learn a lot by reading articles published in *The Nation* over the last 135 years.

The magazine made its debut at a momentous time in American history: July 6, 1865, less than three months after the end of the Civil War. In the September 21, 1865, edition of *The Nation*, E. L. Godkin, co-founder and editor, wrote a lengthy piece on the meaning of the war and what should happen next. A couple of poignant sentences have particular relevance for a present-day American audience:

> The great lesson which we have learned from the war, if we have learned any lesson at all, is that homogeneousness, social as well as political, is the first condition of our national existence. The government, we now know as well as we know anything, cannot be carried on, if any portion of the population which lives under it is legally in degradation, or legally

excluded from the enjoyment of any of the rights and privileges possessed by the rest of the community.

THE PECULIAR INSTITUTION

Godkin was writing about slavery. Of course, no group in the United States today is living in conditions remotely comparable to slaves in the South prior to 1865, but his point about rights and privileges, and the significance he attributes to homogeneity, apply to political and social questions in our time.

Civil and economic rights for particular groups are debated in the media and at

> ### THE IMPORTANCE OF A UNIFIED NATION
>
> *The Civil War began as a struggle to preserve the federal union. Generals Ulysses S. Grant and William Sherman and President Abraham Lincoln each felt war was necessary to preserve the union. It was only later that Lincoln added the elimination of slavery to the list of war aims.*

every level of government. You have probably heard arguments that affirmative action, anti-discrimination laws for gays and lesbians, and rules against sexual harassment will make American society more inclusive by helping to eliminate racism, homophobia, and sexism.

You have likely heard opposing arguments as well: America is coming apart as a result of claims made by group after group for special rights and consideration under the law. The meaning of "nation" is at the heart of this debate, as it was during the time of the Blues and the Grays.

THE SECESSIONISTS

During House deliberations on the impeachment of President Clinton, you may recall commentators noted that Southern members dominated the Republican leadership. To some, their anger and determination was a reminder of the spirit that infused that region in 1860–61, following the election of Abraham Lincoln to the presidency. Here you can see how quickly the Southern states seceded from the Union.

- South Carolina—December 20, 1860

- Mississippi—January 9, 1861

- Florida—January 10, 1861

- Alabama—January 11, 1861

- Georgia—January 19, 1861

- Texas—February 1, 1861

- Virginia—April 17, 1861

- Arkansas—May 6,1861

- North Carolina—May 20, 1861

- Tennessee—June 8, 1861

The Civil War (1861–65) remains the bloodiest conflict in the history of this country. More than 360,000 Union soldiers and 258,000 Confederate troops were killed, with another 275,000 and 100,000 wounded respectively. An estimated 50,000 civilians died in the Confederate states. In the 135 years since the end of the Civil War the United States has not faced a domestic crisis near this magnitude. Today those who advocate "breaking away" are usually fringe militia groups who would have trouble defeating a well-armed police department.

Causes of the War

The institution of slavery plus the growth of agrarian society in the South set the stage for the war. Signs of an inevitable conflict could be seen decades before the war broke out:

- *1820*—A deal put together by Henry Clay, the famous senator from Kentucky, allowed Maine to enter the Union as a free state, and Missouri as a slave state, on March 3, 1820. In addition, slavery would be forever prohibited in states created from the Louisiana Purchase that were north of Missouri's southern border. This Compromise was preempted by a second, the Compromise of 1850, which established the rules governing free and slave states in territories acquired by the United States in the war with Mexico (1846–48).

- *1831*—On August 21, 1831, Nat Turner, a slave raised on a Virginia plantation, and seven other slaves murdered the Travis family, his owners. The group went into the countryside, where they were joined by as many as sixty recruits. For two days they went on a rampage, until most were killed or captured by a well-armed militia. Five—including Turner—were not caught for another six weeks. In November, Turner and sixteen of his followers were hanged.

  In the aftermath of the revolt, as many as two hundred blacks were killed in Virginia by vengeful state and federal troops. Laws were passed forbidding slaves to read and write, as it was believed they were being influenced by the writings of radical abolitionists from the North.

- *1847*—In December, the man many regard as the greatest president in our history took his seat in the House of Representatives. Abraham Lincoln of Illinois launched his career in Congress by making a speech against the Mexican War.

- *1857*—Dred Scott was a slave who had been taken to a variety of army posts in America and the Western territories and had spent two years in the free territory of Minnesota. Scott claimed this time away from slave states meant he was no longer a slave under the Missouri Compromise. He sued for his freedom in 1846.

An eleven-year legal battle culminated in a 7–2 vote against Scott in the Supreme Court. Chief Justice Roger B. Taney, a former slaveowner, issued a hard-line opinion: (a) no black man—free or slave—was a U.S. citizen, which meant that no black man had the right to sue in federal court; and (b) Congress never had the right to ban slavery in territories, on the grounds that that the Constitution protected people from being deprived of life, liberty, or property. "According to Taney, slaves, like cows or goats, were property and could be taken anywhere under U.S. jurisdiction."

The above is from *Don't Know Much About the Civil War* by Kenneth C. Davis.

Slaveholders were delighted with the result of the Dred Scott case; opponents of slavery were out-raged. A few years later the Civil War was over and the Thirteenth Amendment—outlawing slavery in the United States—had been ratified.

• *1859*—Twenty eight years after Nat Turner, a white abolitionist named John Brown led a group of 22 men to Harpers Ferry, Virginia. Brown hoped to lead an insurrection of slaves throughout the South in a great uprising that would rid America of slavery.

But Brown and his followers never got past Harpers Ferry. Federal troops under the command of Robert E. Lee and Jeb Stuart stormed into the area where the group were holding hostages. The troops captured Brown, who was executed six weeks later. The two-day raid on Harpers Ferry resulted in the deaths of four civilians and one marine.

- *1860*—In May, Abraham Lincoln became the Republican nominee for president. The Democratic nominee, John Breckinridge of Kentucky, ran on a pro-slavery platform. Southerners threatened to secede if Lincoln became president. Despite the threat, a plurality of the American public cast their ballots for Lincoln on November 6. Seven weeks after the election, South Carolina, the most rabid state on this issue, voted to leave the Union.

- *1861*—Since South Carolina was the first state to secede, it is fitting that the first shots of the war occurred at Fort Sumter in Charleston Harbor. On April 12, 1861, forty-three Confederate cannons fired on the fort, containing federal troops who had refused to surrender. Though no men were killed in the bombardment, the fort commanders surrendered on April 13. On July 21 Bull Run, the first battle of the war, was fought and Union forces were routed.

- *1862*—Many people on the Northern side expected the war to be over quickly. How could the South possibly compete with the North's advantage in resources and troops? By 1862, that notion had begun to dissipate. Lingering illusions were shattered at Shiloh, Tennessee, in 1862. By the second day of fighting, more than 13,000 Union men had been killed, wounded, or captured; the Confederate total in the three categories was nearly 11,000.

- *1863*—The most famous battle of the war, Gettysburg, and the most famous documents produced by the war, the Emancipation Proclamation and the Gettysburg Address, all occurred in 1863. On January 1 Lincoln issued the Emancipation Proclamation, which freed the slaves in the rebel states—Texas, Louisiana (with some exceptions), Mississippi, Alabama, Florida, Georgia, South Carolina, North Carolina, and Virginia.

THE EMANCIPATION PROCLAMATION

Though the document was only a page or two in length, the Emancipation Proclamation transformed American society forever. It's worth reading.

January 1, 1863

By the President of the United States of America:

A Proclamation

Whereas on the 22nd day of September, A.D. 1862, a proclamation was issued by the President of the United States, containing, among other things, the following, to wit:

"That on the 1st day of January, A.D. 1863, all persons held as slaves within any State or designated part of a State the people whereof shall then be in rebellion against the United States shall be then, thenceforward, and forever free; and the executive government of the United States, including the military and naval authority thereof, will recognize and maintain the freedom of such persons and will do no act or acts to repress such persons, or any of them, in any efforts they may make for their actual freedom.

"That the executive will on the 1st day of January aforesaid, by proclamation, designate the States and parts of States, if any, in which the people thereof, respectively, shall then be in rebellion against the United States; and the fact that any State or the people thereof shall on that day be in good faith represented in the Congress of the United States by members chosen thereto at elections wherein a majority of the qualified voters of such States shall have participated shall, in the absence of strong countervailing testimony, be deemed conclusive evidence that such State and the people thereof are not then in rebellion against the United States."

Now, therefore, I, Abraham Lincoln, President of the United States, by virtue of the power in me vested as

Commander-in-Chief of the Army and Navy of the United States in time of actual armed rebellion against the authority and government of the United States, and as a fit and necessary war measure for suppressing said rebellion, do, on this 1st day of January, A.D. 1863, and in accordance with my purpose so to do, publicly proclaimed for the full period of one hundred days from the day first above mentioned, order and designate as the States and parts of States wherein the people thereof, respectively, are this day in rebellion against the United States the following, to wit:

Arkansas, Texas, Louisiana (except the parishes of St. Bernard, Palquemines, Jefferson, St. John, St. Charles, St. James, Ascension, Assumption, Terrebone, Lafourche, St. Mary, St. Martin, and Orleans, including the city of New Orleans), Mississippi, Alabama, Florida, Georgia, South Carolina, North Carolina, and Virginia (except the forty-eight counties designated as West Virginia, and also the counties of Berkeley, Accomac, Northhampton, Elizabeth City, York, Princess Anne, and Norfolk, including the cities of Norfolk and Portsmouth), and which excepted parts are for the present left precisely as if this proclamation were not issued.

And by virtue of the power and for the purpose aforesaid, I do order and declare that all persons held as slaves within said designated States and parts of States are, and henceforward shall be, free; and that the Executive Government of the United States, including the military and naval authorities thereof, will recognize and maintain the freedom of said persons.

And I hereby enjoin upon the people so declared to be free to abstain from all violence, unless in necessary self-defense; and I recommend to them that, in all cases when allowed, they labor faithfully for reasonable wages.

And I further declare and make known that such persons of suitable condition will be received into the armed service of the United States to garrison forts, positions, stations, and other places, and to man vessels of all sorts in said service.

And upon this act, sincerely believed to be an act of justice, warranted by the Constitution upon military necessity, I invoke the considerate judgment of mankind and the gracious favor of Almighty God.

The order did not apply to 300,000 slaves living in the border states. The Proclamation was of mainly symbolic importance; the rebel states were hardly going to free their slaves. The meaning of the Emancipation Proclamation was clear: Should the South lose the war, its way of life would cease to exist.

In 1868, three years after the Civil War ended, the states ratified the Fourteenth Amendment to the Constitution. The best-known section of the amendment gave citizenship with full rights to all persons born or naturalized in the country, and prohibited the states to pass any law to restrict such rights or deny equal protection.

Along with the Thirteenth Amendment, which outlawed slavery, the Fourteenth Amendment was designed to give slaves and free blacks the rights of other Americans. Jim Crow laws and other forms of discrimination—in the South and to some degree in the North—allowed a century to pass before anything like full equality would be achieved. You can read more about that subject in chapter 15, "The 1960s."

The New Deal

*F*ranklin Delano Roosevelt may be even more popular at the end of the twentieth century than when he was president. That's saying a lot for a man elected to the office *four times.*

FDR: A HERO FOR HIS TIMES (AND OURS)

Roosevelt, who served as chief executive from 1933 to 1945, now has a memorial in Washington—dedicated in May 1997. During the 1980s and 1990s he was praised by Ronald Reagan and Newt Gingrich, conservatives who are usually contemptuous of Democrats and big government.

Yet Roosevelt is a symbol of both. He helped build the Democratic coalition that remains largely intact today—blacks, Jews, labor, the poor—and, with the possible exception of Lyndon Johnson during 1964–65, was the most powerful chief executive of the twentieth century. FDR represented strength in words and action. We remember what he said, and we still live by what he did.

The consensus is that America was lucky to have Roosevelt. He was President during the Depression, our worst economic crisis, and through nearly all of World War II—frightening times.

You have probably heard the often-expressed view that the United States today is lacking in tough, decisive leaders—leaders such as Franklin Delano Roosevelt.

The New Deal, Roosevelt's famous package of economic reforms, and the consequences of World War II continue to have an impact. The following timeline will highlight events during the period 1933–41, when FDR expanded the role of government and changed the nature of American society.

THE GREAT DEPRESSION

Few of us alive at the end of the twentieth century can truly imagine what it was like to live during the Depression. At worst, we've known economic recessions—not the same thing.

- *1929–32*—In the United States this period of time is not called "the depression," but the Great Depression. According to statistics cited in *The Great Depression: America in the 1930s* by T. H. Watkins, 1,352 banks failed in 1930, representing more than $853 million in deposits. In 1931, the number of bank failures rose to 2,294, with deposits approaching $1.7 billion. In 1930, 26,355 businesses failed; the rate of failure, 122 per 10,000, was the highest ever recorded up to that time. At the end of 1931 unemployment had reached 8 million, and within a few months it would climb to 12 million. As Watkins put it: "There had never been such statistics in our history, and there have been none like them since."

- *1929*—Providing an airtight explanation for economic events is a risky business. There is not much on which all economists agree, including the specific causes of the Great Depression. We do know that in October 1929, the price of stocks on the New York Stock Exchange started to fall, and fell some more. Within a month stock prices had declined by about 37 percent. An economic collapse—which became worldwide—followed.

THE NEW DEAL

- *1932*—In 1932, New York governor Franklin D. Roosevelt, a Democrat, was elected President of the United States in a landslide over Herbert Hoover. Roosevelt received 22,800,000 popular votes, to 15,750,000 for Hoover; the margin in the electoral college was 472 to 59. Roosevelt would go on to be elected president in 1936, 1940, and 1944. He died in office in April 1945, at which time Vice President Harry Truman became President.

THE 100 DAYS

The first one hundred days of his administration, known by the catchy title "the Hundred Days," represent the most famous legislative blitz in the history of the country. During that period FDR accomplished the following:

1. *He created the Civilian Conservation Corps, which employed young men from destitute families. The members of the CCC were put to work in various conservation projects in forests and parks. The CCC didn't pay much, but even a little helped families who had nothing.*

2. *He established the Federal Emergency Relief Administration, which made available relief funds for food, clothing, and shelter to the millions of unemployed until they could find jobs or work relief.*

3. *He started the Public Works Administration, which involved hiring private firms to construct buildings, dams, and other vast federal projects.*

4. *Also during this time the Farm Credit Administration was created. The FCA refinanced farm mortgages at low interest rates. Agriculture was devastated during the Great Depression, with the value of all farm property declining from $57.7 billion in 1929 to $51.8 billion in 1931.*

—Watkins, The Great Depression, page 55

- *1933*—Franklin Roosevelt was inaugurated on March 4, 1933. (The Twentieth Amendment to the Constitution, which was ratified in April 1933, changed the inauguration of the president to the current date of January 20.)

- *1935*—Roosevelt did not rest after the hundred days. A number of his most significant and lasting accomplishments occurred later. In 1935, for example, the National Labor Relations Board came into existence. The NLRB remains an important factor in labor relations in this country. The role of the NLRB is to enforce fair practices on the part of labor and management in conducting collective bargaining.

- *1935*—No component of FDR's legacy is as controversial as the establishment of the Social Security program.

As the number of people receiving Social Security has grown, the ratio of workers to beneficiaries has declined significantly as well:

1940—177	1970—3.5
1945—35.7	1975—3.1
1950—13.8	1980—3.2
1955— 8.2	2000—3.2 (projected)
1960— 4.9	2020—2.3 (projected)
1965— 3.9	2030—2.0 (projected)

You can see by these figures, provided by the U.S. Government, that Social Security is an enormously successful program. There are many who would argue that without Social Security benefits, the poverty rate for senior citizens in this country would be astronomical.

In 1999, the Clinton administration began an ambitious program to put Social Security on sound fiscal footing well into the twenty-first century. When you get old—it happens to the best of us—you will be in a better position to either appreciate or denigrate what politicians are doing right now to save Social Security

The Social Security Act provided (1) a federally funded system of old-age insurance beginning at age sixty-five for retired persons, and benefits for dependent survivors of workers who died; and (2) a system of federal aid to the states for pensions for the aged, maternal, and child health services, and aid for crippled children and the blind.

Three years after passage of the Social Security Act, FDR discussed his view on the role of government vis-à-vis the citizenry.

> Government has a final responsibility for the well-being of its citizenship. If private co-operative endeavor fails to provide work for willing hands and relief for the unfortunate, those suffering hardship from no fault of their own have a right to call upon the government for aid; and a government worthy of its name must make fitting response.
>
> —*quoted in* The FDR Years: On Roosevelt and His Legacy, *by William E. Leuchtenberg*

In these anti-tax, anti-government times, could any politician dare be as passionate in defense of the public sector?

- *1937*—Even Roosevelt's admirers have trouble defending his attempt to "pack" the Supreme Court in 1937 with pro–New Deal justices. Frustrated by Court decisions challenging some of his reforms, FDR went to a group of his friends in Congress and convinced them to sponsor legislation permitting a president to appoint as many as six additional justices to the Supreme Court when incumbent justices over seventy did not choose to retire. Bitter opposition in Congress and across American society forced him to abandon the idea before the House could put it to a vote.

The plan to create a more sympathetic Court was an early warning sign of the "Imperial Presidency." Flush with legislative success, and highly popular with the voters, FDR felt he could do anything, including tinkering with the system of checks and balances.

After Roosevelt, presidents seeking to increase the power of the office became a fixture in American politics. During the Cold War, presidents found themselves on top of billions of dollars of weapons, and were fed daily top-secret reports from around the world by the Central Intelligence Agency and the National Security Council. This tempted them to act without consulting Congress.

With Vietnam, for example, Congress never issued a formal declaration of war, which was its right under the Constitution. Though "court-packing" is not in this league, it still represents a blatant effort to give the executive unprecedented power.

- *1941*—A brief mention of Pearl Harbor ("a day that will live in infamy," to quote Roosevelt's famous phrase). Roosevelt had taken a number of steps in the late 1930s and in 1940–41 to counter Japanese moves against China. The most damaging of these was the cutoff of the sale of oil to Japan.

The debate continues whether or not Roosevelt "wanted" war, but it is clear that he recognized Japan as a military threat to American interests in the Pacific. Certainly the Japanese felt war was inevitable, which explains their bombing of Pearl Harbor. On December 8, Congress declared war on Japan. Three days later, Italy and Germany declared war on the United States. By the war's end, America had become a superpower.

ROOSEVELT AND THE MARKET

You're a senior citizen if you lived through the Great Depression, but you might be as young as thirty if you remember the (1987) Great Stock Market Crash.

On October 19, 1987, the Dow Jones Industrial Average fell over 500 points—a decline of almost 25 percent of the market, and double the decline of 1929, the year of the Great Crash. Throughout that Monday evening, television and radio programs made frequent references to bank failures, massive unemployment, and social unrest. Suddenly, the 1930s did not seem very far away.

During the rest of the week millions of Americans monitored the stock market. Even people with zero investments wanted to know what was going to happen on Wall Street. They were reassured. There was no second collapse. One of the chief reasons was that the Securities and Exchange Commission imposed computer trading restrictions, automatically shutting down computerized trading after a set decline. The Securities and Exchange Commission, or SEC, was created by President Franklin Delano Roosevelt in 1934.

This was a year after FDR had started the Federal Deposit Insurance Corporation, or FDIC, which provides insurance on individual bank accounts. Because of the FDIC, the economic consequences of bank failures following the 1987 crash were not as severe as in the 1930s.

A new generation owes its thanks to Franklin Roosevelt.

The 1960s

*T*he 1960s will never go away. Not when it comes to politics. The decade was too important.

The first half of the 1960s was a model of political success. Things got done, and promises were fulfilled. The Civil Rights Acts of 1964 and 1965, the creation of Medicare (1965), the elimination of national quotas on immigration (1965), the birth of the National Endowment for the Arts (1965), the anti-war movement, feminism, and the stirrings of gay liberation, all occurred in that period.

Politicians and commentators sometimes refer to "Vietnam syndrome," which is shorthand for describing a timid foreign policy. The theory: Having lost the war in Vietnam, the military is now extra cautious about sending troops to faraway lands. Each time a crisis looms, the phrase is brought into the debate.

The impact of the Civil Rights movement, which actually began in the late 1950s in the South, is obvious. The success of the movement influenced later demands by Chicanos, women, gays, the handicapped, and other groups, for society to acknowledge *their* rights. "Diversity," "multiculturalism," and "political correctness"—terms made popular in the 1990s—represent a continuation of sixties liberalism. Feminists, gay activists, and ethnic/race-based political groups are still around and are exerting considerable political pressure, especially within the Democratic Party.

THE LEGACY

You can't be neutral about the 1960s. Liberal or conservative must acknowledge it was a decade when many people worked hard for change. And to a remarkable degree they succeeded.

The political legacy of that decade is more than civil rights and Vietnam. The 104th (1995–96) and the 105th Congresses (1997–98) have been preoccupied with what to do about the issues of elimination of national quotas on immigration, Medicare, and the NEA. You can see that the Republican counterrevolution of the 1980s and 1990s is essentially a revolt against the politics of the 1960s— namely, big government.

The concept of 1960s-style activism influenced one group who is otherwise contemptuous of the decade: freshmen Republicans elected to the House in 1994. They called themselves revolutionaries—just like the campus protestors of the 1960s—and they demanded change *now*, just like the campus protestors of the 1960s. The obvious difference between the two is that many more student demonstrators than members of Congress were arrested and put in jail.

Turning Points

- *1962*—The 1960s are often discussed solely on the basis of what made headlines during the last half of the decade. In the case of race relations, that means

ghetto riots, the Black Panthers, and Black Power—
each time, blacks playing the role of the aggressors.
In September, a black student named James
Meredith tried to enroll at the University of
Mississippi. His enrollment sparked rioting in
which two people were killed. Order was restored
only with the arrival of 10,000 federal troops.

- *1963*—Two events took place that remain among
  the most discussed and analyzed in recent
  American history. You have probably read thousands of words about each.

The first was the assassination of President John F.
Kennedy on November 22; the second is the March on
Washington on August 28. Some 250,000 people went to
the Lincoln Memorial that day to hear a variety of speakers talk passionately about civil rights. You are a sixties
trivia champion if you can name any of the speakers
besides Dr. Martin Luther King Jr. who delivered his
famous "I have a dream . . ." speech that day.

- *1964*—President Lyndon Johnson was at the height
  of his political powers in 1964. The first indication
  was the passage of the Civil Rights Act in June.

The President overcame the fierce opposition of
Southern members of Congress to get a bill approved outlawing discrimination in public places and helping to
ensure fair employment and desegregated schools. The
next year Congress—again swayed by Johnson—passed
the Voting Rights Act, which ended literacy tests and poll
taxes. Both had been used to deny blacks the vote in the
South. Along with the war on poverty, these measures
were part of LBJ's ambitious platform, the Great Society.

- *1965*—On August 11, 1965, five days after
  President Johnson signed the voting-rights bill,

rioting broke out in the Watts section of Los Angeles. When it ended, thirty-four people—most of them black residents of Watts and South-Central Los Angeles—were dead.

Watts was the first of the major ghetto riots of the 1960s; Newark and Detroit followed in 1967. The Watts riots captured the attention of the media and government, which had all but ignored the area in the past. Even the reclusive and brilliant novelist Thomas Pynchon wrote a piece on Watts for the *New York Times Magazine* on June 12, 1966.

Ironically, Watts would prove to be a boon to right-wingers. One year after the riot, Ronald Reagan was elected governor of California. This was not a coincidence. Inspired by Reagan's 1966 gubernatorial campaign, law-and-order Republicans taunted Democrats throughout the sixties for supposed permissiveness regarding ghetto riots and campus demonstrations.

This strategy continues today, though now the charge leveled at Democrats is being "soft on crime." After all, riots and demonstrations were not as common in the 1980s and 1990s. (There are a few exceptions, notably the Rodney King riots of 1992.)

- *1965*—At the end of 1965 there were 184,000 troops in Vietnam—some 150,000 more than at the beginning of the year. This was the point where the costs of the war, in men and in dollars, could no longer be easily justified by the government.

With the escalation of American involvement came an escalation of protest. In April 1965, 25,000 students marched in Washington against the war in Vietnam. Two years later 250,000 people marched in New York City. The war in Vietnam and the anti-war movement have had a tremendous, lasting influence on American politics and foreign policy.

- *1968*—There have been several books written about 1968 alone. This year saw the assassinations of Martin Luther King Jr. and Robert Kennedy, the Tet Offensive, demonstrations at Columbia University, and riots in Washington, D.C. *All* the traumas of a traumatic decade came together in 1968.

The violent battle between police and demonstrators at the Democratic National Convention in Chicago in August seems the perfect symbol for the year. Chicago was a vivid reminder of the generational divisions over Vietnam, and it became a major factor in the defeat of Democratic presidential candidate Hubert Humphrey in November 1968. Humphrey lost to Richard Nixon, which was a not-very-sixties way to close out the 1960s. After all, Nixon had lost the presidency to John Kennedy in 1960.

After eight years of Democratic rule, 1961–69, Nixon's victory started the Republican dominance of the White House. From 1969 to 1993 (when Clinton took office) Jimmy Carter (1977–81) was the only Democratic president.

WOMEN'S LIBERATION

The Civil Rights movement of the late 1950s and 1960s was inspired, if not led, by Dr. Martin Luther King Jr. The women's liberation movement of the late 1960s, later known as feminism, was inspired by *The Feminine Mystique* by Betty Friedan. Published in 1963, *The Feminine Mystique* argued that "suburban middle-class housewives were not fulfilled by homemaking and childbearing" (*Leaders from the 1960s: A Biographical Sourcebook of American Activism*, David DeLeon, editor). The book sold three million copies, and was excerpted in all the major women's magazines.

Friedan proved to be as talented an organizer as she was an author. She turned her thoughts into action. In 1966

Friedan and others founded the National Organization for Women (NOW), which today remains the most influential feminist organization in the country. Friedan was NOW's first president, from 1966 to 1969. She wrote the founding statement of the organization: "The purpose of NOW is to take action to bring women into full participation in the mainstream of American society now, exercising all the privileges and responsibilities thereof in truly equal partnership with men" (DeLeon, page 249).

Friedan later became a critic of the extreme aspects of feminism. She objected to some feminists turning equal rights for women into an attack on the "predatory" nature of male heterosexuality.

GAY RIGHTS

Today acknowledgements of homosexuality, partial homosexuality, or homosexual thoughts are all the rage in America. Celebrities, athletes, and even a few brave (or calculating) politicians are playing the game. How different this is from the early 1960s—when Frank Kameny not only came out of the closet, but aggressively and publicly fought for homosexual rights. Kameny is one more example of the way in which the 1960s changed the nature of American society and American politics.

Kameny was a scientific researcher in the army at a time (1957) when "there was a demand for political and sexual conformity" (DeLeon, page 253). This was a consequence of the Cold War, specifically, the fear that homosexuals would be subject to blackmail by enemy spies. When asked about his private life by army security officials, Kameny told them it was none of their business. As a result he was fired from his job.

Kameny decided to form a Washington chapter of the Mattachine Society, a gay-rights organization started in California ten years earlier. The name was taken from medieval court jesters who wore masks, enabling them to articulate unpopular truths. "Kameny, elected the group's first president, was one of the few homosexuals in America willing to appear publicly and use his own name" (DeLeon, page 255).

In the spring and summer of 1965 Kameny organized gay pickets in front of the White House to protest regulations preventing homosexuals from working in government. He also began challenging the American Psychiatric Association's finding that homosexuality was a pathology.

In 1973, the APA removed homosexuality from its list of psychiatric disorders; in 1975, the Civil Service Commission ended the policy of using homosexuality as a reason for disqualification in federal employment. Kameny played an important part in both decisions.

In many ways the gay-rights movement and feminism have become part of the establishment which they rejected and, more importantly, which rejected them. Weekly you hear politicians openly debate issues of importance to gays and women. And pop culture caters to both as never before. Sometimes it seems all of America has come rushing out of the closet.

VIETNAM

Though American troops weren't withdrawn from Vietnam until the 1970s, opposition to the war at the end of the preceding decade was so intense that it transformed the political landscape for the foreseeable future. Vietnam was a hugely unpopular war. It created or fed a supposition on the part of Americans that its leaders couldn't be trusted and that its institutions were corrupt. Even soldiers who risked and lost their lives in combat in that war were (unfairly) held accountable by some. The freedom from suspicion and criticism enjoyed by American officials before the war seemed to vanish once it had been concluded.

Moreover, the war in Vietnam was the first one clearly lost by the United States. The myth of invincibility was shattered—at least for a time—and, clearly, any political figure advocating any foreign-policy adventure was going to have to make a strong case.

Finally, those who were actively or passively involved in the anti-war movement felt vindicated when our troops were withdrawn in the early 1970s. They felt empowered by the idea that a grassroots movement could so radically affect both national and international affairs. Citizen involvement in political affairs has increased since the 1960s.

The Republican Comeback and the Comeback Kid

Y

ou may be wary of the so-called Great Man theory of history, the idea that one person, usually a man, can make an era. Perhaps you believe it's inconsistent with the meaning of this country. We are taught in this country that each of us is special or—to quote the title of a 1970 hit by Sly and the Family Stone—"Everybody Is a Star."

WATERGATE AND NIXON

The resignation of President Nixon—a first in American history—seemed to put an end to the idea of the "Imperial Presidency." Nixon left office because he was almost certain to be removed from office by Congress. The "high crimes and misdemeanors" of which he was accused were identified with political shenanigans performed by operatives working on behalf of the president's reelection in 1972. The downfall of the president was to some degree ascribed to the investigation of "dirty tricks" in the White House by several journalists, most notably two young reporters for the *Washington Post*, Bob Woodward and Carl Bernstein. The power of public officials, already weakened by the growth of citizen unrest in Vietnam, now seemed to be further eroded by the media. And an increasing number of media outlets, eager to scoop one another, have uncovered scandal after scandal about public figures, for the last two decades.

This did not seem to be an era for heroes.

THREE POLITICAL GIANTS

And yet, American politics in the last twenty years of the twentieth century has been dominated by three men: Ronald Reagan, Bill Clinton, and Newt Gingrich. These three have changed the established political order—surely a criterion for historical greatness.

Reagan

Ronald Reagan demonstrated in 1980, and again in 1984, that a right-wing conservative could be elected president of the United States. Up until Reagan's victory over Jimmy Carter in 1980, intelligent people argued that a majority of Americans would not elect someone of his political beliefs. Four years later, when Walter Mondale was crushingingly defeated by Reagan, the triumph of this brand of conservatism was obvious.

Though Reagan could be faulted for advocating fantastic increases in defense spending which helped multiply the national debt, the rather abrupt end of the Cold War with the Soviet Union under his successor George Bush, appeared to many to vindicate his foreign policy.

In 1988, Vice President George Bush, a comparative moderate, defeated his Democratic rival, Michael Dukakis. Republicans had captured the White House in five of six elections. Anguished Democrats asked the question, "When will we ever again elect one of our own as president?" The answer came sooner than they expected.

Clinton

Bill Clinton's victory in 1992 returned a Democrat to the White House and represented the emergence of the "New Democrats,"the centrists of the party. New Democrats called for welfare reform and a reduced role for government on many fronts. Many of these Democrats were also in favor of free trade and opposed to quotas.

The election of Clinton also marked the first time that a person born after World War II—a baby boomer—had been elected president. Clinton's easy reelection in 1996 has now made it seem as if the Democrats have a lock on the presidency.

Gingrich

Election night 1992 was not a happy occasion for Republicans. Not only did their candidate for president lose, but once again Democrats retained control of Congress. Anguished Republicans asked the question, "When will we ever elect a Republican House and/or a Republican Senate?" Again the answer came sooner than expected.

Throughout 1994 Newt Gingrich, a Republican congressman from Georgia, plotted with fellow GOP members of the House, and like-minded consultants and pollsters, to win the House of Representatives. It had been forty years since Republicans had controlled the House. He believed 1994 presented an excellent opportunity for ending the losing streak.

The Republicans' strategy was simple: Use the Democrats' power against them. Attack the Democratic leadership in the House as arrogant, corrupt, and out-of-touch, and blast Clinton on health care and other seemingly ill-conceived policies. In addition, offer a "Contract with America," which would show the public that Republicans intended to move the country forward.

On election day 1994, Republicans won a majority in the House and Senate, one of the more astounding results in modern American elections. Gingrich became Speaker of the House in 1995. Two years later, the GOP lost several seats in the House, but not enough to return to the minority. You could argue that today Republicans have a lock on Congress.

TURNING POINTS

- *1964*—The chapter on the 1960s referred to the power wielded by President Johnson at the beginning of his term. Much of the reason for LBJ's early success stems from the 1964 presidential election.

  Johnson won a huge victory over Barry Goldwater that year. Goldwater was victorious in only six states: five in the South, and his home state of Arizona. It looked as if the right wing of the Republican Party had been destroyed.

  Many journalists believed this to be the case. Robert Novak, the well-known conservative newspaper columnist you may have seen on *Crossfire*, wrote a book about the election called *The Agony of the G.O.P. 1964*. *New York Times* columnist James Reston shared this thought on November 4, 1964: "Barry Goldwater not only lost the Presidential election yesterday but the conservative cause as well. He has wrecked his party for a long time to come. . . ."

  Not quite. Four years after Goldwater lost the presidency, Richard Nixon won, although Nixon was not a conservative of the Goldwater mold. And sixteen years after Goldwater's defeat, Ronald Reagan—who had campaigned for the Arizona senator against LBJ—had a victory every bit as convincing as Johnson's in 1964. Conservatives had finally placed one of their own in the White House.

- *1980*—Ronald Reagan captured forty-three states, trouncing President Jimmy Carter. Reagan won because he had a couple of dream issues on his side—the American hostages in Iran, double-digit inflation at home—and because he had extraordinary charm. His beliefs may have been those of a fire-breathing conservative, but his personality made the message less threatening. Younger conservatives, Gingrich included, were captivated by Reagan's supreme confidence, telegenic appeal, and anti-government theme. Reagan took two contradictory messages—hatred of government and a desire to get elected—and made them compatible.

- *1988*—With his awkward syntax and "aw, shucks" manner, George Bush was far from the ideal campaigner, but he defeated Michael Dukakis in the 1988 presidential election because he kept the Democratic candidate on the defensive with the kinds of issues that had been keeping Democrats on the defensive for twenty years.

  Bush accused Dukakis of being insufficiently patriotic and of coddling criminals. He also disparaged Dukakis as a liberal and "a card-carrying member of the ACLU." Dukakis sealed his own fate when he took an ill-advised ride in a tank. (If you remember nothing else about the 1988 campaign, you probably remember that image.)

  Bill Clinton and other Democrats watched the Dukakis campaign in horror, determined not to make the same mistakes in 1992.

- *1992*—Bill Clinton started the 1992 presidential race on shaky ground, to say the least. The media soon became obsessed with the candidate's sex life and his decision to avoid the draft during the war in Vietnam. For days this was virtually the sum total of what got reported about Clinton. A less determined candidate would have given up. But one of Clinton's great strengths is an ability to dodge bad news and to keep moving toward his goal. He stayed in the race, and grew stronger, sharpening his New Democrat message of personal responsibility and tax relief for the middle class.

President Bush not only had to contend with the most capable Democratic candidate in years, but with a stagnant and slumping economy, and the entry into the race of Ross Perot, a viable third-party challenger. Perot became a sort of ally of Clinton's, attacking Bush much more frequently than the Democrat did. In the end Clinton received only 43 percent of the popular vote, but won 370 electoral votes, 100 over the minimum needed to be elected.

• *1994*—In February 1994, at a Republican retreat in Salisbury, Maryland, House Republicans began a series of discussions on electoral strategy for the November 1994 elections.

CONTRACT WITH AMERICA

According to *Contract with America: The Bold Plan By Representative Newt Gingrich, Representative Dick Armey, and the House Republicans to Change the Nation*, the Salisbury conference produced both the idea of the Contract and an agreement on five principles that defined the Republican Party:

1. Individual liberty

2. Economic opportunity

3. Limited government

4. Personal responsibility

5. Security at home and abroad

The next step was to bring the Contract in line with these core ideals. Here are the ten provisions of the Contract, which was signed September 27, 1994, on the steps of the U.S. Capitol by more than three hundred Republican candidates for the House of Representatives.

1. Balanced-budget amendment and line-item veto

2. Stop violent criminals

3. Welfare reform

4. Strengthen families and protect our kids

5. Tax cuts for families

6. Strong national defense

7. Fairness for senior citizens

8. Roll back government regulations and create jobs

9. Common-sense legal reforms

10. Congressional term limits

The Contract turned out to be more important in setting the Republican agenda than as a campaign tool. Many voters who backed GOP candidates in the 1994 elections had never heard of the Contract, and many of these were less than pleased when they learned the details. By then, however, the GOP had gained control of the House. In a burst of activity that had a number of members of the House spending the night in their offices, the new majority passed much of the Contract within the first few months of the session. Gingrich proved his point— even if the Senate blocked many of the key bills.

- *1996*—Bill Clinton has acquired two nicknames during his political career: "Slick Willie" and "the Comeback Kid." Leaving aside the less flattering title, Clinton has proved the aptness of the other. Devastated by the results of the 1994 elections, Clinton floundered for several months. Nobody gave him much of a chance of being reelected.

The president didn't panic. He waited for House Republicans to make mistakes, and when they did (shutting down the government), he hit them hard. At the same time he reclaimed his status as a New Democrat by signing a tough welfare bill in the summer of 1996. Many columnists and commentators remarked on how Clinton brilliantly (or cynically) borrowed Republican ideas and made them his own. But he won, and, in campaigns, winning is everything.

Deeper into Politics

You vote, you debate elections and issues with your friends. You teach your children the importance of politics.

Is that enough? Yes . . . but. In America, you can always do more, such as giving money to a candidate or candidates. If your check's good and you have obeyed campaign finance laws (more about that later), then your support will be gratefully accepted. Campaigns are expensive. Every little bit counts.

political action committee. You have no idea what it does, or how you can become a member.

Here are some questions you may ask in your pursuit of information.

1. How much is spent on federal elections in the 1990s?

2. Has money always played a role on the electoral process in America?

3. What are the rules governing campaign finance?

4. How can I access campaign spending information? Is it public record?

MONEY, MONEY, MONEY, MONEY

The 1996 presidential election cycle was the most expensive in the history of the United States. According to the Federal Election Commission, from January 1, 1995, through December 31, 1996, national, state, and local Republican Party committees reported federal receipts of $416.5 million. The GOP committees disbursed $408.5 million. These totals represent a 57 percent increase in fund-raising and a 62 percent increase in expenditures since the last presidential election cycle in 1991–92.

The FEC reported that Democratic committees over that same period raised $221.6 million and spent $214.3 million. This represented an increase of 36 percent in receipts and disbursements since 1991–92.

At the end of 1996 the Republicans were left with a debt of $15 million, while the Democrats were $17.4 million in the red.

You read newspapers and watch public-affairs programs on television. You are aware that the increased cost of running for office has fueled criticism of the campaign finance system. With so much money changing hands, there are bound to be problems.

You may have heard that the moneyed classes can buy access to members of Congress or the president; and/or that politicians will sponsor legislation or do other special favors on behalf of generous contributors to their campaign.

You're not sure if it's true or false. Arguments can be made on both sides. What you do know is, a lot of people are dissatisfied with the current system.

Money and Politics

Maybe you've never thought about contributing money to a politician. Charities and business groups may have benefited from your generosity in the past, but when a campaign sends you a fundraising letter, you toss it in the trash. You don't care enough to part with your money.

Still, the day might come when your all-time favorite candidate, a man or woman in whom you have put your faith, is desperately short of funds. The campaign puts out an appeal: *Send Money!* You're torn. You haven't given in the past, but this is different. You decide it's time.

SENDING IN THAT CHECK

You contribute, understanding it takes money to run a campaign. You may not like it, but that's the way the system works. Others don't like the idea, either, but that doesn't stop them from making contributions.

Before sending a check, you do some research. Among the things you discover is that your company operates a

The huge amount spent in 1996 had a political impact in 1997. Two bills and a number of proposals to change the way campaigns are financed were unveiled early in the year. One measure, sponsored by Arizona Republican senator John McCain and Wisconsin Democratic senator Russell Feingold, called for greater restrictions on contributions and spending.

A second, by California Republican congressman John Doolittle, proposed an opposite solution. Doolittle's measure would repeal all limits on individual and PAC (political action committee) contributions.

Outside of Congress, other efforts were undertaken.

The public-interest group Common Cause launched Project Independence, which set a goal of 1,776,000 signatures on a petition urging a vote on campaign finance reform legislation before July 4, 1997. The drive fell just short.

The League of Women Voters Education Fund supported five ideas for campaign reform developed by a group including Norman J. Ornstein of the American Enterprise Institute and Thomas E. Mann of the Brookings Institution.

The plan included providing free TV time for federal candidates, strengthening the Federal Election Commission, which is responsible for enforcing election laws; and providing a tax credit for small contributions from individuals. The League took out a newspaper ad with a number to call for anyone interested in receiving a copy of these proposals.

> The American people cannot afford another election like the one we just had—an election drowning in soft money and poisoned by attack ads. We cannot afford to have the integrity of the system continually undermined by the disastrous combination of an ineffective Federal Election Commission and laws that allow undisclosed millions to be funneled into campaigns.
> —*Becky Cain, chair, League of Women Voters Education Fund, July 21, 1997*

Some argue that the issue of campaign contributions is much ado about nothing. They point out in the context of the American economy, the amount of money given to politicians is minuscule.

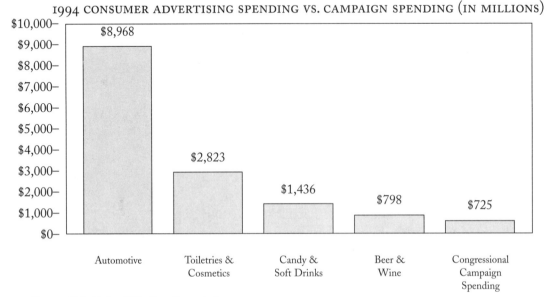

1994 CONSUMER ADVERTISING SPENDING VS. CAMPAIGN SPENDING (IN MILLIONS)

Source: U.S. Federal Election Commission

CAMPAIGN FINANCE REFORM

You might be surprised to know that the problem of money in politics is not new; it started with George Washington.

In her book *Politics and the Power of Money*, author Suzanne M. Coil includes a chapter on the history of campaign finance reform. Here are some of the highlights:

> When George Washington sought election to the Virginia House of Burgesses in 1757, he plied voters with twenty-eight gallons of rum, fifty gallons of rum punch, thirty-four gallons of wine, forty-six gallons of beer, and two gallons of cider. His opponents were quick to accuse him of buying votes (page 33).

When Abraham Lincoln decided to run for Congress in 1846, his supporters raised $200 for his campaign fund. After winning the election, Lincoln returned $199.25 to his contributors, because he did not need the money. He used his own horse to ride to speeches, stayed in the homes of friends, and spent only 75 cents for a barrel of cider (page 36).

The first federal law on campaign financing was enacted on March 2, 1867. The measure was a response to efforts to tie federal jobs to contributions. The text:

No officer or employee of the government shall require or request any workingman in any navy yard to contribute or pay any money for political purposes, nor shall any workingman be removed or discharged for political opinion; and any officer or employee of the government who shall offend against the provisions of this section shall be dismissed from service to the United States (page 36).

> ## MAKING A (FINANCIAL) CONTRIBUTION
>
> *Despite criticisms and complaints, you're still inclined to make a contribution. Your candidate needs help. He said so. If you decide not to write a check, and he loses by a slim margin, you will never forgive yourself.*
>
> *First you've got to know the rules. The campaign staff can clarify some arcane points, but it is your responsibility to learn the basics. It wouldn't be good if your help got you in trouble with federal election authorities.*

According to Coil, this bill did not end the "spoils" system—in which political favors are dispensed to members of the victorious party.

In 1910 Congress passed a bill establishing disclosure requirements for candidates for the House of Representatives. A similar law passed the following year in the Senate.

The legislation also set limits on the amount candidates could spend toward nomination and election. For House candidates, the limit was $5,000; for Senate candidates, $10,000.

The Federal Election Campaign Act of 1971 and Its Amendments

This law (1971) and amendments (1974 and 1979) are the basis for the current system of campaign finance. The key provisions are listed below.

Note: The limits apply to a calendar year unless otherwise stated.

- You may contribute $1,000 per candidate, per election; $20,000 to a national party committee per year; $5,000 to any other political committee per year. The aggregate total of individual contributions cannot exceed $25,000 in a single year.

> **CONTRIBUTIONS ARE PROHIBITED**
>
> - *from foreign nationals, national banks, corporations, and labor unions;*
> - *in cash amounts of more than $100;*
> - *from anonymous contributors of more than $50.*

- A multicandidate political committee can give $5,000 per candidate, per election; $15,000 to a national party committee; $5,000 to any other political committee. A multicandidate committee is defined as having more than 50 contributors.

- Other political committees can give $1,000 per candidate, per election; $20,000 to a national party committee; $5,000 to any other political committee.

- Party committees can supply $1,000 or $5,000 per candidate, per election (depending on whether the committee qualifies as a multicandidate committee); $5,000 to any other political committee. For National Senatorial Campaign Committee, or National Party Committee, or combination of both; $17,500 to Senate candidate, per year, in which election is sought.

American subsidiaries of foreign companies are permitted to make contributions under U.S. election law.

The rules apply to you, the contributor. What limits does the system impose on candidates? Here are some other provisions you—and the candidate—should know.

How the Law Affects the Candidates

- Candidates who accept public funding in presidential elections can contribute up to $50,000 in personal and immediate family funds.

- Presidential primary candidates who have raised at least $5,000 in each of twenty states in contributions from individuals of $250 or less may have contributions of $250 or less matched equally with federal money, up to one-half the primary spending limit. Nominees of major parties in general elections are eligible for public funds in the amount of their spending limit. (Note: The 1976 presidential election was the first publicly funded federal election in U.S. history.)

- All candidates for federal office and all political committees operating in federal elections must file regularly scheduled reports. Presidential candidates and most political committees file with the Federal Election Commission, while House and Senate candidates file with the Clerk of the House and the Secretary of the Senate. However, all federal spending reports are available through the FEC.

- Reports show total cash on hand, receipts, transfers, loans, rebates, refund dividends, and interest. For presidential candidates, the reports include public funds. All contributors donating in excess of $200 per year—and persons to whom expenditures were made in excess of $200 per year—must be identified.

Once you give money to your candidate, you might be curious to know how much the other guy has in his campaign account. The information is as near as your home computer.

The Federal Election Commission now has a computerized disclosure database available twenty-four hours a day, seven days a week.

CONTRIBUTIONS ARE NOT ACCOUNTED FOR

An article by Edward Roeder in the April 14, 1997, issue of The New Republic *was highly critical of the FEC's disclosure policing efforts. According to Roeder, a computer analysis of the FEC's database showed that the National Republican Congressional Committee failed to disclose a first name or first initial for 764 major donors in the 1995–96 election cycle. He said the Democratic National Committee reported no first name for 122 donors during the same period.*

"All in all, in 1996 more than $56 million in large contributions was not properly accounted for by members of Congress, the six major party committees and the two major party presidential campaigns. And that's not counting soft money. If Congress and the Justice Department want to limit their inquiries to clear violations of the law, that $56 million is a good place to start."

—Edward Roeder, "Blank Check," The New Republic,

April 14, 1997, page 19

The FEC's Direct Access Program has information on contributions by individuals, political action committees, and political party committees; financial status reports on all candidates and committees, including latest total receipts, total disbursements, cash on hand, debt amounts, and more. The DAP works on virtually any personal computer equipped with a modem and communications software. The FEC imposes a $20 per hour usage charge. There is no sign-up fee.

For more information contact a DAP specialist through the FEC's toll-free number, (800) 424-9530.

If you take time to study spending reports, you'd like to think the information is complete. You're sufficiently knowledgeable about campaign finance law to know full disclosure is required. So you take the reports at their word. However, some skepticism is in order. The reports are not always 100 percent accurate. For whatever reason—deliberate deception or innocent oversight—candidates or parties have been known to disguise the source of some contributions.

At this point in your study you have a sense of the laws covering contributions in federal (House, Senate, presidential) elections. You are confident that you know what is and what is not permitted. The difference between the rules governing PACs and the rules governing an individual contributor such as yourself are clear.

Yet as you probe more deeply, you may hear about a key Supreme Court ruling that serves as the constitutional foundation for the current system.

Buckley v. Valeo

The Supreme Court's 1976 *Buckley v. Valeo* decision is to campaign finance law what *Roe v. Wade* is to abortion. Nearly every discussion about campaign finance reform somehow gets back to *Buckley v. Valeo*. The decision has devoted defenders and angry accusers.

The *Buckley* decision is often summarized as "money = speech." The Court ruled that in general, expenditure limits were unconstitutional because they imposed direct restraints on the quantity of political speech. Contributing money to a candidate is considered a constitutionally protected form of political expression.

The Court ruled, however, that some limitations were important to counter the appearance of corruption, and to make the system accessible to more than the rich. As a result, the Court upheld the $1,000 per year limitation for individual contributions to individual candidates.

Finally, the Court affirmed the general reporting and disclosure and public financing provisions of campaign finance law.

In the series of Supreme Court cases beginning with the 1976 *Buckley* decision to the 1996 decision in the *Colorado Republican Federal Campaign Committee*, the . . . theme that pervades. . . . is that campaign finance reform affects speech, expression and association, and is thus severely limited by the First Amendment and subject to a standard of strict judicial review by the courts.
—*Thomas M. Durbin, "Campaign Finance: First Amendment Issues and Major Supreme Court Cases," a Congressional Research Service Report for Congress, updated September 17, 1996, page 16*

HARD MONEY AND SOFT MONEY

If you follow elections, you will come across the phrases "soft money" and "hard money." The distinction between the two is extremely important. Campaigns and contributors have come to grief by being unable or unwilling to acknowledge the difference. You need to be very clear on soft money versus hard money before you contribute.

The spending regulations discussed earlier in this chapter apply to so-called hard money. These are funds given directly to a candidate's campaign. Hard money is used expressly to urge the election of a candidate, as in commercials that say "Nixon's the One," "All the Way with LBJ," or "Reelect President Bush."

Note: Hard money can also include certain expenditures that are made, independent of the campaign. These would urge the defeat of a clearly identified candidate. You are endorsing the election of one candidate by blasting his opponent. Some political action committees have been known to use this method of getting across their point of view.

Soft money has been around since the 1940s. In 1943 labor unions were banned from making contributions or expenditures to candidates in federal elections (corporations had been banned from doing so in 1907). To get their voice heard, unions now choose to spend money for related political purposes, such as voter registration drives, "nonpartisan" education, and donations to state and local candidates. Instead of directly helping a candidate, soft money helps the party. Of course, the party can use the funds in a way that ultimately benefits that same candidate, such as sponsoring a voter registration drive in her district.

Soft money is subject to comparatively few regulations or limits. Thus lies its appeal to fund-raisers and contributors—they can do almost anything they want with soft money.

In the past twenty years the major political parties have raised and spent huge amounts of soft money. Indeed, soft money was at the heart of the 1996 Clinton-Gore campaign controversy. The large contributions the Clinton-Gore operation received from foreign or otherwise suspect donors—sometimes hundreds of thousands of dollars per person—was in the form of soft money.

In the 1996 presidential race, soft money was used to fund issue-oriented ads, which had the practical effect of saying, "Vote for Bill Clinton." This is demonstrated by the following example: The Democratic National Committee would release an ad discussing the assault-weapons ban, noting that President Clinton was a strong supporter. People in sympathy with the ban would be given a good reason to vote for Clinton, although the ad never stated, "Reelect the President."

There are people who feel this kind of "issue spending" constitutes a major loophole that enables groups to circumvent the law. But any attempts to change it will invariably run up against the First Amendment guarantees of legitimate political speech.

POLITICAL ACTION COMMITTEES

Every couple of months you receive a notice at work asking you to make a contribution to the office political action committee. You speak to a coworker, who reassures you that contributions are not mandatory. By law you cannot be forced to join the company PAC.

However, you are intrigued. You like your job, and you are becoming more involved with politics every day. Why not give to the PAC?

Again, the first thing you should do is get some background information.

Political action committees, or PACs, are the spawn of federal campaign laws passed in the 1970s. They have since become a tremendously popular device for groups wanting to influence the political process. Their growth in number has matched the huge increase in campaign spending.

GETTING THE FACTS

The toll-free telephone number for the FEC's Public Records Office is (800) 424-9530. The FEC's World Wide Web site is http://www.fec. gov.

The politics of most PACs are self-explanatory, such as the National Rifle Association Victory Fund, the National Education Association Political Action Committee, or the American Bankers Association (BankPAC). You have no doubt where the first stands on gun control, the second stands on merit pay for teachers, and the third stands on regulation of the banking industry: no, no, and no.

Other PACs, however, are not so easy to figure out. For example, can you determine the agenda of Campaign America, the Monday Morning Political Action Committee, the National Committee for an Effective Congress, or National PAC? It's impossible to know without some guidance.

One sure way you can learn more is through FEC records. The FEC will not only answer questions about specific PACs, but will provide computer printout listings and disclosure reports.

Another way of obtaining this information—and more—is by checking campaign spending reports. The secretaries of each state usually have on file reports for state and federal candidates under its jurisdiction. Address all inquiries to the secretaries of state in each state.

Sources for Campaign Spending Data

Alabama
600 Dexter Avenue
Montgomery, AL 36130
TEL: (205) 242-7205
FAX: (205) 242-4993

Alaska
P.O. Box 110015
Juneau, AK 99811
TEL: (907) 465-3520
FAX: (907) 463-5364

Arizona
1700 W. Washington Street
Phoenix, AZ 85007
TEL: (602) 542-0681
FAX: (602) 542-1575

Arkansas
256 State Capitol
Little Rock, AR 72201
TEL: (601) 682-1010
FAX: (501) 682-1284

California
1500 11th Street
Sacramento, CA 95814
TEL: (916) 653-7244
FAX: (916) 653-4620

Colorado
1560 Broadway, Suite 200
Denver, CO 80202
TEL: (303) 894-2200
FAX: (303) 894-2242

Connecticut
State Capitol, Room 104
Hartford, CT 06106
TEL: (203) 566-2739
FAX: (203) 566-6318

Delaware
P.O. Box 898
Dover, DE 19903
TEL: (302) 759-4111
FAX: (302) 739-3811

Florida
Secretary of State
The Capitol
Tallahassee, FL 32399
TEL: (904) 922-0234
FAX: (904) 487-2214

Georgia
State Capitol, Room 214
Atlanta, GA 30394
TEL: (404) 656-2881
FAX: (404) 656-0513

Hawaii
State Capitol, 5th Floor
235 S. Beretania Street
Honolulu, HI 96813
TEL: (808) 586-0255
FAX: (808) 586-0231

Idaho
State House, Room 203
Boise, ID 83720
TEL: (208) 334-2300
FAX: (208) 354-2282

Illinois
213 State House
Springfield, IL 62706
TEL: (217) 782-2201
FAX: (217) 785-0358

Indiana
State House, Room 201
Indianapolis, IN 46204
TEL: (317) 252-6536
FAX: (317) 283-3283

Iowa
1007 E. Grand Avenue
Des Moines, IA 50319
TEL: (515) 281-5204
FAX: (515) 242-5952

Kansas
300 SW 10th Street
Topeka, KS 66612
TEL: (913) 296-4575
FAX: (913) 296-4570

Kentucky
State Capitol, Room 150
700 Capitol Avenue
Frankfort, KY 40601
TEL: (502) 564-3490
FAX: (502) 564-5687

Louisiana
P.O. Box 94125
Baton Rouge, LA 70804
TEL: (504) 342-4479
FAX: (504) 342-5577

Maine
Nash Building, Station #148
Augusta, ME 04333
TEL: (207) 626-8400
FAX: (207) 287-8598

Maryland
Jeffrey Building, 16 Francis Street
Annapolis, MD 21401
TEL: (410) 974-2229
FAX: (410) 974-5190

Massachusetts
Secretary of the Commonwealth
State House, 24 Beacon Street
Boston, MA 02133
TEL: (617) 727-9180
FAX: (617) 742-4722

Michigan
Treasury Building, 1st Floor
490 W. Allegan Street
Lansing, MI 48918
TEL: (517) 373-2510
FAX: (517) 979-0727

Minnesota
Secretary of State
180 State Office Building
100 Constitution Avenue
St. Paul, MN 55155
TEL: (612) 296-2079
FAX: (612) 296-9075

Mississippi
P.O. Box 136
401 Mississippi Street
Jackson, MS 39215
TEL: (601) 359-1350
FAX: (601) 354-5019

Missouri
State Capitol, Room 208
P.O. Box 778
Jefferson City, MO 66101
TEL: (573) 751-4936
FAX: (573) 526-3242

Montana
State Capitol, Room 225
1301 6th Avenue
Helena, MT 59620
TEL: (406) 444-2054
FAX: (406) 444-9976

Nebraska
State Capitol, Suite 2300
P.O. Box 94608
Lincoln, NE 68509
TEL: (402) 471-2554
FAX: (402) 471-3237

Nevada
Capitol Complex
Carson City, NV 89710
TEL: (702) 687-5203
FAX: (702) 687-3471

New Hampshire
204 State House
Concord, NH 03301
TEL: (603) 271-3242
FAX: (603) 271-6316

New Jersey
State House, CN300
Trenton, NJ 08625
TEL: (609) 777-2535
FAX: (609) 292-7665

New Mexico
325 Don Gasper
Santa Fe, NM 87503
TEL: (505) 827-3600
FAX: (505) 827-3634

New York
Department of State
162 Washington Avenue
Albany, NY 12231
TEL: (518) 474-0060
FAX: (518) 474-4765

North Carolina
300 N. Salisbury Street
Raleigh, NC 27603
TEL: (919) 733-5140
FAX: (919) 733-5172

North Dakota
State Capitol, 1st Floor
600 E. Boulevard Avenue
Bismarck, ND 58505
TEL: (701) 328-2900
FAX: (701) 328-2992

Ohio
30 E. Broad Street, 14th Floor
Columbus, OH 43266
TEL: (614) 466-2655
FAX: (614) 644-0649

Oklahoma
State Capitol Building, Suite 101
2300 N. Lincoln Boulevard
Oklahoma City, OK 73105
TEL: (405) 521-3911
FAX: (405) 521-3911

Oregon
136 State Capitol
900 Court Street NE
Salem, OR 97310
TEL: (503) 378-4139
FAX: (503) 373-7414

Pennsylvania
Secretary of the Commonwealth
Department of State
N. Office Building, Room 302
Harrisburg, PA 17120
TEL: (717) 787-7630
FAX: (717) 787-1734

Rhode Island
State House, Room 218
1 Capitol Hill
Providence, RI 12903
TEL: (401) 277-2357
FAX: (401) 277-1356

South Carolina
P.O. Box 11350
Columbia, SC 29211
TEL: (803) 734-2170
FAX: (803) 734-2164

South Dakota
500 E. Capitol Avenue, Suite 204
Pierre, SD 57501
TEL: (605) 773-3557
FAX: (605) 773-6580

Tennessee
State Capitol, 1st Floor
Nashville, TN 37243
TEL: (615) 741-2819
FAX: (615) 741-5962

Texas
1200 S. Congress Avenue, Room 18
P.O. Box 12697
Austin, TX 78711
TEL: (512) 463-5701
FAX: (512) 475-2761

Utah
203 State Capitol
P.O. Box 140111
Salt Lake City, UT 84114
TEL: (801) 538-1520
FAX: (801) 538-1557

Vermont
109 State Street
Montpelier, VT 05609
TEL: (802) 828-2148
FAX: (802) 828-2496

Virginia
Secretary of the Commonwealth
Capitol Square, P.O. Box 2454
Richmond, VA 23201
TEL: (804) 786-2441
FAX: (804) 371-0017

Washington
Secretary of State
Legislative Building, 2nd Floor
P.O. Box 40220
Olympia, WA 98504
TEL: (360) 753-7121
FAX: (360) 586-5629

West Virginia
Building 1, Suite 157K
1900 Kanawha Boulevard E.
Charleston, WV 25305
TEL: (304) 558-6000
FAX: (304) 558-0900

Wisconsin
30 W. Miffin Street, 9th & 10th Floors
Madison, WI 53703
TEL: (608) 266-8888
FAX: (608) 267-6815

Wyoming
Secretary of State
State Capitol
200 W. 24th Street
Cheyenne, WY 82002
TEL: (307) 777-5333
FAX: (307) 777-6217

District of Columbia
District Building, Room 504
441 4th Street NW
Washington, DC 20001
TEL: (202) 727-6306
FAX: (202) 727-3582

American Samoa
Office of the Governor
Pago Pago, AS 96799
TEL: (684) 633-5201
FAX: (684) 693-2269

Guam
Executive Chambers:
1 Adelup Complex
Agana, GU 96910
TEL: (671) 476-9216
FAX: (671) 472-7561

Puerto Rico
Department of State
P.O. Box 9271
San Juan, PR 00904
TEL: (787) 725-4344
FAX: (787) 725-7303

U.S. Virgin Islands
Lieutenant Governor
18 Kongens Gade
Street Thomas, VI 00802
TEL: (809) 774-2991
FAX: (809) 774-6953

If you give money to a political action committee, you will have lots of company. Over the years PACs have been the source of hundreds of millions of dollars for campaigns. During the 1995–96 election cycle, PACs contributed a total of $126.5 million to federal candidates, an increase of almost $17 million over the eighteen-month 1993–94 cycle.

Receipts and disbursements for the top fifty PACs for the 1995–96 election cycle are shown in table 8, page 386.

The champion in both categories is Emily's List, an acronym for "Early Money Is Like Yeast." You may have heard of Emily's List, an organization dedicated to electing pro-choice Democratic women to high office.

The president of Emily's List is Ellen Malcolm, a veteran of Common Cause. According to Malcolm, Emily's List recommends candidates to its 45,000 members. She said more than 65,000 contributions at $95 or less went through Emily's List during the 1995–96 election cycle. Emily's List works only to elect candidates, and is not a lobbying organization.

You started out thinking that money was a necessary evil in electoral politics. After doing some research, you realize the situation is more complicated than that. It's not just fat cats who write checks. Well-meaning people such as yourself also contribute to candidates. You want nothing more than to see your candidate win. You have no desire to buy access.

Your positive assessment, however, does not mean you believe that the system is corruption-proof. You have little doubt that for the right price, some politicians can be bought. You like the idea that there are agencies and organizations monitoring the system. You want to learn more about how these function.

THE WATCHDOGS: COMMON CAUSE AND THE FEC

You probably know about Common Cause. Common Cause was founded in 1970 by John Gardner, a former Secretary of Health, Education, and Welfare. The organization describes itself as campaigning for "open and accountable government in Washington and around the country." Today this non-profit, non-partisan citizens' lobby claims 250,000 members.

Common Cause is best known for its work on campaign finance reform. The current national president, Ann McBride, is frequently quoted in stories involving politics and money. Common Cause also concerns itself with ethical standards for government officials and lobbyists.

In his 1972 book, *In Common Cause*, John Gardner discusses the deleterious effect of money on the political process. It's interesting to note that this was written just before Watergate brought the problem to everyone's attention.

> The most serious obstacle the citizen faces when he sets out to participate is that someone with a lot of money got there first and bought up the public address system. The full-throated voice of money drowns him out. It isn't just that money talks. It talks louder and longer and drowns out the citizen's hoarse whisper.
> —*John Gardner,* In Common Cause

The Federal Election Commission was created as a result of the 1974 amendments to the Federal Election Campaign Act of 1971. It was believed the original act needed teeth; i.e., a commission with enforcement powers.

The FEC is authorized to write regulations and monitor compliance with the Federal Election Campaign Act.

The president of the United States, the Speaker of the House, and the president pro tempore of the Senate each appoint two of the six voting members of the Federal Election Commission. Unless they choose to retire, commissioners are usually reappointed.

Commissioner Joan D. Aikens served from 1975 to 1997. Commissioners Lee Ann Elliot and Danny McDonald were appointed in 1981 and reappointed through April 1999.

According to the FEC, enforcement cases are generated by complaints filed by the public, referrals from other federal and state agencies, and the FEC's own monitoring procedures. Violators are usually assessed a fine.

Many critics have lambasted the FEC for its lax pursuit of funding irregularities. They claim the commission is cozy with those it monitors: Congress and the president.

CAMPAIGN REPORTS

You don't have to depend exclusively on Common Cause or the FEC to track campaign spending. Campaign reports are public record. Here is how you go about getting the material.

1. The Federal Election Commission Public Records Office is open Monday through Friday from 9 A.M. to 5 P.M. All reports filed since April 7, 1972, are available for public inspection and copying. Copies are 5–15 cents per page. The address is 999 E Street NW, Washington, D.C. 20463. The toll-free number is (800) 424-9530. The local Washington number is (202) 219-4140. The fax number is (202) 219-3880.

   Reports can also be obtained by writing the FEC at the above address. The request must include advance payment. MasterCard and Visa are acceptable methods of payment. Checks should be made out to the "Federal Election Commission."

   These documents are on file at the FEC office:

   - statements of candidacy and designation of principal campaign committee

   - statements of organization of political committee

   - candidate authorization of a political committee

- reports of receipts and expenditures

- statements of independent expenditures

- communication costs by corporations, labor organizations, membership organizations, and trade associations

- office accounts

- debt settlement statements

2. Reports filed by candidates for the U.S. House of Representatives and their personal committees are available with the Clerk of the U.S. House of Representatives Office Records and Registrations, Room 1026, Longworth House Office Building, Washington D.C. 20515. The office is open Monday–Friday from 9 A.M.to 5 P.M.

3. Reports filed by U.S. Senate candidates and their personal committees are available in the Secretary of the U.S. Senate Office of Public Records, Hart Senate Office Building, Room 232, Washington D.C. 20510.

Do You Live in California and Use the Internet?

In the spring of 1997 the California State Senate approved a bill that will require prompt online filing of campaign contributions to statewide races like the governorship and ballot-measure committees by 1998. All state legislative offices in California will be covered by 2000. A number of other states, including Hawaii, Virginia, and Washington, have passed similar legislation.

The online system will get the public swift access to the identity of donors. This is especially important in the last two weeks of a competitive campaign, when contributions tend come in at a faster clip. Under the current system, these late contributions don't appear on spending reports until after the election.

Does Money Corrupt?

You don't *have* to give money to a candidate. Should you choose to contribute, it's essential to learn about the campaign finance system. You don't want to make a mistake.

Is the system corrupt? It depends on whom you ask. No politician ever admits running interference or sponsoring legislation for a generous contributor. At the same time, what appears in the media as a quid pro quo could be something completely innocent. Reporters can "spin" stories as well as the best press secretaries.

The truth probably lies somewhere between the views of a diehard cynic and a naive optimist.

CHAPTER RECAP

- Know basic campaign finance rules before you give.

- Money has been a factor in elections since George Washington.

- Post-Watergate reforms set strict limits on individual and PAC contributions.

- You can now get information regarding candidates and their contributors on the Internet.

- Hard money goes directly to a candidate; soft money goes to the party.

- Political action committees are a way for people who work together, or believe the same things, to give to candidates.

- Common Cause monitors campaign finance from the outside; Federal Election Commission members are appointed by congressional leaders and the president.

The Campaign Business

*I*t's late October in an election year. You're at home watching one of your favorite television shows. Time for a commercial. You get up to fix yourself a snack. Before you've taken two steps, the image of a well-known person appears on the screen. It's the challenger for a U.S. Senate seat in your state. He's shaking hands at a shopping center, touring a factory, and frolicking with his family in a beautiful park. You're so enthralled, you forget about food.

THE MEDIA AND THE MESSAGE

An hour later, you're still watching TV. A series of good programs are on. Time for a commercial. You know the routine—off to the kitchen. But suddenly, on the screen is an image of that same guy running for the Senate. Except this time the picture is not flattering. The candidate looks tired, frustrated, and angry. His lovely family is nowhere to be found. An announcer is telling how the man twice failed to pay his taxes, and faced two sexual harassment suits. Can this be the same person? You're too confused to eat.

This is a condensed version of the modern American political campaign. For at least the last several years the big races—president, U.S. Senate, and governor—have been conducted mainly on television. Much of the exposure is through paid campaign commercials, the most effective tool candidates have to score points with the voters.

GETTING RICH OFF CAMPAIGN ADS

The high cost of getting elected—or reelected—is a result of the increasing cost of maintaining a campaign operation. To be competitive, a candidate for Congress or the U.S. Senate must be able to afford direct mail, a personal pollster, radio spots, and, of course, television ads.

Who receives the biggest share of the campaign funds in a major race? Television stations.

According to Competitive Media Reporting, an ad-industry research firm, in 1996 the nation's top seventy-five media markets took in $400 million in political ads. This was up from $300 million in 1992, which was the previous presidential election year.

In Raleigh, North Carolina, alone, Competitive Media Reporting estimated that in 1996 politicians aired more than 18,000 commercials and spent some $8.5 million with local broadcasters.

The reason campaigns rely heavily on television is because commercials are quick, vivid, and one-sided. The candidate says what she wants to say, without the message being distorted by her opponent. Positive ads paint a glowing portrait, often with the aid of a sentimental soundtrack. Negative ads are grainy, harsh, and frequently funny. It's hard for the viewer to separate fact from fiction.

You and your friends may not have the time to follow every campaign on a daily basis in the newspapers. You are the ideal audience for a paid political advertisement. You go to the polls, but your time spent on politics is limited. You pay attention to the commercials.

With the lesser campaigns, especially those for state offices, political advertisements may be your *only* source of information. Sometimes there are just too many races on the same ballot for you to track all of them.

You may know about political consultants. They're the people who run campaigns. Their job is developing strategy, hiring a campaign team, and approving television and radio spots. The consultant's staff often includes a pollster, press secretary, fundraiser, computer maven, general strategist, and campaign manager.

Some consultants get rich running campaigns. Most do not. Ron Faucheux, editor of *Campaigns & Elections*, told *U.S. News and World Report* in 1997 that 90 percent of consultants earn less than $100,000 a year.

The American Association of Political Consultants estimates the industry currently has about 7,000 full-time professionals.

Have you ever watched the emotional press conference of a politician who's just lost an election? It can be extremely painful. Crying is not out of the question. Politicians want badly to win. Indeed, politicians believe they must win. They are in love with the power and prestige of office. For many, this is their reason for being.

There is little more devastating in public life than losing. Bob Dole, who cheerfully rebounded from his 1996 presidential defeat, is an exception. Many candidates "disappear" for months after being defeated at the polls.

A good consultant is worth everything to a politician. An elected official needs someone who can tell him

> **MISSION STATEMENT OF THE AMERICAN ASSOCIATION OF POLITICAL CONSULTANTS (ADOPTED IN 1995)**
>
> *To raise the standards of practice in political consultation, thereby enhancing the political process and improving public confidence in the American political system.*
>
> • *To provide professional guidance, assistance, and education to members as they develop the skills, techniques, and business procedures required for successful political consultation.*
> • *To establish and maintain a high standard of ethical conduct through membership education and the establishment and promotion of a workable Code of Ethics for members.*
> • *To help inform the news media, educational institutions, political organizations, and the general public about the value of political consultation and its contribution to the political process.*
> • *To place particular emphasis on our work in reaching out to involve and educate young people in the art of political consultation and the benefits it brings to the practice of democracy.*

honestly and directly what works and what doesn't. Not all the advice will be heeded, but it's an essential role.

The candidate must have absolute faith that his consultant will lead him to victory. The candidate places his future in the consultant's hands. The consultant and his or her team analyze the electorate and plot strategy while the politician is tending to the duties of the office: voting on bills, appearing at events, meeting with constituents, and so on. The best consultants know what works and what doesn't.

SOME MEMORABLE CAMPAIGN MOMENTS

Like it or not, political campaigns—especially the presidential ones—are part of your life. You could not escape them if you tried. They are ingrained in American pop culture and in American history. Slogans such as "In You're Heart You Know He's Right" (the 1964 Goldwater for President campaign) or the commercial entitled "Morning Again in America" (the 1984 President Reagan reelection campaign) are remembered long after an election is over.

Presidential campaign commercials are like oldies-but-goodies rock'n'roll records. You don't have to be a Beatlemaniac to know who performed "I Want to Hold Your Hand," and you don't have to be a political junkie to know George Bush (and his consultant, Lee Atwater) made good use of a criminal named Willie Horton in the 1988 presidential race.

Hot Times on the Campaign Trail
Do you recall any of these? The embarrassed candidates wish you didn't.

- In 1972, Democratic Primary contender Edmund Muskie appeared to be crying while speaking to supporters in New Hampshire. Muskie was responding to a letter to the editor that claimed his wife used an insulting term for Canadians. Muskie's emotional performance doomed his campaign. He was no longer considered "presidential."

The letter was a fraud. It was written by Donald Segretti, who worked for President Nixon's reelection team. The Nixon campaign had quite a year in 1972. Remember Watergate?

• Those who worked with him say that Ronald Reagan was a superb candidate. Scripted or unscripted, he often knew just what to say.

In the 1980 Republican presidential primary, Reagan and four other candidates were preparing to debate frontrunner George Bush in Nashua, New Hampshire. Bush felt ambushed; he had insisted on a debate with Reagan, and Reagan only.

The moderator, Jon Breen, agreed with Bush. Breen ordered Reagan's microphone turned off. Reagan angrily responded, "I paid for this microphone, Mr. Green [sic]." Now that was presidential.

The crowd went wild, and the exchange was subsequently broadcast on all the network news programs. According to Lou Cannon's book, *President Reagan: The Role of a Lifetime*, it was later revealed that the Reagan campaign had hired the sound technician, who was not about to turn off the Gipper's microphone.

• At a crucial point in the 1984 Democratic presidential primary, Walter Mondale, Gary Hart, and Jesse Jackson came together for a debate. Mondale was reeling from having lost to Hart in several states. Before the campaign, few people took Hart seriously; now he was close to getting the nomination. Mondale needed to hit a home run.

During one of his answers, Mondale attacked Hart for his lack of substance. In fact, said Mondale, Hart's ideas reminded him of the popular television commercial that asked: "Where's the beef?"

With his clever response, which may have been prearranged, Mondale had ridiculed his opponent with a phrase already known to millions. "Where's the beef?" haunted Hart in the '84 campaign, just as a young woman named Donna Rice would haunt him in the '88 campaign.

• Bob Dole had just defeated George Bush in the 1988 Iowa Republican Caucus. That same night Bush and Dole appeared together via satellite on a news program. Dole was asked if he had anything he wanted to say to the vice president.

Bitter, Dole asked Bush to "stop lying about my record." America hates a sore winner even more than a sore loser. Dole dropped in the polls. Bush surged ahead and captured the nomination.

THE RISE OF CONSULTANTS

As you venture further into politics, you will hear more and more about the consultants themselves; who they are, and their list of clients. This is not trivial information. You can learn something about a campaign by knowing something about the consultant. Such information would certainly come in handy if you ever decided to run for office.

The better consultants put their mark on campaigns. One consultant might be known for "going negative," while another is famous for picking the right issues.

Time was, politicians were the stars. The inner circle remained largely anonymous. Now, some consultants are almost as famous as their bosses. The change probably began with James Carville and Mary Matalin. You probably know their story. In 1992, he worked for Bill Clinton, and she worked for George Bush. They dated during the campaign, and married soon after the election. Then they wrote a nationwide bestseller about their experience.

Another well-known political operative is Ed Rollins, who worked on Christine Whitman's 1994 gubernatorial race in New Jersey. Rollins later claimed the campaign had paid black ministers to hold down the black vote. The Whitman group denied the charge, and Rollins recanted. The negative publicity gave Rollins an idea; Why not write a book? So he did. It sold, though not as well as the Carville-Matalin story.

The year 1996 belonged to Dick Morris, President Clinton's chief strategist. Morris was going great until word got out that he had spent many sessions with a prostitute in a Washington hotel. Morris was banished from the campaign.

Why not write a book? He did, and received a reported advance of $2.5 million. *Behind the Oval Office* is considered by many to be the best of the books by consultants. In it, Morris discusses campaign strategies and his relationship with Clinton. Read the book and you will get a good sense of the role and value of such a consultant.

Consultants must come loaded with ideas. Each campaign requires a particular approach. You've followed politics enough to know that voters change their priorities from year to year, or even month to month. A consultant must sense the mood of the electorate.

Morris decided 1996 was the year of living cautiously. Don't be partisan, he advised the president, but rise above the fray. Morris's best-known plan was called "triangulation." Here is his own description:

The president needed to take a position that not only blended the best of each party's views but also transcended them to constitute a third force in the debate.

I blurted out the strategy I proposed in a single word: *triangulate* [his italics]. I found myself shaping my fingers into a triangle, with my thumbs joined at the base and my forefingers raised to meet a point at the top.

Triangulate, create a third position, not just in between the old positions of the two parties but above them as well. Identify a new course that accommodates the needs the Republicans address but does it in a way that is uniquely yours [Clinton's],' I counseled.

—*Dick Morris,* Behind the Oval Office

Consultants don't win elections—candidates do—but consultants play a crucial role.

RUNNING FOR OFFICE

Does all this talk make you want to run for office? Should you move in that direction, it might be a good idea to list the things you need to do to get elected. A detailed list was published in the July 1997 issue of *Campaigns & Elections,* the political-consultant industry's trade publication. Editor Ron Faucheux came up with "The First 25 Steps Every Candidate Should Take." These are reprinted below, with occasional asides from the author of this book.

1. Make a final, irrevocable decision to run.

2. Determine the rationale for your candidacy.

3. Get your résumé in order.

4. Prepare your family.

5. Get your business affairs in order.

6. Carefully check all applicable election laws and set up a legal compliance system—before you accept or spend one penny.

7. Raise seed money. [To cover expenses before you have officially established your campaign.]

8. Get professional help. [Researcher, media consultant, and strategist would be examples of this.]

9. Write a confidential autobiography for in-house use.

10. Take a benchmark poll. [Faucheux said this poll will "provide the road map for your campaign strategy and message."]

11. Develop a fund-raising plan, put the fund-raising team in place, and start asking for money.

12. Tour the geography. [This is obviously more difficult for U.S. Senate candidates than it is for House candidates, but just as necessary.]

13. Learn the issues.

14. Hire personal staff. [Personal assistant and scheduler.]

15. Set up an office.

16. Find a campaign manager.

17. Set up a strategy inner circle.

18. Develop your campaign message.

19. Write a campaign plan.

20. Establish a recognizable "graphic" look. [This applies to brochures, mailings, and photographs of the candidate and his family.]

21. Determine your pre-announcement timetable.

22. Prepare "The Speech" and "The Book." ["The Speech" is the standard speech that the candidate delivers to chambers of commerce and community

groups. It should answer the crucial question, "Why am I running?" "The Book" contains "The Speech" and set answers to anticipated questions. "The Book," which should be with the candidate at all times, contains what will become "The Message." The press is always asking about "The Message."]

23. Get professional candidate training. [This can include reading political biographies, taking college courses on leadership and politics, or attending candidate training seminars.]

24. Create a personal-contact pyramid—and start dialing. [Faucheux breaks this down as super-VIPs, VIPs, priority contacts, and general contacts.]

25. Announce.

—*Ron Faucheux, "The First 25 Steps Every Smart Candidate Should Take,"* Campaigns & Elections, *July 1997, pages 18–24*

WOMEN CANDIDATES

The campaign business is one in which women have been making considerable strides. It makes sense that with more women running for office, more women would be in the business of running women (and some men) for office.

Campaign polling is a field in which women are well-represented. Some of the heavyweights are Linda DiVall, who worked for Bob Dole's 1996 presidential campaign, for Senators Phil Gramm of Texas, and Fred Thompson of Tennessee, and for House Speaker Newt Gingrich; Celinda Lake, who has polled on behalf of Illinois Senator Carol Moseley-Braun; and Kellyanne Fitzpatrick, a Republican pollster and frequent guest on *Politically Incorrect with Bill Maher.*

In 1994, Yale University started the Women's Campaign School, a four-and-a-half-day program held in June to "teach women the political skills, strategies, and tactics to run a winning campaign." The sessions include training in polling, public speaking, scheduling, image, fundraising, ethics, media, and message and slogan. Instructors have included Lynn Martin, former U.S. Secretary of Labor; Anita Perez Ferguson, president of the National Women's Political Caucus; and Ellen Malcolm, founder and president of Emily's List.

> I think that for many years women never really thought it [politics] was a field in which they could achieve. And it was discouraging to constantly be excluded. I think that the last couple of years have really made a dramatic turnaround for women and they are now very accepting of the fact that they can make this work for them.
> —*Julie D. Belaga, founding member of the Women's Campaign School at Yale University, in an interview with the* New York Times *on May 29, 1994*

The Women's Campaign School at Yale University has forty openings for each session. Students come from across the country and throughout the world. Tuition is $750. For more information call (800) 353-2878.

THE COST OF CAMPAIGNS

The following numbers will give you some idea of the high cost of campaigns. New Jersey Democratic Senator Robert Torricelli, who won a hotly contested race in 1996 for Bill Bradley's open seat, spent 80 percent of his $9.2 million campaign fund on television, according to a Torricelli spokesman cited in the April 12, 1997, issue of *National Journal*. While Torricelli's percentage is high, other candidates have spent well over 50 percent of their campaign budget on television.

For more on the issue of politics and money, you might want to refer to the previous chapter.

If the cost of campaigns continues to rise, you will see more and more proposals for reforming the system of campaign finance. Of these, the one that relates directly to the management of campaigns is the call for free television (see page 285). Here are some other ideas.

Paul Taylor left his position as political reporter for the *Washington Post* to become executive director of the Free TV for Straight Talk Coalition. Taylor helped develop a proposal for free electronic media spots to qualified candidates. The idea has attracted the interest of several members of Congress:

> The proposal would require all TV and radio stations to give two hours of time to a bank administered by the Federal Election Commission, which would hand out vouchers to parties and candidates. To qualify, candidates would have to appear in their ads, which could run no more than one minute. The bank would 'relieve the burdens of fund raising,' Taylor said.
>
> —*Eliza Newlin Carney, "Tuning Out Free TV,"*
> National Journal, *April 12, 1997, page 700*

After his reelection in 1996, President Clinton expressed support for the idea of free TV to candidates. In his plan, candidates would receive free TV in exchange for the government granting free digital-spectrum licenses to broadcasters. These licenses are said to be worth billions of dollars.

But broadcasters are hard to sell on this issue. They stand to lose hundreds of millions of dollars if Taylor's plan is adopted. Already the National Association of Broadcasters is mobilized on this issue, and the NAB often gets what it wants.

Free TV proposals could either be adopted by Congress or as the result of independent action by the administration.

Are you disgusted by negative campaign commercials? Do they make you want to walk away from politics? You are not alone. The most frequent criticisms of campaigns in this country involve negative or misleading commercials and the high cost of running for office.

You could think of negative ads as political pornography. The metaphor makes more sense when you realize that there are politicians, pundits, and activists who have urged the adoption of regulations limiting or even banning negative ads. These people say negative ads poison the political environment, which in turn increases voter cynicism.

> **FREE TELEVISION: AN IDEA WHOSE TIME HAS COME?**
>
> *You recall that at the beginning of this chapter there was a discussion of the role of television in modern campaigns, along with the high cost of political advertisements. For a number of years some influential voices have been arguing for free television in political campaigns. The adoption of this proposal would have a profound effect on American campaigns. They would be much cheaper, and probably more competitive.*

As in the case of pornography, the debate over negative commercials has First Amendment implications. Opponents of any regulation argue that curbing or restricting negative commercials is an infringement on the right to freedom of speech. Besides, they say, what defines a negative ad? Is criticizing a candidate's record "negative" in this context? Is pointing out that a candidate misused personal funds "negative"? Doesn't the public have a right to know?

Under the circumstances, it appears any effort to ban or restrict negative ads will result in massive litigation. You will have to accept that negative ads will be around for a long time.

As a voter, your responsibility is to distinguish the valid attacks from low blows in political advertising. To do that, you have to stay informed. The political parties, the media, the respective campaigns, and organizations such as the League of Women Voters can help.

CHAPTER RECAP

- Political advertisements are the most direct way of communicating with voters.

- Political consultants have become wealthier and more famous than ever before.

- Campaign mistakes haunt candidates—as history has shown.

- Running for office requires much thought, preparation, and money.

- A solid political background helps you distinguish between accurate campaign ads and gross distortions.

The Self-Financed

Candidate

You're rich, and you don't know what to do with all your money. You're bored, and you don't know what to do with your life. Faced with those life-changing decisions, a number of men and women in the 1990s chose to run for political office. Do you remember Ross Perot, Michael Huffington, and Al Checchi? They each poured millions of dollars from their personal fortunes into getting elected. Not one of them succeeded. Was that a coincidence?

MONEY AND POWER

Outside of Nelson Rockefeller, who ran for the Republican nomination for president and was governor of New York in the late 1960s and early 1970s, and John F. Kennedy, wealthier Americans have shown little or no interest in running for political office. Writing checks is more their speed. A cynic might say that the point of being rich is to own a politician, not to become one. Certainly the well-to-do tend to give a disproportionate amount of political contributions. A study released in June 1998 entitled

Individual Congressional Campaign Contributors: Wealthy, Conservative and Reform-Minded revealed that a full 46 percent of donors from the 1996 election cycle had an annual family income of $250,000 or more.

Rich people have more disposable income than does the middle class. They may contribute a few thousand bucks to the candidate or candidates of their choice without worrying about putting their family in debt. If nothing else, the money gives them a better shot at getting their calls returned after the election.

Rich and Famous

As we mentioned, in the past rich people only rarely filed to run for a major office. It's hard to know why, but fear may be part of the reason. There is something risky about being rich and asking middle-class and lower-middle-class voters to vote for you. You'd never know beforehand if they would say yes or shout you down.

Remember the Marx Brothers' movies? The rich were in the pictures to be mocked and ridiculed. Groucho in particular toyed with any wealthy man or woman who had the misfortune to make his acquaintance. The same with the Three Stooges. If you're a Stooges fan, you've probably lost track of the number of mansions trashed by Curly, Mo, and Larry. The rich were snobs, while their detractors were hilarious. Humiliating the rich has been a comic device in American pop culture from the Depression era of the 1930s through contemporary sitcoms.

A candidate with tons of money would be exposed to these attitudes day after day on the campaign trail. Could you blame him or her for saying, Who needs it?

But the late 1980s and 1990s have been much better for the image of people with wealth. Programs such as *Lifestyles of the Rich and Famous* and the various celebrity/entertainment news shows envy and admire—rather than scorn—the rich. The reasons for the change are hard to say, although it's quite possible the election of Ronald Reagan as president in 1980 played a part. Reagan was a charming and popular guy with a lot of wealthy buddies. He made it seem okay to be rich, or at least to be in the company of rich people.

It seemed like an irresistible argument, especially during this time of increased campaign spending. Yet something got lost in translation. When the candidates went out on the campaign trial, the issue quickly became their

> **THE CASE FOR A RICH MAN OR WOMAN**
>
> *Each of the high profile self-funded candidates in the 1990s—Perot, Huffington, Harman, and Checchi—campaigned on the notion that they can't be bought or sold like the other politicians. For example, they often pointed out that they didn't need to take PAC money because they had enough dollars of their own, thank you very much. While their opponents would sell out for a thousand here or there, they remained apart from the dirty game of fundraising. They had promised nothing to nobody.*

own money, not the comparatively "clean" source of their contributions. Voters asked some tough questions:

- Why would someone spend millions of his own money just to win political office?

- Where did he or she get the money?

- What's so special about the self-financed candidate?

California has long had a reputation for trend-setting political campaigns. During the 1990s this applied to wealthy people vying for office. In 1994, Michael Huffington spent some $28 million of the family fortune to unseat incumbent Democratic senator Dianne Feinstein. He lost. It's estimated that in the 1998 Democratic gubernatorial primary, Al Checchi spent $40 million, and Jane Harman, $15 million. They both lost.

You've got to have more than a big bank account to get elected these days. If you don't have a strong message or series of messages, get one as soon as possible. Voters want to know where you stand. You insult their intelligence when you reduce the campaign to 30-second spot after 30-second spot.

Checchi's blitz backfired. By the end of the primary season people were sick of seeing his face on TV. And when they weren't seeing his face, they were seeing Jane Harman's. She finished third out of three Democratic candidates.

CHAPTER RECAP

- In the 1990s, the stigma was erased against rich people using their own money to run for political office.

- The man or woman with the most money doesn't always win the race.

- The self-financed candidate makes a pitch to voters that he or she "can't be bought" by special interests.

- Too much money poured into a campaign can lead to overexposure, which turns off many voters.

Media and Politics

*B*etween talk radio, C-SPAN's broadcasts of House and Senate proceedings, *Crossfire* and its clones, the Internet, and the Sunday talk shows, you can follow politics through the media twenty-four hours a day, seven days a week. Nothing on this scale has ever happened in America.

A CACOPHONY OF VOICES

You have an advantage over political novices of generations past. If they were having trouble sleeping, they couldn't turn on C-SPAN in the middle of the night to see the rebroadcast of a Senate hearing on campaign finance or a Washington conference on the presidency and the press. But you can.

You've heard the term "the Information Age" applied to our society. Information moves faster than ever, due primarily to computers, fax machines, and the Internet, and there is more information to process. You must determine for yourself the difference between valid news and junk. They're both out there.

In some ways, . . . the explosion of information technology may be luring Americans away from focusing on Washington. The mass of information available through the Internet leaves many thinking they don't need the president or anybody else in government to tell them what to think about national affairs.

—*Gerald F. Seib, "Many Americans View Washington As a Mess and Just Tune It Out,"* Wall Street Journal, *June 4, 1997, page A8*

The problem is particularly acute with politics. Conspiracy theories, disinformation, unfounded accusations, and distortions are regularly transmitted through Web sites, radio, and television. You can get taken in by slick spokespersons. The political parties and their media friends see the explosion in communications technology as a way of winning the hearts and minds of people like you.

If you know the issues, and are familiar with the American system of government, the chances are good you won't get snookered. You don't want to make decisions based on bogus information heard on some radio show. And you especially don't want to repeat that information to your friends and family. Ignorance can spread like a contagion.

If you have watched political talk shows, you know many of them place a premium on hosts and guests with loud voices and bad manners. While this style is sometimes entertaining, it can breed disgust. Viewers can hear the president, Congress, or the Speaker of the House trashed only so many times before they decide to hell with it, and choose not to vote.

Yet praise of politicians does not come easily to the media. They do not want to appear as cheerleaders, which is neither hip nor adversarial—qualities prized by journalists. Of course, there are times when our leaders deserve scorn and ridicule, but there are other times when kudos are called for. You have to look a lot harder to find them.

Getting involved in politics demands you pay attention. The country and the government are too big to comprehend without help from other sources, and all is not lost. There are excellent stations, columnists, reporters, and magazines that cover politics in America.

THE EDUCATED VOTER?

Is the increase in political programming turning people on to politics, or turning them off? Political junkies have never been happier. But what about everyone else? There is more political information than ever available through the media, yet voter turnout in presidential elections is lower than ever. Is there a connection?

C-SPAN

You will find that C-SPAN is to political people what ESPN is to sports fans: indispensable. Its aims are clear.

- C-SPAN is a public service created by the American Cable television industry . . .

- To provide C-SPAN audiences access to the "live" gavel-to-gavel proceedings of the U.S. House of Representatives and the U.S. Senate, and to other forums where public policy is discussed, debated, and decided—all without editing, commentary, or analysis and with a balanced presentation of points of view;

- To provide elected and appointed officials and others who would influence public policy a direct conduit to the audience without filtering or otherwise distorting their points of view;

- To provide the audience, through the call-in program, direct access to elected officials, other decision makers, and journalists on a frequent and open basis;

- To employ production values that accurately convey the business of government rather than distract from it; and to conduct all other aspects of its operations consistent with these principles.

One of the trade secrets of punditry is that saluting pols for doing the best they can doesn't attract as much notice as calling them to account for imperfection. It's also not as satisfying.

—*Matthew Miller, "Pols Are Indispensable, Pundits Aren't,"* Los Angeles Times, *August 6, 1997, page B10*

Great Moments in C-SPAN History

- *March 19, 1979*—C-SPAN begins broadcasting the House of Representatives live to 3.5 million households.

- *January 6, 1981*—C-SPAN adds gavel-to-gavel coverage of congressional hearings to its program schedule.

- *September 13, 1982*—C-SPAN begins 24-hour-a-day programming.

- *June 2, 1986*—C-SPAN 2 cablecasts live proceedings of the U.S. Senate during a television test period.

- *July 29, 1986*—U.S. Senate votes to allow televised coverage of its proceedings.

- *1992*—C-SPAN provides more than 1,200 hours of election coverage from January through November.

- *April 15, 1996*—C-SPAN offers audio coverage of the House and Senate on the Internet.

- *January 1997*—C-SPAN offers Live video Web coverage of the House and Senate on the Internet.

Source: timeline provided by C-SPAN

THE CHARM OF C-SPAN

C-SPAN may not make politics fun, but it does make it interesting. Whenever you're in the mood to see your leaders in action, you should watch proceedings of the House and Senate, as well as congressional committee hearings. You can learn a lot about Congress and its members by watching C-SPAN. You'll know you're hooked when you can identify the men and women of the House and Senate by their voices.

C-SPAN's quasi-professional production values are part of its appeal. This is one-camera, open-mike political coverage. In an age when candidates are packaged for television, C-SPAN's casual style is refreshing. (At the daily White House press briefing, for example, viewers see the press secretary but none of the reporters.)

PRINT JOURNALISM

With all the talk about news media, are newspapers obsolete? Not when it comes to political coverage. You can neither expect nor insist that TV and radio do as good a job as newspapers or magazines in this area. Major newspapers are better-equipped to provide the depth that political reporting requires. You cannot be an informed voter by restricting your intake to broadcast media; you must read as well.

Newspapers continue to place a high priority on political stories. Washington is bursting with reporters. Small and mid-sized newspapers cover Congress just as, if not more, closely than many of the major urban dailies. After all, in smaller cities the local member of Congress is the most powerful politician around.

Papers with Washington bureaus include the *Courier* (Potsdam-Massena, New York) *Observer*, the *Hemet* (California) *News*, and the *Henderson* (Kentucky) *Gleaner*. Alabama has eight papers with D.C. bureaus; Michigan, sixteen; and Florida, twenty-one.

Of course, the reporters from the big and/or respected publications command the biggest audience. In its April 5, 1997, issue, *National Journal*, a highly regarded political magazine, selected Washington's twenty-five most influential (print and broadcast) journalists. You might want to look for their stories and opinion pieces in the future:

EROSION OF TRUST AND INTEREST

A major survey (of 1,211 adults, 18 years of age and over) conducted by the Pew Research Center in 1997 found only 26 percent of Americans said they enjoyed watching the news "a great deal." That was down from 42 percent in 1985. The favorable rating for large newspapers dropped from 53 percent in 1992 to 41 percent in 1997.

The poll also revealed that 56 percent of the public believed news stories are often inaccurate (Jack Nelson, "Major News Media Trusted Less, Poll Says," Los Angeles Times, March 21, 1997). These statistics are no excuse to become a hermit. Use them to hone your own critical skills. Face it, no viable alternatives exist to acquiring political news through the media.

1. Jill Abramson, reporter for the *New York Times*

2. David Broder, op-ed columnist for the *Washington Post*

3. Ronald Brownstein, political reporter for the *Los Angeles Times*

4. E. J. Dionne Jr., columnist for the *Washington Post*

5. Maureen Dowd, op-ed columnist for the *New York Times*

6. Leonard Downie Jr., executive editor of the *Washington Post*

7. Jeff Gerth, investigative reporter for the *New York Times*

8. Paul Gigot, op-ed columnist and editorial writer for the *Wall Street Journal*

9. Al Kamen, federal-page columnist for the *Washington Post*

10. Michael Kelly, contributor to the *National Journal*

11. Larry King, host, CNN's *Larry King Live*

12. William Kristol, editor of the *Weekly Standard*

13. Howard Kurtz, media reporter of the *Washington Post*

14. Brian Lamb, chairman of C-SPAN

15. Jim Lehrer, executive editor of *The NewsHour with Jim Lehrer*

16. Doyle McManus, Washington bureau chief of the *Los Angeles Times*

17. Robert Novak, syndicated columnist

18. Robert Pear, social-policy reporter for the *New York Times*

19. Wesley Pruden, editor-in-chief of the *Washington Times*

20. Cokie Roberts, congressional reporter for National Public Radio and co-host of ABC's *This Week*

21. David Rogers, congressional reporter for the *Wall Street Journal*

22. Tim Russert, Washington bureau chief for NBC News and host of *Meet the Press*

23. William Safire, *New York Times* op-ed columnist

24. George F. Will, syndicated columnist and ABC News analyst

25. Bob Woodward, assistant managing editor for investigations, the *Washington Post*

Not surprisingly, the *Washington Post* and the *New York Times* dominate the top twenty-five. These are generally regarded as best at covering Washington politics. Close behind on this list—and in the view of many experts—are the *Los Angeles Times* and the *Wall Street Journal*.

Newspapers are not perfect. Approach them with that same critical distance that you exercise with television or radio talk shows. Indeed, newspapers in the 1990s are becoming more like television. The inordinate amount of attention paid by political reporters to so-called character issues, which really means adultery and sexual harassment, is an example. Editors and reporters are troubled by the trend, but don't seem to know when or how to stop.

Political Magazines

When you begin to read magazines devoted to politics, you'll know you're addicted. These publications are not intended for the casual, on-again, off-again follower of campaigns, politicians, and issues. They are highly opinionated, and they assume a level of expertise on the part of the audience. It takes time and effort to read them.

Time, Newsweek, and *U.S. News & World Report* are not part of this group for three primary reasons:

> *Virtually all thinking journalists are concerned that we are in a time of crisis about the status of journalism, because of the confusion about the mission of journalism, the emergence of new technologies and the organization of the press.*
>
> —*Bill Kovach, curator of the Nieman Foundation at Harvard, quoted in Iver Peterson's July 21, 1997, "Media" column in the* New York Times

1. They officially avoid taking sides in political issues;

2. they target a general audience; and

3. they cover much more than politics and the arts.

On the other hand, *The New Republic*, *The Nation*, *The American Spectator*, *George*, *National Review*, and *The Weekly Standard* are purely political, and eager to let you know what they think. Their goal seems to be either to get you to change your mind, or to reinforce any opinions that you already hold. It's deeply gratifying to read a talented writer expressing a point of view that is in accord with yours.

Below are brief descriptions of six of the best-known political magazines currently on the market.

- *The American Spectator*—Like the U.S. economy, *The American Spectator* has thrived under President Clinton. The magazine has aggressively pursued the many scandals or potential scandals associated with the Clinton administration. Its articles have been periodically referenced by print and broadcast reports. *The American Spectator* is politically conservative, but it does not automatically condemn everything involving Democrats. It also criticizes its own. The monthly detests Clinton more for who he is than for what he believes.

   You will have fun with sections at the front of the magazine, which tend to be sarcastic items about questionable sexual-harassment suits, experiments in education, or other examples of liberal excess.

   The feature articles tend to run long, however, and you're ready to quit after three pages, while the story continues for five.

- *George* had the most famous editor in the world: John F. Kennedy Jr. It's the first political monthly to say that there is no division between politics and pop culture in American society. The theme is conveyed through its covers—often beautiful women draped in some variation of "political" garb—and in many of its articles, which tend toward exposé, rather than opinion. *George* takes the laudable position that there is never a dull moment in politics, but there are some dull moments in *George*—features that fail to deliver after thousands of words. But this is offset by superb reporting—*George* has scoops, lively interviews, and sparkling graphics.

- *The Nation*—*The Nation*'s chief assets are two columnists transplanted to the U.S. from the United Kingdom: Alexander Cockburn and Christopher Hitchens, who alternate each week. My guess is you will find yourself agreeing more with Hitchens than with Cockburn, whose visceral disgust at capitalism and whoever happens to be in power in Washington can grow a bit weary. Both are superb writers who often pick subjects the pack of establishment pundits is unaware of or chooses to ignore.

  The Nation remains unabashedly liberal, even leftist, at a time when most of America isn't. The editors deserve credit for remaining true to the magazine's 130-year tradition. The only problem with the *Nation*, or any publication that adheres closely to a particular worldview, is that you can usually predict where it will come down on an issue. If you agree with the magazine's stance, you'll think it's great.

- *National Review*—Founded in the 1950s by William F. Buckley, one of the giants of post–World War II American conservatism, *National Review* has endured the movement's bad times (Kennedy and Johnson), flourished during the good times (Nixon and Reagan), and plowed a steady course in uncertain times (Bush and Clinton). The magazine has a more civilized tone than *The American Spectator,* but is just as angered and/or bemused by liberals. If you prefer intellectual conservatism, *National Review* will be to your liking. If you're not a conservative, but can appreciate good writing, you might want to pick up the magazine as well.

- *The New Republic* seems to take pride in occupying the political center. The magazine might slam affirmative action and right-wing efforts to cut back on environmental regulations, or run negative profiles of Jesse Jackson one week and Trent Lott the next. It's predictably unpredictable—except in the case of Israel, which receives unfailing support.

  The New Republic has the best arts section by far of any of the other magazines mentioned in this section, and the articles tend to be just the right length. Fans of *The New Republic* have claimed throughout the Clinton years that it's the most widely read political journal in Washington; a centrist magazine during the reign of a centrist administration.

- *The Weekly Standard*—Its format is similar to *The New Republic*'s , but its politics are strictly conservative. *The Weekly Standard* was started in the mid-1990s by media mogul Rupert Murdoch, who obviously believed the market would support another magazine that favored the right.

  But *The Weekly Standard* is more than a digest of conservative opinion. Its reporters dig for interesting stories and write well. Like *The New Republic*, *The Weekly Standard* has a good mix of short and longer articles. The magazine's politics are generally pro-Republican, but the GOP has also received sharp criticism within its pages.

BROADCAST JOURNALISM

Despite the decline in the number of people who watch the evening news, it's probably safe to say that you and the people you know catch it at least once a week, but you probably don't watch solely for its coverage of politics. If you do, you're wasting your time; there are days when a thirty-minute newscast will not include any political stories. With health, fitness, lifestyle, gender, children, and other topics crowding the agenda, politics is far from a sure thing.

Then again, it's not the news that makes politics interesting on television, but John McLaughlin, Tony Snow, Tim Russert, or Robert Novak, a few of the hosts and participants on the political chat shows. The growth of such programs is good news for people who are just coming to politics, or can't get enough of politics. They are entertaining and, at times, informative. These programs deal in political issues more than the personalities of the political elite, which tend to be explored in lifestyle articles for newspapers or feature stories in publications such as *Vanity Fair*. You will usually learn something of value from watching these shows.

The Ten Best Political Chat Shows on Television

Cable channels are largely responsible for the increase in these political chat shows. The long-running network programs—*Face the Nation, Meet the Press, Nightline,* and *This Week with Sam Donaldson and Cokie Roberts*—have been joined by *Crossfire, Capital Gang,* and *Fox News Sunday*.

When was the last time you overheard a group of people debating the size of the Pentagon's budget, the effect of soft money on campaigns, or whether Congress should grant most-favored nation status to China? It's not that these discussions never occur in "the real world," but they are infrequent and irregular. There is no set place—salon, dinner party, outdoor cafe, club—where people such as yourself can gather on a regular basis in the U.S. and talk about politics. Otherwise, we would be hearing about it on the evening news or reading about it in the *New York Times*.

But what you do know is that every weekend brings a glut of discussion/argument shows about politics. For those needing a political "fix," satisfaction comes on Saturdays and Sundays. Below is a ranking of some of the television programs devoted to politics. The ranking goes from best to worst.

- *Fox News Sunday*—Here is a show that has managed to strike a balance between sober discussion and high-pitched argument. The host, Tony Snow, asks good questions in a way that is neither condescending, petulant, nor rude. Occasionally Snow fumbles his words, but that is probably due to lack of experience with television.

  Another plus is the regular participation of Fox political correspondent Brit Hume, whose questions are much more intelligent and relevant here than the ones he usually poses during presidential press conferences.

- *Meet the Press*—There is something self-important and smug about the host, Tim Russert, but no one is better at keeping a political show in motion. Russert fires a lot of queries at his guests, but allows them to answer without interruption. He knows that strictly political questions will elicit valuable information; there is no need to go for the sensational. This is in his favor when guests who made news the previous week are deciding where they will appear on Sunday morning.

- *This Week* was a good show with David Brinkley, and remains a good show without him. The guests are first-rate (British prime minister Tony Blair

gave *This Week* his first American television interview) and the questions are solid. On key subjects
This Week fills in the gaps left by television and,
increasingly, the newspapers in their coverage of
politics. In addition, Sam Donaldson has toned
down his abrasive style, which was the only reason
not to watch the program in the past.

• The host of *Washington Week in Review*, Gwen
Ifill, has less to do than any other political talk-
show host on television. Ifill sets the scene at the
beginning, and then fades into the background as
the panelists question each other about their own
areas of expertise. It's a welcome change from the
other shows. *Washington Week in Review* continues
to adhere to the belief that there is an audience that
watches political discussions to learn something, not
to cheer or laugh. I think they're right.

• *Face the Nation*—This show gets points on the title
alone. *Face the Nation* sounds so dramatic, like
politicians on trial. The implication is that the lies
stop here; America is paying attention.

    Of course, politicians can spin on *Face the
Nation* as well as on any other program. Still, the
show features good guests and good discussion. It
has not succumbed to the pump-up-the-volume
style of the newer programs.

• *Crossfire*—The first of the "argumentative" shows,
Crossfire can sometimes make a frat party seem
sedate. The hosts and guests have been known to
yell, interrupt, threaten, and cajole. One is tempted
to ask, "Who's in charge here?"

    But *Crossfire* features an impressive range of
topics, and a surprising number of interesting
guests. Perhaps an appearance on *Crossfire* is
their catharsis.

- *McLaughlin Group*—For whom should we feel the most pity? The director, who has to decide which of five people shouting at once should be shown on camera, or the guests, who endure host John McLaughlin's barks and bites like bemused children? This is either a truly silly show or the only sitcom about politics on television. The fact that it's eminently watchable does not necessarily mean it's good.

- *Nightline*—At one time this was the best political program on TV. However, the changes in *Nightline* over the last few years are a perfect example of network television's overreaction to cable. Rather than having faith enough in the host and the format to hold out and weather the storm, *Nightline* experienced something of a nervous breakdown in the mid-1990s, and began doing too many shows on tabloid-driven sex scandals, O. J. Simpson, and media coverage of same.

  Come home, *Nightline*.

- *Capital Gang*—It's a tough call, but I think this is the show on which Robert Novak is most obnoxious. That wouldn't be so bad, except the three other regular guests engage him in ridiculous, predictable banter. We know Novak is far to the right. We know the others think he's nuts. Can we please move on?

Some Choice Political Sites on the Internet

- http: //www.yahoo.com/headlines/politics/

- allpolitics.com (This is CNN.)

- http://events.yahoo.com/Government/Politics

- http://www.hotwired.com/netizen (*Wired* magazine's political guide.)

- http://www.vote-smart.org/ (Non-partisan database.)

- http://www.cq.com (*Congressional Quarterly*)

- slate.com (Microsoft; Michael Kinsley oversees Microsoft's politics venture.)

- politics.com

- http://www.policywonk.com/index.html (Tools and resources for policy mavens.)

- http://www.penncen.com/psotd/ (Political site of the day.)

- http://www.DonaldJTrump2000.com

- http://www.crp.org/ (Center for Responsive Politics—this site monitors the flow of contributions to parties, candidates, and Congress.)

- http://info.lib.uh.edu/politics/markind.htm (The marketplace of political ideas.)

Political Parties

- http://www.lp.org (Libertarians)

- http://www.democrats.org/

- http://www.rnc.org/

- http://www.vote.com/

This list was compiled by Ellen Fitzmaurice, president of Mindworx in North Hollywood, California.

FROM INSIDER TO OUTSIDER

You've probably noticed that an increasing number of journalists and politicos are trading places. In the past few years the list includes George Stephanopoulos, who went from being Bill Clinton's senior adviser to a position with ABC News; Susan Molinari, who resigned her seat in Congress to become a Saturday-morning news anchor for CBS; and Sidney Blumenthal, who left the *New Yorker* for a job with Clinton.

The number of high-profile job changes has caused some to worry that only a fuzzy line now separates journalism from politics. Can Stephanopoulos remain objective in discussing the Clinton administration? Will Molinari slant the news in favor of her former Republican colleagues? What trade secrets is Blumenthal taking with him to the White House? Do you trust Stephanopoulous and Molinari to keep their obvious biases out of their reporting?

It's one thing for a football player–turned–sports commentator to speak fondly of his former team. After all, sports is fun. But it's quite another for a former politician or political aide to root for his "team." This is the latest twist in the always fascinating world of politics and media relations.

When you find yourself impatient for the next issue of *The New Republic*, or counting the minutes before *Meet the Press*, you'll know you've arrived. Politics has become your passion. You must learn more.

Don't be alarmed if your early moves in the world of politics and civic involvement eventually lead to this point. It's hard not to get caught up in the excitement of voting, the satisfaction of volunteering, the buzz of community activism, the rush of a good political argument, or the drama of a close race.

Getting involved is not only good for your country, it's good for you!

CHAPTER RECAP

- Learn to separate the valuable political information from the junk.

- Be wary of the tendency of journalists to always criticize politicians.

- The evening news seems to spend less time now covering politics.

- Watching C-SPAN can be an important part of your political education.

Lobbyists and
Special Interests

Next time you're in Washington, stroll through the corridors of any congressional building on a midweek afternoon. You will inevitably see small groups of people patiently waiting outside the offices of members of the House and Senate. Some of them will be constituents dropping by between trips to the historic sites of Washington and Virginia. The congressman or congresswoman will invite these folks in to say hello, chat with them about life in D.C. and back home, and pose for pictures. It's all over in a few minutes.

THE OPERATIVES

The other groups have come to the Capitol for much more than a photo and small talk. They have business to discuss with members of Congress. Maybe they are asking for support for or opposition to a pending bill, or maybe they simply want an exchange of views on politics and policy. At times as many as fifteen in a single party will crowd into a congressperson's office to make their pitch. Rarely

IN THIS CHAPTER:

• *Lobbyists and their role*

• *Rules every lobbyist must know*

• *Lobbyists and money*

• *What's special about special interests?*

• *The impact of lobbyists and special interests on the political process*

• *Can politics survive with lobbyists and special interests? Can politics survive without them?*

do they get more than thirty minutes; the daily schedules of members of Congress are routinely filled with meetings, hearings, interviews, and working breakfasts, working lunches, working dinners. The 12- to 15-hour day is a fact of life in Washington, for elected officials and staff.

We've just described lobbying as practiced in the political arena. Of course, the concept of lobbying applies to daily life as well. When you ask your boss for a raise, making the argument that you have many good ideas and work very hard, you are lobbying her. When your kids tell you they want to stay up late to watch a particular program, they are lobbying you. If your kids are successful lobbyists, they will be bleary-eyed the next morning.

It's not all that different in politics. Lobbyists from the public and private sector, non-profit corporations, and big business, descend on Washington to get the members of Congress to listen to and accept their positions. Persuasion is the goal. The only significant difference between AT&T's person on the Hill and your children is, that the AT&T man or woman is getting paid for lobbying.

Lobbying

The Center for Responsive Politics has a very good starting definition of lobbying: "paying individuals to influence Congress or the executive branch." The definition certainly applies to the stereotypical Washington lobbyist, the person who wears expensive clothes, has a way with words, is absolutely determined to get what he or she wants, and is well-compensated by the client. It also applies to those less-flashy lobbyists who ask members of Congress to support an environmental program or additional school funding. Yet even in politics, this definition doesn't cover everybody. When you call your congressman or congresswoman and say vote against Bill *X* or in favor of Bill *Y*, you're lobbying him or her. But you're certainly not a lobbyist in the sense that Washington thinks of lobbyists.

Professional lobbyists have a product to sell. Like the typical salesmen, they go door-to-door (only a slight exaggeration) on the Hill, peddling a product they want the members to buy. One crucial difference, of course, is that they are not selling to the American public, but to the American public's elected representatives. Another is that the product is not a physical object, but an idea, a philosophy, a point of view.

But the approach is very similar. Like salesmen, lobbyists must demonstrate absolute confidence in their product, even if deep down they don't believe a word of it. Corner a lobbyist late at night, over drinks in a hotel bar, and maybe you'll get him or her to admit that it's all a big game. The insurance lobbyist might confess that rates are indeed exorbitant, the woman representing the NRA might let it slip that guns do kill people, too. However, any internal conflicts must be put aside when working the halls of Congress. Then the attitude is more like, My client, right or wrong.

The very idea of D.C.-style lobbying disgusts many people, inside and outside the Beltway. What they choose to see are a bunch of overpaid manipulators who will do anything and everything to make Congress bend to their will. This is an oversimplification, but one that's easily exploited by the "inside the Beltway" haters. You have probably heard talk-radio hosts or read columnists who lambaste lobbyists for being entrenched in the corrupt culture of Washington. In large part, it was public outrage that led to passage of the Lobbying Disclosure Act of 1995. The Act will be discussed in more detail later.

It's certainly true that lobbyists work on behalf of narrow (special) interests. You can obviously assume that what they want for their clients—and what their clients want— is not always in the best interests of the rest of us. At the end of the chapter we will take a brief look at the negative perception of lobbyists and special interests. Like fat-cat contributors and PACs, lobbyists are considered by reformers and people such as you or your friends to be symptomatic of what's wrong with Washington.

Where to Gather Information on Lobbyists

The Lobbying Disclosure Act of 1995 requires that lobbyists register with either the Clerk of the House of Representatives or the Secretary of the Senate. The Clerk of the House and Secretary of the Senate also receive and maintain the semiannual financial reports filed by lobbyists. This information is available for public inspection at two locations. If you're in Washington and you've got some time to kill, you could do worse than visiting either of these places.

EVEN LOBBYISTS NEED FRIENDS

It probably comes as no surprise that lobbyists have lobbyists. The American League of Lobbyists, based in Alexandria, Virginia, counts among its duties monitoring lobby legislation and improving the public image of lobbyists. The League's telephone number is (703) 960-3011.

Clerk of the House of Representatives
Legislative Resource Center
B106 Cannon House Office Building
Washington, D.C. 20515-0515
TEL: (202) 226-5200
FAX: (202) 225-7781

Secretary of the Senate
Office of Public Records
232 Hart Senate Office Building
Washington, D.C. 20150
TEL: (202) 224-0322
FAX: (202) 224-1851

What Lobbyists Do

Take away the lobbyists, and Washington would be a quieter, less crowded place. One main thoroughfare in the city—K Street, to be precise—is inhabited almost exclusively by lobbying firms. "K Street" is shorthand for the lobbyists' ghetto. Lobbyists are to Washington what production companies are to Los Angeles: omnipresent.

Not that this should come as a surprise to you. Lobbying is a high-stakes game. Companies can lose or gain millions of dollars according to what happens in the House and the Senate. If lobbyists are to be believed, the fate of entire industries can sometimes rest on the success or defeat of a bill. While that might be putting it a bit strongly, certainly Congress can and does take action that has a profound impact on different segments of society or sectors of the economy. Your own company may at this very moment be monitoring legislation that could affect the livelihood of you and your co-workers.

Earlier we took a brief look at groups that come to Washington to meet with a member of Congress about specific areas of concern. These groups can represent anything from the Beer Distributors of America to a state university system. When you take that walk through a congressional building or take a break in your hotel lobby, glance at the identification tags on the members of the various trade associations. Just about any industry you can think of—and some you've probably never heard of—have lobbyists based in Washington.

The Center for Responsive Politics, a Washington-based organization that studies politics and money, has defined a number of terms pertaining to lobbying and lobbyists:

- Under the Lobbying Disclosure Act of 1995, a *lobbyist* is someone who spends more than 20 percent of his or her time for a particular client in lobbying activities; has multiple contacts with legislative staff, members of Congress, or high-level executive-branch officials; and works for a client that pays more than $5,000 over six months for lobbying.

- *Lobbying activities* include contacts with legislative staff, members of Congress, or high-ranking executive-branch officials, or any efforts to facilitate these contacts.

- *Registration and registration update*—A lobbying firm or organization that employs its own lobbyists must register with the Clerk of the House or the Secretary of the Senate within 45 days, either after a lobbyist is hired, or when the lobbyist contacts a member of Congress, congressional committee staff, the president, the vice president, or other high-ranking official of the executive branch.

- *Issue areas*—The Disclosure Act requires lobbyists to list the general issues on which they lobby.

Any person that does not remedy a "defective filing" within 60 days after being notified by the Clerk of the House or the Secretary of the Senate, or fails to comply with other provisions of the Act, can be fined up to $50,000.

The Byrd Amendment, passed in 1989, made it illegal to use federal money to lobby for contracts, grants, and loans. This mainly affects the non-profit organizations around the country that inundate Washington with requests for funding.

A book entitled *The Interest Group Connection: Electioneering, Lobbying and Policymaking in Washington*, edited by Herrnson, Shaiko, and Wilcox, includes a chapter on non-profits. The author, Howard Marlowe, of the lobbying firm Marlowe and Company, points out that non-profit lobbyists can sometimes be too sure of their product, diminishing their effectiveness. "When you know what the truth is, you do not have to work to convince others that you are right," said Marlowe.

THE REVOLVING DOOR

It probably won't come as a surprise to you that former members of Congress and the executive branch often make excellent lobbyists. Going in, they have two extraordinary advantages over most outsiders: immediate access to powerful members of the House and Senate or the administration, and years of mastering the tricky world of legislation. You might find that more ex-politicians become lobbyists than ex-ballplayers become color-commentators. Why shouldn't they move into lobbying? The job pays extremely well and keeps them in the thick of the political action, which they crave. Remember the saying, "Old soldiers never die, they just fade away"? Well, old politicians never die, but neither do they fade away. They become lobbyists.

In recent years Congress has taken a closer look at the so-called revolving door between the House and Senate and lobbying firms. The members decided to act after a number of their colleagues were going straight from being elected officials to being lobbyists, creating the appearance that they had been using their positions in Congress or the executive branch to set themselves up for the big bucks later. This was not in the best interests of the public, said Congress.

New rules require an ex-member of Congress or the executive branch to wait at least a year before registering as a lobbyist. Presumably this is a sufficient amount of time between the two jobs. In reality it's harder to tell. After all, the major firms continue to hire ex-politicians such as Bob Dole and Ann Richards. The one-year rule certainly did not hurt Dole's marketability; he is reportedly paid several hundred thousand dollars.

Are you looking for a job? Do you like politics? Do you like Washington, D.C.? Oh, and one more thing. Would you like the chance to make a lot of money? Then have we got a job for you. I think you know what it is.

Lobbying Firms

The biggest lobbying firms earn millions of dollars every year. The biggest firms hand out millions every year, as well. We're not talking philanthropy here, but political contributions. The campaign funds are a thank-you for support in the past, and a way of garnering support for the future. Lobbyists are paid to deliver for their clients, but they can't deliver unless they have the "cooperation" of a majority of the Congress.

On the following page is a table that details the numbers on the top twenty heavy-hitters in the lobbying business. These statistics, which cover the first six months of 1997, are provided by the Center for Responsible Politics.

WHAT'S SO SPECIAL ABOUT SPECIAL INTERESTS?

If you heard the term "special interests" outside of politics, you probably wouldn't think it's a bad thing. Quite the opposite. We think of special interests as those which we hold near and dear: family, education, clean air and water, and safe streets. There are casual interests and then there are special interests. What could be wrong with having a special interest in something?

Plenty, if you follow congressional campaigns, C-SPAN floor debates, or the political talk shows. Here the term takes on a different meaning. "Captive of special interests" or "beholden to special interests" are among the most common insults rival politicians throw at each other. The implication is twofold:

1. The accused cares little for the desires of the majority. He or she would rather satisfy an aggressive clique that has unusual access to Congress than the rest of us.

2. Special interests buy and sell politicians, who are only too eager to be bought and sold.

MAJOR LOBBYISTS (1997)

Lobbying Firm	Income Earned	Contributions
1. Verner, Lipfert, et al.	$8,443,000	$682,754
2. Cassidy & Assoc., Inc.	$8,310,429	$551,579
3. Patton Boggs, LLP	$5,040,000	$283,706
4. Atkin, Gump, et al.	$4,820,000	$709,024
5. Preston, Gates, et al.	$4,130,000	$259,199
6. Hogan & Hartson	$3,299,549	$243,870
7. Williams & Jensen	$3,280,000	$459,628
8. Washington Counsel	$3,095,000	$18,870
9. R. Duffy Wall & Assoc.	$2,560,000	$92,687
10. Black, Kelly, et al.	$2,550,000	$34,550
11. Johnson, Smity, et al.	$2,510,000	$109,980
12. Van Scoyoc Assoc., Inc.	$2,450,000	$78,100
13. Timmons & Co.	$2,300,000	$156,118
14. O'Connor & Hannan	$2,180,957	$180,600
15. Swidler & Berlin	$2,080,000	$104,358
16. Barbour, Griffith & Rogers	$2,060,000	$64,248
17. Dutko Group, Inc.	$2,031,000	$80,296
18. Podestra Assoc., Inc.	$1,920,000	$152,859
19. Alcalde & Fay	$1,850,000	$31,682
20. Oldaker, Ryan, et al.	$1,840,000	$88,060

Source: Center for Responsive Politics

The standard response is either to say it's not true, or to point out that the opponent is much worse when it comes to cooperating with special interests. But no politician can afford to disregard the charge. The ballot box is the best revenge for voters who believe they're being ignored.

WHAT IS A SPECIAL INTEREST?

It's tempting to say you'll know one when you see one. As we just discussed, "special interests" is a derogatory term that has become part of the standard political vocabulary. No group will ever admit to being a special interest, and most groups would vehemently deny it.

Still, you can make a pretty good guess about what is or is not a special interest by keeping in mind this basic fact: Special interests advance an agenda that serves their own members above all. This is not always a bad thing. A gay-and-lesbian group fighting job discrimination is clearly a special interest; a heterosexual female or a hetero-sexual male would not directly benefit if the group succeeds in its aims, but at the same time, a legitimate battle against job discrimination is something many heterosexuals would embrace. A medium-sized firm seeking congressional protection from a massive and bullying competitor might arouse sympathy from you and others who have no stake, financial or emotional, in the company. Yet this, too, is clearly a special interest.

It's those greedy special interests that give the rest a bad name—such as the rich businessman who wants an unheard-of tax break, or the big industry that is obsessed with eliminating environmental regulations in order to increase its already massive profits. The best lobbyists are hired, and tens, if not hundreds, of thousands of dollars in campaign contributions are made in an all-out effort to win. No, you won't find many people who are rooting for these kinds of special interests to succeed.

Are Special Interests and Lobbyists Ruining Politics?

You will have to decide. The fact that the question gets asked at all is a good indication that more than a few people believe the answer is yes. It's their firm belief that politicians respond most of all to special interests, to lobbyists, and to the money that both bring to the table. The rest of us are left to fume on the sidelines.

While this assessment may have some validity, you have to keep in mind a couple of points: The first is that special interests and lobbyists are not inherently evil. They are participants in a system that takes a broad view of legitimate political participation. As you read in chapter 18, "The Campaign Business," campaign contributions—within prescribed limits—are a legal form of political expression. The second is that special interests and lobbyists regard politics as more than a civic duty; it's at the very core of their existence, a do-or-die challenge.

This book has attempted to show how and why you should participate in American politics at every level. Take that same idea and apply it here. You can fault lobbyists for their tactics, or special interests for their myopic view of the world, but can you fault them for getting involved?

CHAPTER RECAP

- Lobbyists walk the halls of Congress every day.

- Professional lobbyists are paid for their work, some of them very handsomely.

- Public outcry against lobbyists and the Washington scene led to regulations passed by Congress in 1995.

- Special interests are often perceived as being opposed to the majority will.

Although the term 'lobbying' may have developed a somewhat sinister and pejorative connotation over the years, the activities involved in lobbying are intertwined with fundamental First Amendment rights of speech, association and petition, and may facilitate the exchange of important information and ideas between the government and private parties.

—*"Legal and Congressional Ethics Standards of Relevance to Those Who Lobby Congress,"* CRS Report, *March 5, 1996*

- Lobbyists and special interests are a fundamental part of American democracy.

- Despite the growth of news media, newspapers and journals of opinion are still important conveyors of information about politics.

- Though they strive to entertain, the television talk shows are often quite informative.

Where Do You Stand?—Political Parties and Ideology

Y ou've analyzed the issues, you've studied the candidates. You are feeling comfortable with politics. You can more than hold your own in a political argument. You not only vote, but look forward to voting.

A PROFILE OF YOURSELF

You tend to vote for people rather than parties. You hear a candidate speak in person or on television, you like what he or she stands for, and that determines how you vote. For you, voting is conducted on a case-by-case basis, especially in the major races.

You are not alone. Party affiliation is not what it once was in America. Democrats and Republicans today feel no regret about crossing party lines to support the candidate of their choice. Elected officials occasionally switch parties. Senator Wayne Morse of Oregon did so in the sixties. Senator Ben Nighthorse Campbell of Colorado did the same thing a few years ago. If voters went strictly by party, the Republicans could never capture the White

House—there are more registered Democrats than Republicans. Yet Ronald Reagan and George Bush were elected with the support of many Democratic voters.

When you register to vote, you are asked to indicate your political party preference. This is not a decision you should take lightly. If you usually agree with the Republicans, then you probably want to select the GOP. If you like the Democrats' platform, then the Democratic Party should be your choice. And if both parties leave you cold, you can always pick the "decline to state" category. But do your homework first.

This chapter will discuss the two major parties, including their history, presidential platforms, and beliefs. The second part deals with the ideology of liberals, centrists, and conservatives. It's certain that you will be asked at least once where you fit in these categories. Politics is big on labels.

Your choice of political party is an indication of your own beliefs and priorities. A Republican voter most likely abhors taxes and is indifferent or hostile to the idea of subsidizing the underclass. A Democratic voter probably thinks government has a responsibility to assist the less fortunate. And though Democrats aren't fond of taxes, they would raise them if it meant saving key programs.

Beyond that, it's hard to generalize. Some Republicans would ban abortion outright, but a majority think that women have the right to choose. Some Democrats are strong supporters of affirmative action, others feel the program is counterproductive and has run its course. Some Republicans believe in school prayer; others think it's unconstitutional. Some Democrats are in favor of free trade; others prefer some form of protection. As these examples indicate, each party has internal differences.

You can learn more about the major parties by contacting state party headquarters.

THE BIG TENT

The two parties are not monolithic. In political circles, it's not enough to label yourself a Democrat or a Republican. What matters is the kind of Democrat or Republican that you claim to be. Bill Clinton called himself a "New Democrat," which was a clever way of saying, I'm not liberal, I'm not conservative, and I represent the future. In the 2000 presidential race, Republican frontrunner George W. Bush added a new category, "compassionate conservative," to describe his political philosophy. He repeated the phrase at every campaign stop, just so we would get the point.

The Democratic Party includes moderate Democrats, liberal Democrats, conservative Democrats, Reagan Democrats, and "New Democrats." The Republican Party includes moderate Republicans, right-wing Republicans, liberal Republicans, and conservative Republicans. You might put yourself in one or more of these groups.

You could also choose to register independent. In primary elections, independents can request either the Democratic or Republican ballot. Or you could align yourself with one of the minor parties, the Greens, the Socialist Worker's Party, the Libertarians, or Ross Perot's Reform Party. Nothing says you have to join either the Democrats or the Republicans, though the political system certainly encourages it.

THE DEMOCRATS

Following are ten important dates in Democratic Party history. (Information provided by the Democratic National Committee.)

- *1792*—Democrats are organized by Thomas Jefferson as a Congressional Caucus to fight for the Bill of Rights and against the elite Populist Party.

Here's what one well-known Democrat had to say about Democrats:

"We are, in short, a party reflecting character as well as calculation, values as well as interests, moral as well as material goals, and human as well as statistical projections, and we must continue to be so."

—*Theodore C. Sorensen,* Why I Am a Democrat

- *1798*—The Democrats become "the party of the common man" and are officially called the Democratic-Republicans.

- *1800*—Jefferson is elected as the first Democratic president.

- *1840*—Official name becomes the Democratic Party.

- *1860*—The Democratic Party formally splits over slavery.

- *1870s*—The party's Southern base is disenfranchised by the Civil War and Reconstruction.

- *1920s*—Democrats are divided over the issue of Prohibition.

- *1932*—Franklin Delano Roosevelt is elected, and creates a Democratic Party coalition of blacks, Jews, and the poor.

- *1964-65*—Lyndon Johnson's Great Society.

- *1984*—Geraldine Ferraro becomes the first woman ever nominated for vice president. She shares the Democratic ticket with Walter Mondale.

WHAT DEMOCRATS BELIEVE

As you have probably gathered, no two Democrats are exactly alike. (No two Republicans are exactly alike, either, but that's for later.) No definitive statement of party beliefs will please everybody, nor apply to everybody.

The best and most comprehensive statement of official Democratic or Republican positions is the party platform. The platform addresses everything, not only the hot-button issues regularly covered in the media. The platform is put together every presidential election year by a committee consisting of dedicated party members from across the country.

The 1996 Democratic National Platform was divided into four sections: Opportunity; Responsibility; Security, Freedom, and Peace; and Community.

Below are some highlights of each:

Opportunity

1. Balance the budget by 2002, while protecting Medicaid, Medicare, education, and the environment.

2. Increase access to quality, affordable health care; help unemployed workers get health insurance between jobs.

3. Expand public school choice and promote public charter schools.

4. Pass GI Bill for America's workers, to provide skill grants that let workers choose the training that's right for them.

Responsibility

1. Prosecute serious violent juveniles as adults.

2. Cut the federal workforce by 240,000 positions, making it the smallest in thirty years.

3. Enact a constitutional amendment to protect the rights of crime victims.

4. Keep the abortion rate coming down, by making abortion less necessary and more rare, not more difficult and more dangerous.

Security, Freedom, and Peace

1. Outlaw poison gas forever by ratifying the Chemical Weapons Convention.

2. Keep working to shut off foreign drug flows and to eradicate foreign drug crops.

3. Give law enforcement the most powerful tools available to fight terrorism.

4. Fully fund the Pentagon's five-year defense plan, including a 40 percent real increase in weapons modernization by 2001.

Community

1. Continue efforts to stamp out discrimination and hatred of every kind.

2. Further accelerate clean-up of toxic waste sites.

3. Provide flextime so workers can choose whether to take overtime as wages or time off.

4. Continue America's leadership in meeting environmental challenges that transcend national borders.

*—1996 Democratic National Platform, published by the
Democratic National Committee*

What you have just read is a sample of Democratic Party goals and objectives during Bill Clinton's second term. It might be worthwhile to check this list again in the year 2000, when the next platform is being debated.

The Democratic National Committee

You will undoubtedly encounter something called the Democratic National Committee in reading about party politics. The Democratic National Committee, or DNC, is the governing body of the Democratic Party. The DNC has 431 members, who are either elected, appointed, or serve by

virtue of a party political office. The DNC receives and disperses campaign contributions for the Democratic Party.

Should you want to become a member of the DNC,
you need to contact your state or territory's Democratic
Party for information. The DNC usually meets twice a
year, in the spring and fall. In presidential election years, it
meets once, following the national convention.

As a member, you will

- vote on all resolutions and amendments to the charter and bylaws of the party;

- serve as a delegate to the Democratic National
  Convention; and

- serve as a local leader promoting the ideals of the
  Democratic National Party.

Perhaps you are one of the many Democrats who consider themselves centrists. (Oddly enough, similarly posi-
tioned Republicans prefer the term "middle of the road.")
You think the liberal wing of the party is out-of-touch, and
you think the conservative wing has betrayed the party's
basic principles. There is an organization for people like you.

The Democratic Leadership Council

Disgusted by their party's performance in recent presidential elections, a group of angry and ambitious Democrats
formed the Democratic Leadership Council in 1985. The
DLC, a non-profit organization, cast itself as a fresh and
mainstream alternative to the excesses of sixties liberalism.
So nobody misses the point, the DLC calls its magazine
The New Democrat.

The DLC became a magnet for Democratic politicians
seeking to represent the views of moderates. One of them was
Bill Clinton. In 1990 Clinton took over as DLC chairman;
two years later he was elected president of the United States.

The DLC and its think tank, The Progressive Policy Institute, continue to exert a strong influence on the political debate in this country. The DLC occupies the middle, a place where many voters feel most comfortable.

The five tenets of the New Democrat philosophy are:

1. The private sector, not government, should be the primary engine for economic growth and opportunity.

2. The values that most Americans share—liberty of conscience, individual responsibility, tolerance, work, faith, family, and community—should be embodied in the polices of our government.

3. America needs a renewed ethic of civic responsibility in which people who receive government assistance have an obligation to give something back to the country.

4. In foreign policy, America should lead other nations toward democracy and market economies.

5. As advocates of activist government, we need to reinvent government so that it is both more responsive to those it serves, and more accountable to taxpayers who pay for it.

THE REPUBLICANS

Some key dates in Republican Party history. (From the Republican National Committee info pack.)

- *1854*—The first public meeting of the nascent Republican Party. The party was formed in strong opposition to slavery.

- *1860*—Abraham Lincoln, a Republican, is elected president of the United States. Lincoln was elected a mere six years after the birth of the party.

Alameda County Library
Alameda County Registrar of Voters & the League of Women Voters
invite you to join your friends and neighbors at the library and watch the **2012**

PRESIDENTIAL DEBATES

All programs 5:15 – 8:30 p.m.
5:15 p.m. Doors open
5:45 – 7:30 p.m.   Live televised debate
7:30 – 8: 30 p.m. Facilitated comments

Refreshments served

Wednesday, 10/3
First Presidential Debate
Castro Valley Library
Dublin Library
Union City Library

Thursday, 10/11
Vice Presidential Debate
Castro Valley Library

Tuesday, 10/16
Second Presidential Debate
Albany Library
Castro Valley Library
Newark Library

Monday, 10/22
Third Presidential Debate
Castro Valley Library
Dublin Library
Fremont Main Library
San Lorenzo Library

President Barack Obama

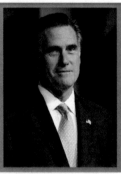

Governor Mitt Romney

Albany Library
1247 Marin Ave.
510-526-3720

Castro Valley Library
3600 Norbridge Ave.
510-667-7900

Dublin Library
200 Civic Plaza Dr.
925-828-1315

Vice President Joseph Biden

Congressman Paul Ryan

For more
election information visit:
http://guides.aclibrary.org/elections

Community Partners (in alphabetical order):

American Association of University Women
Castro Valley Unified School District
City of Albany
City of Fremont
Eden Area Chamber of Commerce
Fremont Family Resource Center
Fremont Unified School District
Friends of the Albany Library
Friends of the Castro Valley Library
Friends of the Fremont Libraries
Friends of the Union City Library
League of Women Voters of Fremont, Newark, and Union City
League of Women Voters of the Eden Area
Newark Library League
New Haven Adult School
Office of Alameda County Supervisor Nate Miley, District 4
Ohlone College

Fremont Main Library
2400 Stevenson Blvd.
510-745-1401

Newark Library
6300 Civic Terrace Ave.
510-795-2627

San Lorenzo Library
395 Paseo Grande
510-670-6283

Union City Library
34007 Alvarado-Niles Rd.
510-745-1464

LEAGUE OF
WOMEN VOTERS

ALAMEDA COUNTY
Registrar of Voters

Library is wheelchair accessible.
For special accommodations, please make request
at least 7 working days in advance.
Voice (call appropriate branch) / TTY 888-663-0660

Alameda County
LIBRARY
...Infinite possibilities

all library programs are FREE

www.aclibrary.org

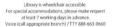

- *1868*—Civil War hero Ulysses S. Grant is nominated for president by the Republican Party. Grant won the presidency in 1868 and 1872.

- *1884*—Republicans lose the White House for the first time in twenty-four years. They regain it with the election of Benjamin Harrison in 1888.

- *1896–1912*—William McKinley (1896–1901), Theodore Roosevelt (1901–1908), and William Taft (1908–1912) give the Republicans three presidents in a row.

- *1937*—Marion E. Martin named first assistant chairman of the Republican National Committee. This began a tradition where the RNC chairman and co-chairman must be of the opposite sex.

- *1952*—Dwight Eisenhower elected president, ending twenty years of Democratic rule.

- *1984*—Ronald Reagan receives the largest Republican landslide in American history.

- *1994*—Republicans regain control of Congress for the first time in forty years. The party maintains control after the 1996 elections.

The Republican Party is often referred to as the Grand Old Party, or GOP. According to the RNC, that term probably originated with headline writers in the 1870s and 1880s. The irony is that the Democratic Party is actually twenty-two years *older* than the Republican Party.

WHAT REPUBLICANS BELIEVE

The 1996 GOP platform, titled *Restoring the American Dream*, is 107 pages long, and crammed with ideas and policies. As was suggested with the Democrats, you might want to take another look at the GOP 1996 platform in the year 2000 to judge for yourself if the party has stuck to its ideals. Among the highlights of the 1996 GOP platform:

- A balanced budget and lower taxes go hand in hand.

- Tax relief is the only way to return the economy to the growth rates our country enjoyed from World War II to the election of Bill Clinton.

- Support for a national missile defense system for all fifty states by 2003.

- Support for the official recognition of English as the nation's common language.

- Legal immigrants should depend for assistance on their sponsors, and not on the American taxpayer.

- Support for the Defense of Marriage Act, which prevents states from being forced to recognize same-sex unions.

- Elimination of the Departments of Commerce, Housing and Urban Development, Education, and Energy.

The Republican National Committee

- The Republican National Committee, the governing body of the Republican Party, consists of 165 members from all fifty states.

- The RNC supports Republican candidates at the national and local levels.

- Since 1918 the RNC has been permanently based in Washington, D.C.

- The national committeeman, committeewoman, and state party chairman are all elected to four-year terms.

- The RNC receives and disperses contributions to the Republican Party.

LEFT, RIGHT, OR OUT-THERE

Sometimes it's not enough to belong to a party. Your friends want to know: Are you a liberal or a conservative? Think before you respond.

Liberalism and Liberals

Liberals and conservatives are not necessarily more consistent in their beliefs than are Republicans and Democrats. In other words, you might fit the definition of a liberal on some issues, and the definition of a conservative on others.

A liberal might be liberal on government spending ("More is better"), but conservative on gender or sexuality issues ("Keep your hands to yourself"). A conservative might be conservative on defense ("More is better"), but liberal on questions of personal freedom ("To each his own"). Distinguishing between "liberal" and "conservative" can be tricky. Once you have picked a political party—or at least given it some serious thought—you can turn your attention to ideology. In many ways your ideology is a more accurate reading of your beliefs than your party affiliation is. Ideology is not how you vote, but what you believe. And that goes to the core of who you are as a political person.

You have probably noticed that liberals have had a tough time in the 1990s. Nobody wants to be a liberal anymore—not even liberals. A politician who's labeled "liberal" by his opponent, immediately denies the charge. If the description sticks, it can turn victory into defeat, as Michael Dukakis discovered in the 1988 presidential race. "Liberal" has become a dirty word in some circles.

Conservatism

Conservative politicians have no qualms being called conservatives. In fact, they welcome it. The word does not have the negative connotations associated with "liberal." Ronald Reagan made it cool to be a conservative.

As conservatism has gained in popularity, it has become increasingly hard to define. Everyone wants to be known as conservative. Consequently, many people with many varied beliefs call themselves conservatives. There are also neoconservatives—a large portion of whom are former Democrats—and ultraconservatives, a media term for the Christian right, America Firsters, and foreign-policy hawks.

THREE DEFINITIONS OF LIBERALISM AND LIBERALS

Do any of these sound good to you?

Liberalism represents more than anything a way of thinking and feeling, a commitment of citizens to the future and to one another, an optimistic attitude that has the courage to put its money and its reputation where its mouth is.

—David Barash, The 'L' Word

A liberal is one who believes in more government action to meet individual needs.

—William Safire, Safire's Political Dictionary

The liberals believe that no rulers are wise enough to plan the destiny of mankind. They maintain therefore that the power of government must be limited, and that beyond those limits government must protect the freedom of men.

—Walter Lippmann, James Lare, and Clinton Rossiter, eds.,
The Essential Lippmann

You should note the contradiction between the definitions of William Safire and Walter Lippmann. Safire was writing in the 1980s and 1990s, Lippmann in 1915. Today Lippmann's definition seems more applicable to conservatives. Yet there are areas where liberals want a limited government role, such issues as abortion and artistic expression. Again this shows how hard it is to pin down the terms "liberal" and "conservative."

Two Definitions of Conservatism

Do you recognize yourself in either of these definitions?

Russell Kirk, who died in 1994, was a leader in twentieth-century American conservative thought. In 1987 he offered this description of a conservative:

He believes, to begin with, that there endures a moral order natural for mankind. He has found human nature to be a mixture of good and evil, and that it may not be perfected. He defends custom, habit, common sense.

Kirk later added:

He supports the institutions of private property and a competitive economy. He knows that sound government, repressing violence and fraud, providing for the common good, is necessary for the survival of civilization. He assumes that politics is the art of the possible, not the path to Zion.

> —*Louis Filler*, Dictionary of American Conservatism: The
> First Complete Guide to Issues, People, Events, and
> Organizations

Backward and Upward: The New Conservative Writing is a collection of articles by youngish (under forty-five) writers published in 1996. In the introduction, David Brooks talks about the attitudes of conservatives in the 1990s:

Conservative writers are more likely to be attuned with and approving of popular culture. There has been an increased concern with happiness, pleasure and even sensuality.

> —*David Brooks, editor,* Backward and Upward:
> The New Conservative Writing

Here is Brooks on conservatism and politics:

What conservatism can point out is that virtue cannot be developed in a country where people are constantly asking government to do things for them, and where social standards are designed to tame, pacify and stifle.

These are some good definitions of conservatism. Among the recent political figures who proudly call themselves conservatives are Ronald Reagan, Newt Gingrich, Jack Kemp, and Dan Quayle. One of the major figures in post–World War II conservatism is William F. Buckley, whose magazine, *National Review*, was discussed in chapter 20, "Media and Politics." For decades Buckley hosted an interview program on public television called *Firing Line*, which featured well-known guests from all across the political spectrum. The witty host, however, was usually the star of the show.

Libertarianism

It is sometimes hard to know where conservatism ends and libertarianism begins. Certainly many of the contributors to *Backward and Upward* express Libertarian-like views. At the same time, the oath required for membership in the national Libertarian Party, which was founded in 1972, would probably be acceptable to conservatives, even liberals:

> I hereby certify that I do not believe in or advocate the initiation of force or fraud as a means of achieving political or social goals.

In his book *What It Means to Be a Libertarian*, Charles Murray offers this:

> A person who is making an honest living and minding his own business isn't hurting me. He isn't forcing me to do anything. I as an individual don't have the right to force him to do anything. A hundred of his neighbors acting as a mob don't have that right. The government shouldn't have that right either, except for stringently limited functions, imposed under stringently limited conditions.
> —*Charles Murray*, What It Means to Be a Libertarian

These two examples give a general idea of what constitutes libertarianism. But what about specifics?

An excellent source is Harry Browne, the 1996 Libertarian candidate for president of the United States. In *Why Government Doesn't Work,* Browne revealed what he would do on his first day in the White House. It's enough to make FDR's "100 Days" seem lethargic by comparison.

> On my first day in office, by Executive Order, I will personally:
>> Pardon everyone who has been convicted solely on a federal tax-evasion charge, order the immediate release of those in prison, and restore their civil and voting rights.
>> Pardon everyone who has been convicted solely on a federal non-violent drug charge, order the immediate release of those in prison, and restore their civil and voting rights.

Browne isn't finished. Before the clock strikes midnight on Day One of the Browne presidency, he will

- end federal affirmative action;

- bring an immediate end to all federal asset-forfeiture cases;

- order the removal of all American troops from foreign soil;

- order the removal of all American troops from United Nations operations.

And then he'll go to bed.

The Reform Party

You probably recall that in the 1992 presidential election, Ross Perot's Reform Party did remarkably well. A large number of voters responded to the party's message of balancing the federal budget, paying off the national debt, reforming campaign fund-raising, and term limits for members of Congress. In 1993, Ross Perot himself led the fight against the North American Free Trade Agreement (NAFTA).

Even more remarkable was the Reform Party's success in winning the Minnesota governorship against two strong contenders from the major parties. The victor? A professional wrestler, Jesse ("The Body") Ventura.

Selecting a political party is not the most important decision you will make in your life, but it's not trivial, either. Becoming active in politics means finding an outlet for your political beliefs. Parties can play a pivotal role.

Your ideology is a reflection of what does and does not matter in your world. There are things that get conservatives angry that barely register with liberals. Liberals are sensitive to some issues that conservatives ignore.

Defining yourself as a liberal or a conservative is tantamount to crossing a threshold. It means politics matter in your life, they occupy your thoughts and your time.

CHAPTER RECAP

- Choosing a political party, or registering as an independent, is not to be regarded lightly.

- Democrats and Republicans differ on core policy issues, such as government support for the underclass.

- Check in the year 2000 whether Democrats and Republicans met the goals outlined in their respective 1996 platforms.

- The Democratic and Republican National Committees are a huge source of funds for each party.

- In the 1960s, being liberal was cool and being conservative was not. In the 1990s, the reverse is true.

- Libertarians are on the front lines in the fight against taxes of any kind, and are in favor of unlimited personal freedoms.

The Declaration of Independence

*A*ction of Second Continental Congress, July 4, 1776. The unanimous Declaration of the thirteen United States of America.

WHEN in the Course of human Events, it becomes necessary for one People to dissolve the Political Bands which have connected them with another, and to assume among the Powers of the Earth, the separate and equal Station to which the Laws of Nature and of Nature's God entitle them, a decent Respect to the Opinions of Mankind requires that they should declare the causes which impel them to the Separation.

WE hold these Truths to be self-evident, that all Men are created equal, that they are endowed by their Creator with certain unalienable Rights, that among these are Life, Liberty, and the Pursuit of Happiness—That to secure these Rights, Governments are instituted among Men, deriving their just Powers from the Consent of the Governed, that whenever any Form of Government becomes destructive of these Ends, it is the Right of the People to alter or to abolish it, and to institute new

Government, laying its Foundation on such Principles, and organizing its Powers in such Form, as to them shall seem most likely to effect their Safety and Happiness. Prudence, indeed, will dictate that Governments long established should not be changed for light and transient Causes; and accordingly all Experience hath shown, that Mankind are more disposed to suffer, while Evils are sufferable, than to right themselves by abolishing the Forms to which they are accustomed. But when a long Train of Abuses and Usurpations, pursuing invariably the same Object, evinces a Design to reduce them under absolute Despotism, it is their Right, it is their Duty, to throw off such Government, and to provide new Guards for their future Security. Such has been the patient Sufferance of these Colonies; and such is now the Necessity which constrains them to alter their former Systems of Government. The History of the present King of Great Britain is a History of repeated Injuries and Usurpations, all having in direct Object the Establishment of an absolute Tyranny over these States. To prove this, let Facts be submitted to a candid World.

HE has refused his Assent to Laws, the most wholesome and necessary for the public Good.

HE has forbidden his Governors to pass Laws of immediate and pressing Importance, unless suspended in their Operation till his Assent should be obtained; and when so suspended, he has utterly neglected to attend to them.

HE has refused to pass other Laws for the Accommodation of large Districts of People, unless those People would relinquish the Right of Representation in the Legislature, a Right inestimable to them, and formidable to Tyrants only.

HE has called together Legislative Bodies at Places unusual, uncomfortable, and distant from the Depository of their public Records, for the sole Purpose of fatiguing them into Compliance with his Measures.

HE has dissolved Representative Houses repeatedly, for opposing with manly Firmness his Invasions on the Rights of the People.

HE has refused for a long Time, after such Dissolutions, to cause others to be elected; whereby the Legislative Powers, incapable of Annihilation, have returned to the People at large for their exercise; the State remaining in the meantime exposed to all the Dangers of Invasion from without, and Convulsions within.

HE has endeavoured to prevent the Population of these States; for that Purpose obstructing the Laws for Naturalization of Foreigners; refusing to pass others to encourage their Migrations hither, and raising the Conditions of new Appropriations of Lands.

HE has obstructed the Administration of Justice, by refusing his Assent to Laws for establishing Judiciary Powers.

HE has made Judges dependent on his Will alone, for the Tenure of their Offices, and the Amount and Payment of their Salaries.

HE has erected a Multitude of new Offices, and sent hither Swarms of Officers to harrass our People, and eat out their Substance.

HE has kept among us, in Times of Peace, Standing Armies, without the consent of our Legislature.

HE has affected to render the Military independent of and superior to the Civil Power.

HE has combined with others to subject us to a Jurisdiction foreign to our Constitution, and unacknowledged by our Laws; giving his Assent to their Acts of pretended Legislation:

FOR quartering large Bodies of Armed Troops among us;

FOR protecting them, by a mock Trial, from Punishment for any Murders which they should commit on the Inhabitants of these States;

FOR cutting off our Trade with all Parts of the World;

FOR imposing Taxes on us without our Consent;

FOR depriving us, in many Cases, of the Benefits of Trial by Jury;

FOR transporting us beyond Seas to be tried for pretended Offenses;

FOR abolishing the free System of English Laws in a neighbouring Province, establishing therein an arbitrary Government, and enlarging its Boundaries, so as to render it at once an Example and fit Instrument for introducing the same absolute Rule into these Colonies;

FOR taking away our Charters, abolishing our most valuable Laws, and altering fundamentally the Forms of our Governments;

FOR suspending our own Legislatures, and declaring themselves invested with Power to legislate for us in all Cases whatsoever.

HE has abdicated Government here, by declaring us out of his Protection and waging War against us.

HE has plundered our Seas, ravaged our Coasts, burnt our Towns, and destroyed the Lives of our People.

HE is, at this Time, transporting large Armies of foreign Mercenaries to compleat the Works of Death, Desolation, and Tyranny, already begun with circumstances of Cruelty and Perfidy, scarcely paralleled in the most barbarous Ages, and totally unworthy the Head of a civilized Nation.

HE has constrained our fellow Citizens taken Captive on the high Seas to bear Arms against their Country, to become the Executioners of their Friends and Brethren, or to fall themselves by their Hands.

HE has excited domestic Insurrections amongst us, and has endeavoured to bring on the Inhabitants of our Frontiers, the merciless Indian Savages, whose known Rule of Warfare is an undistinguished Destruction of all Ages, Sexes and Conditions.

IN every stage of these Oppressions we have Petitioned for Redress in the most humble Terms. Our repeated Petitions have been answered only by repeated Injury. A Prince, whose Character is thus marked by every act which may define a Tyrant, is unfit to be the Ruler of a free People.

NOR have we been wanting in Attentions to our British Brethren. We have warned them from Time to Time of Attempts by their Legislature to extend an unwarrantable Jurisdiction over us. We have reminded them of the Circumstances of our Emigration and Settlement here. We have appealed to their native Justice and Magnanimity, and we have conjured them by the Ties of our common Kindred to disavow these Usurpations, which, would inevitably interrupt our Connections and Correspondence. They too have been deaf to the Voice of Justice and of Consanguinity. We must, therefore, acquiesce in the Necessity, which denounces our Separation, and hold them, as we hold the rest of Mankind, Enemies in War, in Peace, Friends.

WE, therefore, the Representatives of the UNITED STATES OF AMERICA, in GENERAL CONGRESS, Assembled, appealing to the Supreme Judge of the World for the Rectitude of our Intentions, do, in the Name, and by Authority of the good People of these Colonies, solemnly Publish and Declare, That these United Colonies are, and of Right ought to be, FREE AND INDEPENDENT STATES; that they are absolved from all Allegiance to the British Crown, and that all political Connection between them and the State of Great Britain is and ought to be totally dissolved; and that as FREE AND INDEPENDENT STATES, they have full Power to levy War, conclude Peace, contract Alliances, establish Commerce, and to do all other Acts and Things which INDEPENDENT STATES may of right do. And for the support of this Declaration, with a firm Reliance on the Protection of divine Providence, we mutually pledge to each other our Lives, our Fortunes, and our sacred Honor.

The Constitution of the United States (Including Amendments)

WE THE PEOPLE of the United States, in Order to form a more perfect Union, establish Justice, insure domestic Tranquility, provide for the common defense, promote the general Welfare, and secure the Blessings of Liberty to ourselves and our Posterity, do ordain and establish this Constitution for the United States of America.

ARTICLE I

SECTION 1. All legislative Powers herein granted shall be vested in a Congress of the United States, which shall consist of a Senate and House of Representatives.

SECTION 2. The House of Representatives shall be composed of Members chosen every second Year by the People of the several States, and the Electors in each State shall have the Qualifications requisite for Electors of the most numerous Branch of the State Legislature.

No Person shall be a Representative who shall not have attained to the Age of twenty-five Years, and been seven Years a Citizen of the United States, and who shall not, when elected, be an Inhabitant of that State in which he shall be chosen.

Representatives and direct Taxes shall be apportioned among the several States which may be included within this Union, according to their respective Numbers, which shall be determined by adding to the whole Number of free Persons, including those bound to Service for a Term of Years, and excluding Indians not taxed, three-fifths of all other Persons.[1] The actual Enumeration shall be made within three Years after the first Meeting of the Congress of the United States, and within every subsequent Term of ten Years, in such Manner as they shall by Law direct. The number of Representatives shall not exceed one for every thirty Thousand, but each State shall have at Least one Representative; and until such enumeration shall be made, the State of New Hampshire shall be entitled to choose three, Massachusetts eight, Rhode-Island and Providence Plantations one, Connecticut five, New York six, New Jersey four, Pennsylvania eight, Delaware one, Maryland six, Virginia ten, North Carolina five, South Carolina five, and Georgia three.

When vacancies happen in the Representation from any State, the Executive Authority thereof shall issue Writs of Election to fill such Vacancies.

The House of Representatives shall choose their Speaker and other Officers; and shall have the sole Power of Impeachment.

SECTION 3. The Senate of the United States shall be composed of two Senators from each State, chosen by the Legislature thereof,[2] for six Years; and each Senator shall have one Vote.

Immediately after they shall be assembled in Consequence of the first Election, they shall be divided as equally as may be into three Classes. The Seats of the Senators of the first Class shall be vacated at the Expiration of the second Year, of the second Class at the Expiration of the fourth Year, and of the third Class at the Expiration of the sixth Year, so that one-third may be chosen every second

Year; and if Vacancies happen by Resignation, or otherwise, during the Recess of the Legislature of any State, the Executive thereof may make temporary Appointments until the next Meeting of the Legislature, which shall then fill such Vacancies.[3]

No Person shall be a Senator who shall not have attained to the Age of thirty Years, and been nine Years a Citizen of the United States, and who shall not, when elected, be an Inhabitant of that State for which he shall be chosen.

The Vice President of the United States shall be President of the Senate, but shall have no Vote, unless they be equally divided.

The Senate shall choose their other Officers, and also a President pro tempore, in the Absence of the Vice President, or when he shall exercise the Office of President of the United States.

The Senate shall have the sole Power to try all Impeachments. When sitting for that Purpose, they shall be on Oath or Affirmation. When the President of the United States is tried, the Chief Justice shall preside. And no Person shall be convicted without the Concurrence of two-thirds of the Members present.

Judgment in Cases of Impeachment shall not extend further than to removal from Office, and disqualification to hold and enjoy any Office of honor, Trust or Profit under the United States; but the Party convicted shall nevertheless be liable and subject to Indictment, Trial, Judgment, and Punishment, according to Law.

SECTION 4. The Times, Places and Manner of holding Elections for Senators and Representatives, shall be prescribed in each State by the Legislature thereof; but the Congress may at any time by Law make or alter such Regulations, except as to the Places of choosing Senators.

The Congress shall assemble at least once in every Year, and such Meeting shall be on the first Monday in December,[4] unless they shall by Law appoint a different Day.

SECTION 5. Each House shall be the Judge of the Elections, Returns, and Qualifications of its own Members, and a Majority of each shall constitute a Quorum to do Business; but a smaller Number may adjourn from day to day, and may be authorized to compel the Attendance of absent Members, in such Manner, and under such Penalties as each House may provide.

Each House may determine the Rules of its Proceedings, punish its Members for disorderly Behavior, and, with the Concurrence of two-thirds, expel a Member.

Each House shall keep a Journal of its Proceedings, and from time to time publish the same, excepting such Parts as may in their Judgment require Secrecy; and the Yeas and Nays of the Members of either House on any question shall, at the Desire of one-fifth of those Present, be entered on the Journal.

Neither House, during the Session of Congress, shall, without the Consent of the other, adjourn for more than three days, nor to any other Place than that in which the two Houses shall be sitting.

SECTION 6. The Senators and Representatives shall receive a Compensation for their Services, to be ascertained by Law, and paid out of the Treasury of the United States. They shall in all Cases, except Treason, Felony, and Breach of the Peace, be privileged from Arrest during their Attendance at the Session of their respective Houses, and in going to and returning from the same; and for any Speech or Debate in either House, they shall not be questioned in any other Place.

No Senator or Representative shall, during the Time for which he was elected, be appointed to any civil Office under the Authority of the United States, which shall have been created, or the Emoluments whereof shall have been increased during such time; and no Person holding any Office under the United States, shall be a Member of either House during his Continuance in Office.[5]

SECTION 7. All Bills for raising Revenue shall originate in the House of Representatives; but the Senate may propose or concur with Amendments as on other Bills.

Every Bill which shall have passed the House of Representatives and the Senate, shall, before it becomes a Law, be presented to the President of the United States. If he approves he shall sign it, but if not he shall return it, with his Objections to that House in which it shall have originated, who shall enter the Objections at large on their Journal, and proceed to reconsider it. If after such Reconsideration two-thirds of that House shall agree to pass the Bill, it shall be sent, together with the Objections, to the other House, by which it shall likewise be reconsidered, and if approved by two-thirds of that House, it shall become a Law. But in all such Cases the Votes of both Houses shall be determined by Yeas and Nays, and the Names of the Persons voting for and against the Bill shall be entered on the Journal of each House respectively. If any Bill shall not be returned by the President within ten Days (Sundays excepted) after it shall have been presented to him, the Same shall be a Law, in like Manner as if he had signed it, unless the Congress by their Adjournment prevent its Return, in which Case it shall not be a Law.

Every Order, Resolution, or Vote to which the Concurrence of the Senate and House of Representatives may be necessary (except on a question of Adjournment) shall be presented to the President of the United States; and before the Same shall take Effect, shall be approved by him, or being disapproved by him, shall be repassed by two-thirds of the Senate and House of Representatives, according to the Rules and Limitations prescribed in the Case of a Bill.

SECTION 8. The Congress shall have Power to lay and collect Taxes, Duties, Imposts, and Excises, to pay the Debts and provide for the common Defense and general Welfare of the United States; but all Duties, Imposts and Excises shall be uniform throughout the United States;

To borrow Money on the credit of the United States;

To regulate Commerce with foreign Nations, and among the several States, and with the Indian Tribes;

To establish a uniform Rule of Naturalization, and uniform Laws on the subject of Bankruptcies throughout the United States;

To coin Money, regulate the Value thereof, and of foreign Coin, and fix the Standard of Weights and Measures;

To provide for the Punishment of counterfeiting the Securities and current Coin of the United States;

To establish Post Offices and post Roads;

To promote the Progress of Science and useful Arts, by securing for limited Times to Authors and Inventors the exclusive Right to their respective Writings and Discoveries;

To constitute Tribunals inferior to the Supreme Court;

To define and punish Piracies and Felonies committed on the high Seas, and Offenses against the Law of Nations;

To declare War, grant Letters of Marque and Reprisal, and make Rules concerning Captures on Land and Water;

To raise and support Armies, but no Appropriation of Money to that Use shall be for a longer Term than two Years;

To provide and maintain a Navy;

To make Rules for the Government and Regulation of the land and naval Forces;

To provide for calling forth the Militia to execute the Laws of the Union, suppress Insurrections, and repel Invasions;

To provide for organizing, arming, and diciplining, the Militia, and for governing such Part of them as may be employed in the Service of the United States, reserving to the States respectively, the Appointment of the Officers, and the Authority of training the Militia according to the discipline prescribed by Congress;

To exercise exclusive Legislation in all Cases whatsoever, over such District (not exceeding ten Miles square) as may, by Cession of particular States, and the Acceptance of Congress, become the Seat of the Government of the United States, and to exercise like Authority over all Places purchased by the Consent of the Legislature of the State in which the Same shall be, for the Erection of Forts, Magazines, Arsenals, dockyards, and other needful Buildings;—And

To make all Laws which shall be necessary and proper for carrying into Execution the foregoing Powers, and all other Powers vested by this Constitution in the Government of the United States, or in any Department or Officer thereof.

SECTION 9. The Migration or Importation of such Persons as any of the States now existing shall think proper to admit, shall not be prohibited by the Congress prior to the Year one thousand eight hundred and eight, but a Tax or duty may be imposed on such Importation, not exceeding ten dollars for each Person.

The Privilege of the Writ of Habeas Corpus shall not be suspended, unless when in Cases of Rebellion or Invasion the public Safety may require it.

No Bill of Attainder or ex post facto Law shall be passed.

No Capitation, or other direct Tax shall be laid, unless in Proportion to the Census or Enumeration herein before directed to be taken.

No Tax or Duty shall be laid on articles exported from any State.

No Preference shall be given by any Regulation of Commerce or Revenue to the Ports of one State over those of another: nor shall Vessels bound to, or from, one State, be obliged to enter, clear, or pay Duties in another.

No Money shall be drawn from the Treasury, but in Consequence of Appropriations made by Law; and a regular Statement and Account of the Receipts and Expenditures of all public Money shall be published from time to time.

No Title of Nobility shall be granted by the United States. And no Person holding any Office of Profit or Trust under them, shall, without the Consent of the Congress, accept of any present, Emolument, Office, or Title, of any kind whatever, from any King, Prince, or foreign State.

SECTION 10. No State shall enter into any Treaty, Alliance, or Confederation; grant Letters of Marque and Reprisal; coin Money; emit Bills of Credit; make any Thing but gold and silver Coin a Tender in Payment of Debts; pass any Bill of Attainder, ex post facto Law, or Law impairing the Obligation of Contracts, or grant any Title of Nobility.

No State shall, without the Consent of the Congress, lay any Imposts or Duties on Imports or Exports, except what may be absolutely necessary for executing its inspection Laws: and the net Produce of all Duties and Imposts, laid by any State[6] on Imports or Exports, shall be for the Use of the Treasury of the United States; and all such Laws shall be subject to the Revision and Control of the Congress.

No State shall, without the Consent of Congress, lay any Duty of Tonnage, keep Troops, or Ships of War in time of Peace, enter into any Agreement or Compact with another State, or with a foreign Power, or engage in War, unless actually invaded, or in such imminent Danger as will not admit of delay.

ARTICLE II

SECTION 1. The executive Power shall be vested in a President of the United States of America. He shall hold his Office during the Term of four Years, and, together with the Vice President, chosen for the same Term, be elected, as follows:

Each State shall appoint, in such Manner as the Legislature thereof may direct, a Number of Electors, equal to the whole Number of Senators and Representatives to which the State may be entitled in the Congress; but no Senator or Representative, or Person holding an Office of Trust or Profit under the United States, shall be appointed an Elector.

The Electors shall meet in their respective States, and vote by Ballot for two Persons, of whom one at least shall not be an Inhabitant of the same State with themselves. And they shall make a List of all the Persons voted for, and of the Number of Votes for each; which List they shall sign and certify, and transmit sealed to the Seat of the Government of the United States, directed to the President of the Senate. The President of the Senate shall, in the Presence of the Senate and House of Representatives, open all the Certificates, and the Votes shall then be counted. The Person having the greatest Number of Votes shall be the President, if such Number be a Majority of the whole Number of Electors appointed; and if there be more than one who have such Majority, and have an equal Number of Votes, then the House of Representatives shall immediately choose by Ballot one of them for President; and if no Persons have a Majority, then from the five highest on the List the said House shall in like Manner choose the President. But in choosing the President, the Votes shall be taken by States, the Representation from each State having one Vote; A quorum for this Purpose shall consist of a Member or Members from two-thirds of the States, and a Majority of all the States shall be necessary to a Choice. In every Case, after the Choice of the President, the Person having the greatest Number of Votes of the Electors shall be the Vice

President. But if there should remain two or more who have equal Votes, the Senate shall choose from them by Ballot the Vice President.[7]

The Congress may determine the Time of choosing the Electors, and the Day on which they shall give their Votes; which Day shall be the same throughout the United States.

No Person except a natural born Citizen, or a Citizen of the United States, at the time of the Adoption of this Constitution, shall be eligible to the Office of President; neither shall any person be eligible to that Office who shall not have attained to the Age of thirty-five Years, and been fourteen Years a Resident within the United States.

In Case of the Removal of the President from Office, or of his Death, Resignation, or Inability to discharge the Powers and Duties of the said Office, the Same shall devolve on the Vice President, and the Congress may by Law provide for the Case of Removal, Death, Resignation, or Inability, both of the President and Vice President, declaring what Officer shall then act as President, and such Officer shall act accordingly, until the Disability be removed, or a President shall be elected.[8]

The President shall, at stated Times, receive for his Services, a Compensation, which shall neither be increased nor diminished during the Period for which he shall have been elected, and he shall not receive within that Period any other Emolument from the United States, or any of them.

Before he enter on the Execution of his Office, he shall take the following Oath or Affirmation:—"I do solemnly swear (or affirm) that I will faithfully execute the Office of President of the United States, and will to the best of my Ability, preserve, protect, and defend the Constitution of the United States."

SECTION 2. The President shall be Commander in Chief of the Army and Navy of the United States, and of the Militia of the several States, when called into the actual Service of the United States; he may require the Opinion, in writing, of the principal Officer in each of the executive Departments, upon any Subject relating to the Duties of their respective Offices, and he shall have Power to grant Reprieves and Pardons for Offenses against the United States, except in Cases of Impeachment.

He shall have Power, by and with the Advice and Consent of the Senate, to make Treaties, provided two-thirds of the Senators present concur; and he shall nominate, and by and with the Advice and Consent of the Senate, shall appoint Ambassadors, other public Ministers and Consuls, Judges of the Supreme Court, and all other Officers of the United States, whose Appointments are not herein otherwise provided for, and which shall be established by Law: but the Congress may by Law vest the Appointment of such inferior Officers, as they think proper, in the President alone, in the Courts of Law, or in the Heads of Departments.

The President shall have Power to fill up all Vacancies that may happen during the Recess of the Senate, by granting Commissions which shall expire at the End of their next Session.

SECTION 3. He shall from time to time give to the Congress Information of the State of the Union, and recommend to their Consideration such Measures as he shall judge necessary and expedient; he may, on extraordinary Occasions, convene both Houses, or either of them, and in Case of Disagreement between them, with Respect to the Time of Adjournment, he may adjourn them to such Time as he shall think proper; he shall receive Ambassadors and other public Ministers; he shall take Care that the Laws be faithfully executed, and shall Commission all the Officers of the United States.

SECTION 4. The President, Vice President, and all civil Officers of the United States, shall be removed from

Office on Impeachment for, and Conviction of, Treason, Bribery, or other high Crimes and Misdemeanors.

ARTICLE III

SECTION 1. The judicial Power of the United States, shall be vested in one Supreme Court, and in such inferior Courts as the Congress may from time to time ordain and establish. The Judges both of the supreme and inferior Courts, shall hold their Offices during good Behavior, and shall, at stated Times, receive for their Services, a Compensation, which shall not be diminished during their Continuance in Office.

SECTION 2. The judicial Power shall extend to all Cases, in Law and Equity, arising under this Constitution, the Laws of the United States, and Treaties made, or which shall be made, under their Authority;—to all Cases affecting Ambassadors, other public Ministers and Consuls;—to all Cases of admiralty and maritime Jurisdiction;—to Controversies to which the United States shall be a Party;—to Controversies between two or more State;—between a State and Citizens of another State; between Citizens of different States;—between Citizens of the same State claiming Lands under Grants of different States; and between a State, or the Citizens thereof, and foreign States, Citizens, or Subjects.[9]

In all Cases affecting Ambassadors, other public Ministers and Consuls, and those in which a State shall be a Party, the Supreme Court shall have original Jurisdiction. In all the other Cases before mentioned, the Supreme Court shall have appellate Jurisdiction, both as to Law and Fact, with such Exceptions, and under such Regulations as the Congress shall make.

The Trial of all Crimes, except in Cases of Impeachment; shall be by Jury; and such Trial shall be held in the State where the said Crimes shall have been committed; but when not committed within any State, the

Trial shall be at such Place or Places as the Congress may by Law have directed.

SECTION 3. Treason against the United States, shall consist only in levying War against them, or in adhering to their Enemies, giving them Aid and Comfort. No Person shall be convicted of Treason unless on the Testimony of two Witnesses to the same overt Act, or on Confession in open Court.

The Congress shall have Power to declare the Punishment of Treason, but no Attainder of Treason shall work Corruption of Blood, or Forfeiture except during the Life of the Person attainted.

ARTICLE IV

SECTION 1. Full Faith and Credit shall be given in each State to the public Acts, Records, and judicial Proceedings of every other State. And the Congress may by general Laws prescribe the Manner in which such Acts, Records, and Proceedings shall be proved, and the Effect thereof.

SECTION 2. The Citizens of each State shall be entitled to all Privileges and Immunities of Citizens in the several States.

A Person charged in any State with Treason, Felony, or other Crime, who shall flee from Justice, and be found in another State, shall on Demand of the executive Authority of the State from which he fled, be delivered up, to be removed to the State having Jurisdiction of the Crime.

No Person held to Service or Labour in one State, under the Laws thereof, escaping into another, shall, in Consequence of any Law or Regulation therein, be discharged from such Service or Labour, but shall be delivered up on Claim of the Party to whom such Service or Labour may be due. (This section is nullified by the Thirteenth Amendment.)

SECTION 3. New States may be admitted by the Congress into this Union; but no new State shall be formed or erected within the Jurisdiction of any other State; nor any State be formed by the Junction of two or more States, or Parts of States, without the Consent of the Legislatures of the States concerned as well as of the Congress.

The Congress shall have Power to dispose of and make all needful Rules and Regulations respecting the Territory or other Property belonging to the United States; and nothing in this Constitution shall be so construed as to Prejudice any Claims of the United States, or of any particular State.

SECTION 4. The United States shall guarantee to every State in this Union a Republican Form of Government, and shall protect each of them against Invasion; and on Application of the Legislature, or of the Executive (when the Legislature cannot be convened) against domestic Violence.

ARTICLE V

The Congress, whenever two-thirds of both Houses shall deem it necessary, shall propose Amendments to this Constitution, or on the Application of the Legislatures of two-thirds of the several States, shall call a Convention for proposing Amendments, which, in either Case, shall be valid to all Intents and Purposes, as Part of this Constitution, when ratified by the Legislatures of three-fourths of the several States, or by Conventions in three-fourths thereof, as the one or the other Mode of Ratification may be proposed by the Congress; Provided that no Amendment which may be made prior to the Year One thousand eight hundred and eight shall in any Manner affect the first and fourth Clauses in the Ninth Section of the First Article; and that no State, without its Consent, shall be deprived of its equal Suffrage in the Senate.

ARTICLE VI

All Debts contracted and Engagements entered into, before the Adoption of this Constitution, shall be as valid against the United States under this Constitution, as under the Confederation.

This Constitution, and the Laws of the United States which shall be made in Pursuance thereof; and all Treaties made, or which shall be made, under the Authority of the United States, shall be the supreme Law of the Land; and the Judges in every State shall be bound thereby, any Thing in the Constitution or Laws of any State to the Contrary notwithstanding.

The Senators and Representatives before mentioned, and the Members of the several State Legislatures, and all executive and judicial Officers, both of the United States and of the several States, shall be bound by Oath or Affirmation, to support this Constitution; but no religious Test shall ever be required as a Qualification to any Office or public Trust under the United States.

ARTICLE VII

The Ratification of the Conventions of nine States, shall be sufficient for the Establishment of this Constitution between the States so ratifying the Same.

Done in Convention by the Unanimous Consent of the States present the Seventeenth Day of September in the Year of our Lord one thousand seven hundred and Eighty-seven and of the Independence of the United States of America the Twelfth. In Witness whereof We have hereunto subscribed our Names,

GEORGE WASHINGTON—*President* and deputy from Virginia

(Signed also by the deputies of twelve States.)

Delaware
George Read
Gunning Bedford Jr.

John Dickinson
Richard Bassett
Jacob Broom

Maryland
James McHenry
Dan of St. Thomas Jenifer
Daniel Carroll

Virginia
John Blair
James Madison Jr.

North Carolina
William Blount
Richard Dobbs Spaight
Hugh Williamson

South Carolina
John Rutledge
Charles Cotesworth Pinckney
Pierce Butler

New Hampshire
John Langdon
Nicholas Gilman

Massachusetts
Nathaniel Gorham
Rufus King

Connecticut
William Samuel Johnson
Roger Sherman

New York
Alexander Hamilton

New Jersey
William Livingston
David Brearley
William Paterson
Jonathan Dayton

Pennsylvania
Benjamin Franklin
Thomas Mifflin
Robert Morris
George Clymer,
Thomas FitzSimons
Jared Ingersoll
James Wilson
Gouverneur Morris

Georgia
William Few
Abraham Baldwin

Attest William Jackson Secretary

THE BILL OF RIGHTS

Motion to Ratify Bill of Rights

(The Bill of Rights is made up of the first ten amendments to the Consitution. They were sent to the states for ratification and added to the Consitution as a block. Guaranteeing the rights of citizens under the powerful federal government, they are considered an essential element of the basic document.)

In Convention Monday
September 17th 1787

Present
The States of

New Hampshire, Massachusetts, Connecticut, Mr. Hamilton from New York, New Jersey, Pennsylvania, Delaware, Maryland, Virginia, North Carolina, South Carolina and Georgia.

Resolved,

That the preceeding Constitution be laid before the United States in Congress assembled, and that it is the Opinion of this Convention, that it should afterwards be submitted to a Convention of Delegates, chosen in each State by the People thereof, under the Recommendation of its Legislature, for their Assent and Ratification; and that each Convention assenting to, and ratifying the Same, should give Notice thereof to the United States in Congress assembled. Resolved, That it is the Opinion of this Convention, that as soon as the Conventions of nine States shall have ratified this Constitution, the United States in Congress assembled should fix a Day on which Electors should be appointed by the States which shall have ratified the same, and a Day on which the Electors should assemble to vote for the President, and the Time and Place for commencing Proceedings under this Constitution. That after such Publication the Electors should be appointed, and the Senators and Representatives elected: That the Electors should meet on the Day fixed for the Election of the President, and should transmit their Votes certified, signed, sealed and directed, as the Constitution requires, to the Secretary of the United States in Congress assembled, that the Senators and Representatives should convene at the Time and Place assigned; that the Senators should appoint a President of the Senate, for the sole Purpose of receiving, opening and counting the Votes for President; and, that after he shall be chosen, the Congress, together with the President, should, without Delay, proceed to execute this Constitution.

By the unanimous Order of the Convention

G. WASHINGTON—*President*

W. JACKSON—*Secretary*

Congress of the United States
begun and held at the city of New York,
on Wednesday the fourth of March,
one thousand seven hundred and eighty-nine

THE Conventions of a number of the States, having at the time of their adopting the Constitution, expressed a desire, in order to prevent misconstruction or abuse of its powers, that further declaratory and restrictive clauses should be added: And as extending the ground of public confidence in the Government, will best ensure the beneficent ends of its institution:

RESOLVED by the Senate and House of Representatives of the United States of America, in Congress assembled, two-thirds of both Houses concurring, that the following Articles be proposed to the Legislatures of the several States, as Amendments to the Constitution of the United States, all or any of which Articles, when ratified by three-fourths of the said Legislatures, to be valid to all intents and purposes, as part of the said Constitution; viz.

ARTICLES in addition to, and Amendment of the Constitution of the United States of America, proposed by Congress, and ratified by the Legislatures of the several States, pursuant to the fifth Article of the original Constitution.

FREDERICK AUGUSTUS MUHLENBERG
Speaker of the House of Representatives

JOHN ADAMS, *Vice President of the United States, and President of the Senate*

ATTEST,
JOHN BECKLEY, *Clerk of the House of Representatives*
SAM. A. OTIS, *Secretary of the Senate*

(On September 25, 1789, Congress transmitted to the state legislatures twelve proposed amendments, two of which, having to do with congressional representation and congressional pay, were not adopted. The remaining ten amendments became the Bill of Rights.)

The Bill of Rights

AMENDMENT I [10]

Congress shall make no law respecting an establishment of religion, or prohibiting the free exercise thereof; or abridging the freedom of speech, or of the press; or the right of the people peaceably to assemble, and to petition the Government for a redress of grievances.

AMENDMENT II

A well regulated Militia, being necessary to the security of a free State, the right of the people to keep and bear Arms, shall not be infringed.

AMENDMENT III

No Soldier shall, in time of peace be quartered in any house, without the consent of the Owner, nor in time of war, but in a manner to be prescribed by law.

AMENDMENT IV

The right of the people to be secure in their persons, houses, papers, and effects, against unreasonable searches and seizures, shall not be violated, and no Warrants shall issue, but upon probable cause, supported by Oath or affirmation, and particularly describing the place to be searched, and the persons or things to be seized.

AMENDMENT V

No person shall be held to answer for a capital, or otherwise infamous crime, unless on a presentment or indictment of a Grand Jury, except in cases arising in the land or naval forces, or in the Militia, when in actual service in time of War or public danger; nor shall any person be subject for the same offense to be twice put in jeopardy of life or limb; nor shall be compelled in any criminal case to be a witness against himself, nor be deprived of life, liberty or property, without due process of law; nor shall private property be taken for public use without just compensation.

AMENDMENT VI

In all criminal prosecutions, the accused shall enjoy the right to a speedy and public trial, by an impartial jury of the State and district wherein the crime shall have been committed, which district shall have been previously ascertained by law, and to be informed of the nature and cause of the accusation; to be confronted with the witnesses against him; to have compulsory process or obtaining witnesses in his favor, and to have the assistance of counsel for his defense.

AMENDMENT VII

In Suits at common law, where the value in controversy shall exceed twenty dollars, the right of trial by jury shall be preserved, and no fact tried by a jury shall be otherwise reexamined in any Court of the United States, than according to the rules of the common law.

AMENDMENT VIII

Excessive bail shall not be required, nor excessive fines imposed, nor cruel and unusual punishments inflicted.

AMENDMENT IX

The enumeration in the Constitution, of certain rights, shall not be construed to deny or disparage others retained by the people.

AMENDMENT X

The powers not delegated to the United States by the Constitution, nor prohibited by it to the States, are reserved to the States respectively, or to the people.

Subsequent Amendments

AMENDMENT XI [11]

The Judicial power of the United States shall not be construed to extend to any suit in law or equity, commenced or prosecuted against one of the United States by Citizens of another State, or by Citizens or Subjects of any Foreign State.

AMENDMENT XII [12]

The Electors shall meet in their respective States, and vote by ballot for President and Vice President, one of whom, at least, shall not be an inhabitant of the same state with themselves; they shall name in their ballots the person voted for as President, and in distinct ballots the person voted for as Vice President, and they shall make distinct lists of all persons voted for as President, and of all persons voted for as Vice President, and of the number of votes for each, which lists they shall sign and certify, and transmit sealed to the seat of the government of the United States, directed to the President of the Senate;—The

President of the Senate shall, in the presence of the Senate and House of Representatives, open all the certificates and the votes shall then be counted;—The person having the greatest number of votes for President, shall be the President, if such number be a majority of the whole number of Electors appointed; and if no person have such majority, then from the persons having the highest numbers not exceeding three on the list of those voted for as President, the House of Representatives shall choose immediately by ballot, the President. But in choosing the President, the votes shall be taken by States, the representation from each state having one vote; a quorum for this purpose shall consist of a member or members from two-thirds of the States, and a majority of all the States shall be necessary to a choice. And if the House of Representatives shall not choose a President whenever the right of choice shall devolve upon them, before the fourth day of March next following, then the Vice President shall act as President, as in the case of the death or other constitutional disability of the President.[13]—The person having the greatest number of votes as Vice President, shall be the Vice President, if such number be a majority of the whole number of Electors appointed, and if no person have a majority, then from the two highest numbers on the list, the Senate shall choose the Vice President; a quorum for the purpose shall consist of two-thirds of the whole number of Senators, and a majority of the whole number shall be necessary to a choice. But no person constitutionally ineligible to the office of President shall be eligible to that of Vice President of the United States.

AMENDMENT XIII [14]

SECTION 1. Neither slavery nor involuntary servitude, except as a punishment for crime whereof the party shall have been duly convicted, shall exist within the United States, or any place subject to their jurisdiction.

SECTION 2. Congress shall have power to enforce this article by appropriate legislation.

AMENDMENT XIV [15]

SECTION 1. All persons born or naturalized in the United States and subject to the jurisdiction thereof, are citizens of the United States and of the State wherein they reside. No State shall make or enforce any law which shall abridge the privileges or immunities of citizens of the United States; nor shall any State deprive any person of life, liberty, or property, without due process of law; nor deny to any person within its jurisdiction the equal protection of the laws.

SECTION 2. Representatives shall be apportioned among the several States according to their respective numbers, counting the whole number of persons in each State, excluding Indians not taxed. But when the right to vote at any election for the choice of electors for President and Vice President of the United States, Representatives in Congress, the Executive and Judicial officers of a State, or the members of the Legislature thereof, is denied to any of the male inhabitants of such State, being twenty-one years of age, and citizens of the United States, or in any way abridged, except for participation in rebellion, or other crime, the basis of representation therein shall be reduced in the proportion which the number of such male citizens shall bear to the whole number of male citizens twenty-one years of age in such State.

SECTION 3. No person shall be a Senator or Representative in Congress, or elector of President and Vice President, or hold any office, civil or military, under the United States, or under any State, who, having previously taken an oath, as a member of Congress, or as an officer of the United States, or as a member of any State legislature, or as an executive or judicial officer of any State, to support the Constitution of the United States, shall have engaged in insurrection or rebellion against the same, or given aid or comfort to the enemies thereof. But Congress may by a vote of two-thirds of each House, remove such disability.

SECTION 4. The validity of the public debt of the United States, authorized by law, including debts incurred for payment of pensions and bounties for services in suppressing insurrection or rebellion, shall not be questioned. But neither the United States nor any State shall assume or pay any debt or obligation incurred in aid of insurrection or rebellion against the United States, or any claim for the loss or emancipation of any slave; but all such debts, obligations and claims shall be held illegal and void.

SECTION 5. The Congress shall have power to enforce, by appropriate legislation, the provisions of this article.

AMENDMENT XV [16]

SECTION 1. The right of citizens of the United States to vote shall not be denied or abridged by the United States or by any State on account of race, color, or previous condition of servitude.

SECTION 2. The Congress shall have power to enforce this article by appropriate legislation.

AMENDMENT XVI [17]

The Congress shall have power to lay and collect taxes on incomes, from whatever source derived, without apportionment among the several States, and without regard to any census or enumeration.

AMENDMENT XVII [18]

SECTION 1. The Senate of the United States shall be composed of two Senators from each State, elected by the people thereof, for six years; and each Senator shall have one vote. The electors in each State shall have the qualifcations requisite for electors of the most numerous branch of the State legislatures.

SECTION 2. When vacancies happen in the representation of any State in the Senate, the executive authority of such State shall issue writs of election to fill such vacancies: *Provided,* That the legislature of any State may empower the executive thereof to make temporary appointments until the people fill the vacancies by election as the legislature may direct.

SECTION 3. This amendment shall not be so construed as to affect the election or term of any Senator chosen before it becomes valid as part of the Constitution.

AMENDMENT XVIII [19]

SECTION 1. After one year from the ratification of this article the manufacture, sale, or transportation of intoxicating liquors within, the importation thereof into, or the exportation thereof from the United States and all territory subject to the jurisdiction thereof for beverage purposes is hereby prohibited.

SECTION 2. The Congress and the several States shall have concurrent power to enforce this article by appropriate legislation.

SECTION 3. This article shall be inoperative unless it shall have been ratified as an amendment to the Constitution by the legislatures of the several States, as provided in the Constitution, within seven years from the date of the submission hereof to the States by the Congress.

AMENDMENT XIX [20]

SECTION 1. The right of citizens of the United States to vote shall not be denied or abridged by the United States or by any State on account of sex.

SECTION 2. Congress shall have power to enforce this article by appropriate legislation.

AMENDMENT XX [21]

SECTION 1. The terms of the President and Vice President shall end at noon on the twentieth day of

January, and the terms of Senators and Representatives at noon on the 3rd day of January, of the years in which such terms would have ended if this article had not been ratified; and the terms of their successors shall then begin.

SECTION 2. The Congress shall assemble at least once in every year, and such meeting shall begin at noon on the 3rd day of January, unless they shall by law appoint a different day.

SECTION 3. If, at the time fixed for the beginning of the term of the President, the President elect shall have died, the Vice President elect shall become President. If a President shall not have been chosen before the time fixed for the beginning of his term, or if the President elect shall have failed to qualify, then the Vice President elect shall act as President until a President shall have qualified; and the Congress may by law provide for the case wherein neither a President elect nor a Vice President elect shall have qualified, declaring who shall then act as President, or the manner in which one who is to act shall be selected, and such person shall act accordingly until a President or Vice President shall have qualified.

SECTION 4. The Congress may by law provide for the case of the death of any of the persons from whom the House of Representatives may choose a President whenever the right of choice shall have devolved upon them, and for the case of the death of any of the persons from whom the Senate may choose a Vice President whenever the right of choice shall have devolved upon them.

SECTION 5. Sections 1 and 2 shall take effect on the 15th day of October following the ratification of this article.

SECTION 6. This article shall be inoperative unless it shall have been ratified as an amendment to the Constitution by the legislatures of three-fourths of the several States within seven years from the date of its submission.

AMENDMENT XXI [22]

SECTION 1. The eighteenth article of amendment to the Constitution of the United States is hereby repealed.

SECTION 2. The transportation or importation into any State, Territory, or possession of the United States for delivery or use therein of intoxicating liquors, in violation of the laws thereof, is hereby prohibited.

SECTION 3. This article shall be inoperative unless it shall have been ratified as an amendment to the Constitution by conventions in the several States, as provided in the Constitution, within seven years from the date of the submission hereof to the States by the Congress.

AMENDMENT XXII [23]

SECTION 1. No person shall be elected to the office of the President more than twice, and no person who has held the office of President, or acted as President, for more than two years of a term to which some other person was elected President shall be elected to the office of the President more than once. But this article shall not apply to any person holding the office of President when this article was proposed by the Congress, and shall not prevent any person who may be holding the office of President, or acting as President, during the term within which this article becomes operative from holding the office of President or acting as President during the remainder of such term.

SECTION 2. This article shall be inoperative unless it shall have been ratified as an amendment to the Constitution by the legislatures of three-fourths of the several States within seven years from the date of its submission to the States by the Congress.

AMENDMENT XXIII [24]

SECTION 1. The District constituting the seat of Government of the United States shall appoint in such manner as the Congress may direct:

A number of electors of President and Vice President equal to the whole number of Senators and Representatives in Congress to which the District would be entitled if it were a State, but in no event more than the least populous State; they shall be in addition to those appointed by the States, but they shall be considered, for the purposes of the election of President and Vice President, to be electors appointed by a State; and they shall meet in the District and perform such duties as provided by the twelfth article of amendment.

SECTION 2. The Congress shall have power to enforce this article by appropriate legislation.

AMENDMENT XXIV [25]

SECTION 1. The right of citizens of the United States to vote in any primary or other election for President or Vice President, for electors for President or Vice President, or for Senator or Representative in Congress, shall not be denied or abridged by the United States or any State by reason of failure to pay any poll tax or other tax.

SECTION 2. The Congress shall have power to enforce this article by appropriate legislation.

AMENDMENT XXV [26]

SECTION 1. In case of the removal of the President from office or of his death or resignation, the Vice President shall become President.

SECTION 2. Whenever there is a vacancy in the office of the Vice President, the President shall nominate a Vice President who shall take office upon confirmation by a majority vote of both Houses of Congress.

SECTION 3. Whenever the President transmits to the President pro tempore of the Senate and the Speaker of the House of Representatives his written declaration that he is unable to discharge the powers and duties of his office, and until he transmits to them a written declaration to the contrary, such powers and duties shall be discharged by the Vice President as Acting President.

SECTION 4. Whenever the Vice President and a majority of either the principal officers of the executive departments or of such other body as Congress may by law provide, transmit to the President pro tempore of the Senate and the Speaker of the House of Representatives their written declaration that the President is unable to discharge the powers and duties of his office, the Vice President shall immediately assume the powers and duties of the office as Acting President.

Thereafter, when the President transmits to the President pro tempore of the Senate and the Speaker of the House of Representatives his written declaration that no inability exists, he shall resume the powers and duties of his office unless the Vice President and a majority of either the principal officers of the executive department or of such other body as Congress may by law provide, transmit within four days to the President pro tempore of the Senate and the Speaker of the House of Representatives their written declaration that the President is unable to discharge the powers and duties of his office. Thereupon Congress shall decide the issue, assembling within forty-eight hours for that purpose if not in session. If the Congress, within twenty-one days after receipt of the latter written declaration, or, if Congress is not in session, within twenty-one days after Congress is required to assemble, determines by two-thirds vote of both Houses that the President is unable to discharge the powers and duties of his office, the Vice President shall continue to discharge the same as Acting President; otherwise, the President shall resume the powers and duties of his office.

AMENDMENT XXVI [27]

SECTION 1. The right of citizens of the United States, who are eighteen years of age or older, to vote shall not be denied or abridged by the United States or by any State on account of age.

SECTION 2. The Congress shall have power to enforce this article by appropriate legislation.

AMENDMENT XXVII [28]

No law, varying the compensation for the services of the Senators and Representatives, shall take effect, until an election of Representatives shall have intervened.

---

1. Changed by Section 2 of the Fourteenth Amendment.
2. Changed by the Seventeenth Amendment.
3. Changed by the Seventeenth Amendment.
4. Changed by the Twentieth Amendment.
5. Changed by the Seventeenth Amendment.
6. See Sixteenth Amendment.
7. Changed by the Twelfth Amendment.
8. Changed by the Twenty-Fifth Amendment.
9. Changed by the Eleventh Amendment.
10. The first ten Amendments (Bill of Rights) were ratified effective December 15, 1791.
11. The Eleventh Amendment was ratified February 7, 1795.
12. The Twelfth Amendment was ratified June 15, 1804.
13. Superseded by Section 3 of the Twentieth Amendment.
14. The Thirteenth Amendment was ratified December 6, 1865.
15. The Fourteenth Amendment was ratified July 9, 1868.
16. The Fifteenth Amendment was ratified February 3, 1870.
17. The Sixteenth Amendment was ratified February 3, 1913.
18. The Seventeenth Amendment was ratified April 8, 1913.
19. The Eighteenth Amendment was ratified January 16, 1919. It was repealed by the Twenty-First Amendment, December 5, 1933.
20. The Nineteenth Amendment was ratified August 18, 1920.
21. The Twentieth Amendment was ratified January 23, 1933.
22. The Twenty-First Amendment was ratified December 5, 1933.
23. The Twenty-Second Amendment was ratified February 27, 1951.

24. The Twenty-Third Amendment was ratified March 29, 1961.
25. The Twenty-Fourth Amendment was ratified January 23, 1964.
26. The Twenty-Fifth Amendment was ratified February 10, 1967.
27. The Twenty-Sixth Amendment was ratified July 1, 1971.
28. Congress submitted the text of this Amendment to the States as part of the proposed Bill of Rights on September 25, 1789. The Amendment was not ratified with the first ten Amendments which became effective on December 15, 1791. The Twenty-Seventh Amendment was ratified on May 7, 1992, by the vote of Michigan.

Tables

TABLE I: MAJOR FOREIGN-POLICY TREATIES (REJECTED)

Date of Vote	Country	Vote, Yea–Nay	Subject
March 9, 1815	Colombia	0–40	Suppression of African slave trade
June 11, 1836	Switzerland	14–23	Personal and property rights
June 8, 1844	Texas	16–35	Annexation
June 15, 1844	German Zollverein	26–18	Reciprocity
May 31, 1860	Mexico	18–27	Transit and commercial rights
June 27, 1860	Spain	26–17	Cuban claims commission
April 13, 1869	Great Britain	1–54	Arbitration of claims
June 1, 1870	Hawaii	20–19	Reciprocity
June 30, 1870	Dominican Republic	28–28	Annexation
Jan. 29, 1885	Nicaragua	32–23	Interoceanic canal
April 20, 1886	Mexico	32–26	Mining claims
Aug. 21, 1888	Great Britain	27–30	Fishing rights
Feb. 1, 1889	Great Britain	15–38	Extradition
May 5, 1897	Great Britain	43–26	Arbitration
March 19, 1920	Multilateral	49–35	Treaty of Versailles
Jan. 18, 1927	Turkey	50–34	Commercial rights
March 14, 1934	Canada	46–42	St. Lawrence Seaway
Jan. 29, 1935	Multilateral	52–36	World Court
May 26, 1960	Multilateral	49–30	Law of the Sea convention
March 8, 1983	Multilateral	50–42	Montreal aviation protocol
October 13, 1999	Multilateral	51–48	Nuclear Test Ban Treaty

Source: Senate Historical Office

TABLE 2: SALARIES OF FEDERAL ELECTED OFFICIALS: 1789-1993

Year	President	Vice President	Percent of President's Salary	Cabinet Members
1789	$25,000	$5,000	20.00	$3,500
1799				5,000
1819				6,000
1853		8,000	32.00	8,000
1855				
1856				
1866				
1871				
1873	50,000	10,000	20.00	10,000
1874		8,000	16.00	8,000
1903				
1907		12,000	24.00	12,000
1909	75,000	12,000	16.00	12,000
1911				
1925		15,000	20.00	15,000
1926				
1946		20,000	26.60	
1947				
1949	100,000	30,000	30.00	22,500
1955		35,000	35.00	
1956				25,000
1964		43,000	43.00	
1965				
1969	200,000	62,500	31.25	60,000
1975		65,600	32.80	63,000
1976				66,000
1977		75,000	37.50	
1979		79,125	39.56	69,630
1980				
1981				
1982		91,000	45.50	80,100
1984		94,600	47.30	83,300
1985		97,900	48.95	86,200
1987		115,000	57.50	99,500
1990		124,000	62.00	107,300
1991		160,600	80.30	138,900
1992		166,200	83.10	142,800
1993		171,500	85.75	148,400

*House and Senate salaries varied during these years; the higher salary is used in this table.

Percent of President's Salary	Chief Justice	Percent of President's Salary	Members of Congress	Percent of President's Salary
14.00	$4,000	16.00		
20.00				
24.00	5,000	20.00		
32.00				
	6,500	26.00		
			$3,000	12.00
			5,000	20.00
	8,500	34.00		
20.00	10,500	21.00	7,500	15.00
16.00			5,000	10.00
	13,000	26.00		
24.00				
16.00	13,000	17.00	7,500	10.00
	15,000	20.00		
20.00			10,000	13.30
	20,500	27.00		
	25,500	34.00		
			12,500	16.67
22.50	25,500	25.50	12,500	12.50
	35,500	35.50	22,500	22.50
25.00				
	40,000	40.00	35,000	35.00
		30.00		30.00
30.00	62,500	31.25	42,500	21.25
31.50	65,600	32.80	44,600	22.30
33.00	68,800	34.40		
	75,000	37.50	57,500	28.75
34.82	84,700	42.35	60,662	30.33
	92,400	46.20		
	96,800	48.40		
40.05	100,700	50.35	69,800*	34.90
41.65	104,700	52.35	72,600	36.30
43.10	108,400	54.20	75,100	37.55
49.75	115,000	57.50	89,500	44.75
53.65	124,000	62.00	98,400*	49.20
69.45	160,600	80.30	125,100*	62.55
71.90	166,200	83.10	129,500	64.75
74.20	171,500	85.75	133,600	66.80

Prepared by Saron Stiver Gressle

TABLE 3: PRESIDENTIAL ASSASSINATION ATTEMPTS

Date of Assault	Victim	Location
30 Jan 1835	Andrew Jackson	Washington, DC
14 Apr 1865	Abraham Lincoln	Washington, DC
2 Jul 1881	James A. Garfield	Washington, DC
6 Sep 1901	William McKinley	Buffalo, NY
14 Oct 1912	Theodore Roosevelt *candidate*	Milwaukee, WI
15 Feb 1933	Franklin D. Roosevelt *president-elect*	Miami, FL
1 Nov 1950	Harry S. Truman	Washington, DC
22 Nov 1963	John F. Kennedy	Dallas, TX
4 Jun 1968	Robert F. Kennedy *candidate*	Los Angeles, CA
15 May 1972	George C. Wallace *candidate*	Laurel, MD
5 Sep 1975	Gerald Ford	Sacramento, CA
22 Sep 1975	Gerald Ford	San Francisco, CA
30 Mar 1981	Ronald Reagan	Washington, DC

Source: Levy and Fisher, eds., Encyclopedia of the American Presidency, *Volume 1, A–D*

Method of Attack and Result	*Assailant, Professed or Alleged Reason, and Result*
pistol, misfired	Richard Lawrence: said Jackson was preventing him from obtaining large sums of money; declared insane
pistol, killed	John Wilkes Booth: revenge for defeat of Confederacy; killed
pistol, killed	Charles Guiteau: disgruntled office seeker; convicted and executed
pistol, killed	Leon F. Czolgosz: anarchist ideology; convicted and executed
pistol, wounded	John Schrank: had vision that McKinley wanted him to avenge his death; declared insane
pistol, missed but killed Anton Cermak, mayor of Chicago	Giuseppe Zangara: hated rulers and capitalists; convicted
automatic weapons, prevented from shooting at Truman	Oscar Collazo and Grisello Torresola: espoused Puerto Rican independence; convicted and imprisoned
rifle, killed	Lee Harvey Oswald: motive unknown; killed
pistol, killed	Sirhan Sirhan: opposed Kennedy's stand on Arab-Israeli conflict; convicted and imprisoned
pistol, wounded	Arthur Bremer: motive unknown; convicted and imprisoned
pistol, misfired	Lynette Alice ("Squeaky") Fromme: follower of Charles Manson; convicted and imprisoned
pistol, missed	Sara Jane Moore: revolutionary ideology; convicted and imprisoned
pistol, wounded	John W. Hinkley Jr.: motive unknown; found not guilty by reason of insanity; confined to mental institution

TABLE 4: PRESIDENTIAL VETOES

President	All bills vetoed	Regular vetoed	Pocket vetoed	Vetoes overridden
Washington	2	2	0	0
Madison	7	5	2	0
Monroe	1	1	0	0
Jackson	12	5	7	0
Van Buren	1	0	1	0
Tyler	10	6	4	1
Polk	3	2	1	0
Pierce	9	9	0	5
Buchanan	7	4	3	0
Lincoln	7	2	5	0
A. Johnson	29	21	8	15
Grant	93	45	48	4
Hayes	13	12	1	1
Arthur	12	4	8	1
Cleveland (*first term*)	414	304	110	2
B. Harrison	44	19	25	1
Cleveland (*second term*)	170	42	125	1
McKinley	42	6	36	0
T. Roosevelt	82	42	40	1
Taft	39	30	9	1
Wilson	44	33	11	6
Harding	6	5	1	0
Coolidge	50	20	30	4
Hoover	37	21	16	3
F. D. Roosevelt	635	372	263	9
Truman	250	180	70	12
Eisenhower	181	73	108	2
Kennedy	21	12	9	0
Johnson	30	16	14	0
Nixon	43	26	17	7
Ford	66	48	18	12
Carter	31	13	18	2
Reagan	78	39	39	9
Bush	44	29	15	1

(There were no vetoes during the adminstrations of Presidents John Adams, Jefferson, John Quincy Adams, W. H. Hamilton, Taylor, Fillmore, or Garfield.)

TABLE 5: RESULTS OF THE 103RD, 104TH, AND 105TH CONGRESSES

House (Jan. 3–March 31)	*105th*	*104th*	*103rd*
Days in session	27	53	35
Hours in session	133	486	189
Pages in Congressional Record	1,289	4,032	1,183
Public bills enacted into law	6	0	4
Measures passed, total	82	111	87
Measures reported, total	40	94	48
Conference reports	0	2	1
Measures pending on calendar	11	16	6
Measures introduced, total	1,453	1,636	1,973
Yea-and-nay votes	44	62	81
Recorded votes	25	209	42
Bills vetoed	0	0	0
Vetoes overridden	0	0	0
Senate (Jan. 3–March 31)	*105th*	*104th*	*103rd*
Days in session	37	59	40
Hours in session	226	488	271
Pages in Congressional Record	2,759	5,023	4,179
Public bills enacted into law	2	5	6
Measures passed, total	50	77	89
Measures reported, total	30	40	54
Conference reports	0	0	0
Measures pending on calendar	21	30	21
Measures introduced, total	622	795	870
Yea-and-nay votes	35	128	93
Bills vetoed	0	0	0

Source: Congressional Record

TABLE 6: HOW A BILL BECOMES A LAW

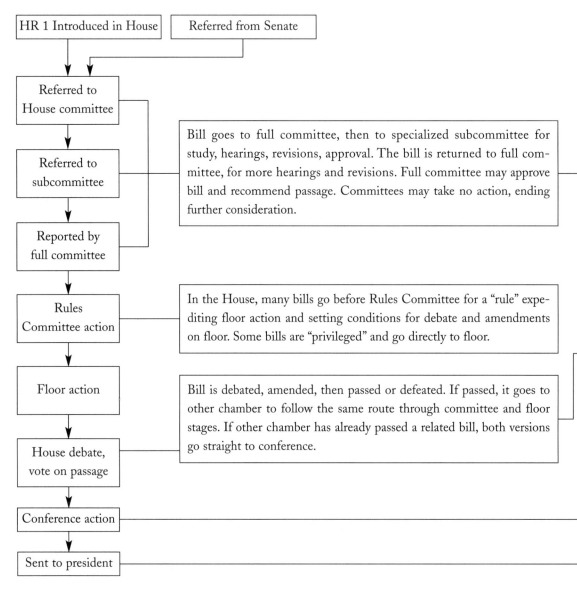

| HR 1 Introduced in House | Referred from Senate |

Referred to House committee

Referred to subcommittee

Bill goes to full committee, then to specialized subcommittee for study, hearings, revisions, approval. The bill is returned to full committee, for more hearings and revisions. Full committee may approve bill and recommend passage. Committees may take no action, ending further consideration.

Reported by full committee

Rules Committee action

In the House, many bills go before Rules Committee for a "rule" expediting floor action and setting conditions for debate and amendments on floor. Some bills are "privileged" and go directly to floor.

Floor action

Bill is debated, amended, then passed or defeated. If passed, it goes to other chamber to follow the same route through committee and floor stages. If other chamber has already passed a related bill, both versions go straight to conference.

House debate, vote on passage

Conference action

Sent to president

This shows typical ways in which proposed legislation is enacted into law. The process is illustrated with two hypothetical bills, House bill No. 1 (HR 1) and Senate

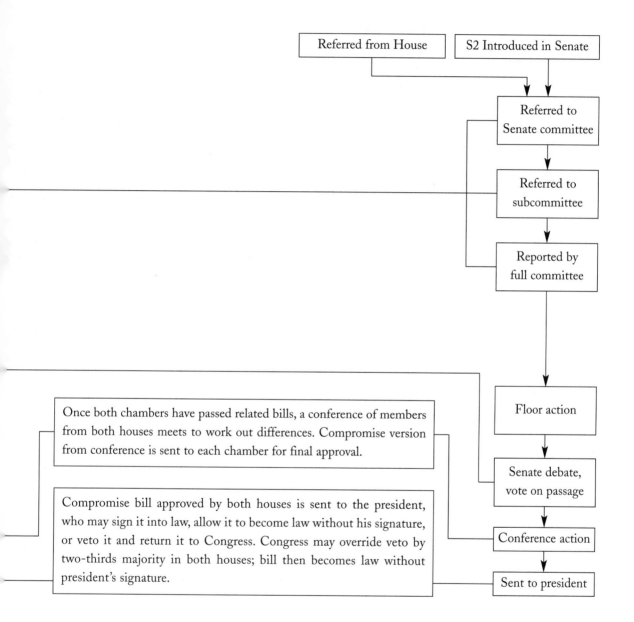

| Referred from House | S2 Introduced in Senate |

Referred to
Senate committee

Referred to
subcommittee

Reported by
full committee

Floor action

Once both chambers have passed related bills, a conference of members from both houses meets to work out differences. Compromise version from conference is sent to each chamber for final approval.

Senate debate,
vote on passage

Compromise bill approved by both houses is sent to the president, who may sign it into law, allow it to become law without his signature, or veto it and return it to Congress. Congress may override veto by two-thirds majority in both houses; bill then becomes law without president's signature.

Conference action

Sent to president

bill No. 2 (S 2). Bills must be passed by both houses in identical form before they can be sent to the president. They can be killed at any point.

TABLE 7: PAC COUNT—1974 TO JULY 1996 (COMMITTEE TYPE)

Date	Corporate	Labor	Trade/Membership/Health
12/31/74	89	201	318*
11/24/75**	139	226	357*
05/10/76***	294	246	452*
12/31/76	433	224	489*
12/31/77	550	234	438
12/31/78	785	217	453
08/15/79	885	226	483
12/31/79	950	240	514
07/01/80	1,107	255	544
12/31/80	1,206	297	576
07/01/81	1,253	303	579
12/31/81	1,329	318	614
07/01/82	1,417	350	627
12/31/82	1,469	380	649
07/01/83	1,514	379	664
12/31/83	1,538	378	643
07/01/84	1,642	381	662
12/31/84	1,682	394	698
07/01/85	1,687	393	694
12/31/85	1,710	388	695
07/01/86	1,734	386	707
12/31/86	1,744	384	745
07/01/87	1,762	377	795
12/31/87	1,775	364	865
07/01/88	1,806	355	766
12/31/88	1,816	354	786
07/01/89	1,802	349	831
12/31/89	1,796	349	777
07/01/90	1,782	346	753
12/31/90	1,795	346	774
07/01/91	1,745	339	749
12/31/91	1,738	338	742
07/01/92	1,731	344	759
12/31/92	1,735	347	770
07/01/93	1,715	338	767
12/31/93	1,789	337	761
07/01/94	1,666	336	777
12/31/94	1,660	333	792
07/01/95	1,670	334	804
12/31/95	1,674	334	815
07/01/96	1,645	332	829

*For 1974–76, these numbers represent all other PACs—no further categorization is available
**On November 24, 1975, the Commission issued Advisory Opinion 1975-23 "SUNPAC."

Non-Connected	Cooperative	Corp. Without Stock	Total
			608
			722
			992
			1,146
110	8	20	1,360
162	12	24	1,653
206	13	27	1,840
247	17	32	2,000
309	23	41	2,279
374	42	56	2,551
441	38	64	2,678
531	41	68	2,901
628	45	82	3,149
723	47	103	3,371
740	50	114	3,461
793	51	122	3,525
940	53	125	3,803
1,053	52	130	4,009
1,039	54	133	4,000
1,003	54	142	3,992
1,063	56	146	4,092
1,077	56	151	4,157
967	56	152	4,109
957	59	145	4,165
1,066	60	143	4,196
1,115	59	138	4,268
1,051	58	143	4,234
1,060	59	137	4,178
1,115	58	139	4,193
1,062	59	136	4,172
1,096	57	137	4,123
1,083	57	136	4,094
1,091	56	144	4,125
1,145	56	142	4,195
1,011	55	139	4,025
1,121	56	146	4,210
963	53	138	3,933
980	53	136	3,954
1,002	43	129	3,982
1,020	44	129	4,016
1,058	43	126	4,033

***On May 11, 1976, Federal Election Campaign Act Amendments of 1976 (PL 94-283) were enacted.
Source: Federal Election Committee

TABLE 8: TOP 50 PACS—RECEIPTS
JANUARY 1, 1995–JUNE 30, 1996

RANK	NAME	RECEIPTS
1	Emily's List	$9,388,631
2	Democratic Republican Independent Voter Education Committee	$6,900,158
3	American Federation of State, County, & Municipal Employees—P E O P L E, Qualified	$4,998,227
4	American Medical Association Political Action Committee	$3,577,743
5	UAW Voluntary Community Action Program (UAW-V-CAP)	$3,573,858
6	National Education Association Political Action Committee	$3,155,672
7	NRA Political Victory Fund	$3,271,300
8	Association of Trial Lawyers of America Political Action Committee	$3,260,235
9	Dealers Election Action Committee of the National Automobile Dealers Association (NADA)	$2,639,029
10	Machinists Non-Partisan Political League	$2,549,778
11	Active Ballot Club, A Dept of Unified Food & Commercial Workers Int'l Union	$2,243,071
12	American Telephone & Telegraph Company Political Action Committee (AT&T PAC)	$2,143,173
13	International Brotherhood of Electrical Workers Committee on Political Education	$2,002,042
14	Transportation Political Education League	$1,931,805
15	Voice of Teachers for Education/Committee on Political Education of NY State Untd Teachers (VOTE/COPE)	$1,930,477
16	CWA-COPE Political Contributions Committee	$1,929,182
17	United Parcel Service of America, Inc., Political Action Committee (UPS PAC)	$1,922,317
18	Campaign America	$1,907,624
19	American Federation of Teachers Committee on Political Education	$1,861,314
20	Committee on Letter Carriers Political Education (Letter Carriers Political Action Fund)	$1,751,279
21	Women's Campaign Fund, Inc.	$1,718,759
22	Laborers' Political League	$1,713,949
23	National Association of Life Underwriters Political Action Committee	$1,177,328
24	National Committee for an Effective Congress	$1,501,509

RANK	NAME	RECEIPTS
25	Americans for Free International Trade Political Action Committee, Inc.	$1,467,189
26	National Association of Retired Federal Employees Political Action Committee (NARFE-PAC)	$1,404,519
27	National Beer Wholesalers' Association Political Action Committee (NBWA PAC)	$1,359,259
28	Black America's Political Action Committee	$1,342,926
29	New York State Laborers Political Action Committee	$1,337,008
30	Carpenters Legislative Improvement Committee, United Brotherhood of Carpenters & Joiners of America	$1,303,065
31	Build Political Action Committee of the National Association of Home Builders	$1,295,396
32	United Steelworkers of America Political Action Fund	$1,266,326
33	American Dental Political Action Committee	$1,265,242
34	Federal Express Corporation Political Action Committee (FEPAC)	$1,221,371
35	Seafarers Political Activity Donation (SPAD)	$1,133,396
36	Lockheed Martin Employees Political Action Committee	$1,119,581
37	Texas Medical Association Political Action Committee	$1,116,756
38	Banc One PAC	$1,089,983
39	Ernst & Young Political Action Committee	$1,074,242
40	National Committee to Preserve Social Security and Medicare PAC	$1,061,637
41	New Republican Majority Fund	$1,617,530
42	American Bankers Association BankPAC	$1,016,444
43	Team Ameritech Political Action Committee	$1,009,110
44	United Association Political Action Committee	$1,002,888
45	United Pacific Fund for Effective Government	$1,002,456
46	Sheet Metal Workers International Association Political Action League (PAL)	$1,001,411
47	Voters for Choice/Friends of Family Planning	$1,000,376
48	Realtors Political Action Committee	$992,245
49	Monday Morning Political Action Committee	$990,291
50	National PAC	$976,318

Source: Federal Election Commission

TABLE 9: THE BUDGET PROCESS

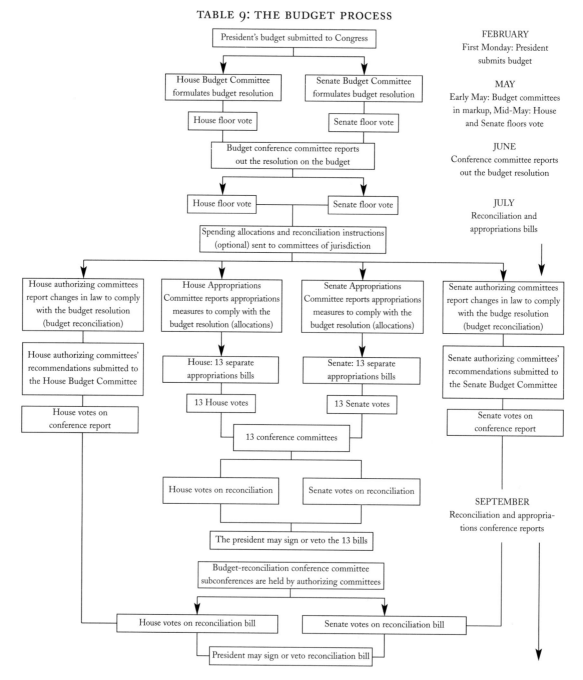

President's budget submitted to Congress

House Budget Committee formulates budget resolution

Senate Budget Committee formulates budget resolution

House floor vote

Senate floor vote

Budget conference committee reports out the resolution on the budget

House floor vote

Senate floor vote

Spending allocations and reconciliation instructions (optional) sent to committees of jurisdiction

House authorizing committees report changes in law to comply with the budget resolution (budget reconciliation)

House Appropriations Committee reports appropriations measures to comply with the budget resolution (allocations)

Senate Appropriations Committee reports appropriations measures to comply with the budget resolution (allocations)

Senate authorizing committees report changes in law to comply with the budge resolution (budget reconciliation)

House authorizing committees' recommendations submitted to the House Budget Committee

House: 13 separate appropriations bills

Senate: 13 separate appropriations bills

Senate authorizing committees' recommendations submitted to the Senate Budget Committee

House votes on conference report

13 House votes

13 Senate votes

Senate votes on conference report

13 conference committees

House votes on reconciliation

Senate votes on reconciliation

The president may sign or veto the 13 bills

Budget-reconciliation conference committee subconferences are held by authorizing committees

House votes on reconciliation bill

Senate votes on reconciliation bill

President may sign or veto reconciliation bill

FEBRUARY
First Monday: President submits budget

MAY
Early May: Budget committees in markup, Mid-May: House and Senate floors vote

JUNE
Conference committee reports out the budget resolution

JULY
Reconciliation and appropriations bills

SEPTEMBER
Reconciliation and appropriations conference reports

Source: Congressional Quarterly Weekly Report, May 13, 1995, page 1305

Answers to Quizzes

Answers to INS Questionnaire (page 66)

1. Red, white, and blue
2. Fifty
3. White
4. One for each state in the Union
5. Thirteen
6. Red and white
7. They represent the thirteen original states.
8. Fifty
9. Independence Day
10. July 4
11. England
12. England
13. George Washington
14. William Jefferson Clinton

15. Al Gore

16. The Electoral College

17. Vice President

18. Four years

19. The supreme law of the land

20. Yes

21. Amendments

22. Twenty-seven

23. Three

24. Legislative, Executive, and Judicial

25. Congress

26. Congress

27. The Senate and the House of Representatives

28. To make laws

29. The people

30. 100

31. (Variable)

32. Six years

33. 435

34. Two years

35. The President, Cabinet, and departments under the Cabinet members

36. The Supreme Court

37. To interpret laws

38. The Constitution

39. The first ten amendments to the Constitution

40. (Variable)

41. (Variable)

42. The Speaker of the House of Representatives

43. William H. Rehnquist

44. Connecticut, New Hampshire, New York, New Jersey, Massachusetts, Pennsylvania, Delaware, Virginia, North Carolina, South Carolina, Georgia, Rhode Island, and Maryland.

45. Patrick Henry

46. Britain, Canada, Australia, New Zealand, Russia, China, France

47. Alaska

48. Two

49. A civil-rights leader

50. (Variable)

51. Must be a natural-born U.S. citizen; must be at least thirty-five years old by the time he/she will serve; must have lived in the U.S. for at least fourteen years

52. Two from each state

53. The President

54. Nine

55. For religious freedom

56. Governor

57. Mayor

58. Thanksgiving

59. Thomas Jefferson

60. July 4, 1776

61. That all men are created equal

62. "The Star-Spangled Banner"

63. Francis Scott Key

64. The Bill of Rights

65. Eighteen

66. The President

67. The Supreme Court

68. Abraham Lincoln

69. Freed many slaves

70. The Cabinet

71. George Washington

72. Hawaii

73. The American Indians

74. The *Mayflower*

75. Colonies

76. (1) The right of freedom of speech, press, religion, peaceable assembly to request change of government; (2) The right to bear arms; (3) The government may not quarter, or house, soldiers in private homes during peacetime without the owners' consent; (4) The government may not search or take a person's property without a warrant; (5) A person may not be tried twice by the same jurisdiction for the same crime and cannot be forced to testify against him/herself; (6) A person

charged with a crime still has many rights,
including the right to a fair trial and to be
represented by a lawyer; (7) The right to jury
trial by his/her peers in most cases; (8) Protects
people against excessive or unreasonable fines
or cruel and unusual punishment; (9)The
people have rights other than those mentioned
in the Constitution; (10) Any power not given
to the Federal government by the Constitution is
a power reserved either to the states or the people.

77. The Congress

78. Fifteenth, Nineteenth, Twenty-Fourth, or
Twenty-Sixth

79. Abraham Lincoln

80. 1787

81. The Bill of Rights

82. For countries to discuss world problems; to
provide economic aid to countries; occasionally, to
take action.

83. In the Capitol in Washington, D.C.

84. Everyone's (citizens and non-citizens living in
the United States)

85. The Preamble

86. Vote for the candidate of your choice; travel with
a U.S. passport; serve on a jury; apply for Federal
employment opportunities, etc.

87. The right to vote

88. The place where Congress meets

89. The President's official residence

90. Washington, D.C. (1600 Pennsylvania Avenue NW)

91. The White House

92. Freedom of speech, freedom of press, freedom of religion, peaceable assembly, and requesting changes in the government

93. The President

94. George Washington

95. November

96. January

97. There is no limit.

98. There is no limit.

99. Democratic and Republican

100. Fifty

(*Source: The Immigration and Naturalization Service*)

Answers to Who's in Charge? (page 88)

1. A city committee usually consists of members of the council. Larger cities might have several committees covering public safety, the environment, parks, and so on. Committee members vote on issues prior to their being heard by the full council.

2. The Department of Motor Vehicles is administered by the state.

3. Trash removal is administered by the city, or county if you live in an unincorporated area.

4. Zoning matters usually fall under the jurisdiction of a city planning commission.

5. Jails are city and county; prisons are state or federal.

6. The federal government does not administer welfare checks. County government administers welfare checks.

7. County and city commissions consist of political appointees. After a commission takes action, the matter goes to the government entity. It's not uncommon for cities to have commissions that oversee libraries, parks, fire, and police.

8. Broken stoplights are a city matter, unless they are on unincorporated county property.

9. Aircraft noise is handled at the federal level. The Federal Aviation Administration (FAA) is the sole government agency that oversees airports in the United States. Call your congressman for help with airport-related matters.

10. Arts funding can be obtained at the federal level through the National Endowment for the Arts— although its resources are dwindling. State, county, and municipal governments often provide funding for the arts as well.

Answers to Supreme Court Quiz (page 188)

1. B) John Jay

2. C) Jimmy Carter

3. D) George Washington

4. A) William O. Douglas

5. A) Oliver Wendell Holmes

6. D) Thurgood Marshall

7. D) Ronald Reagan

8. C) New York

9. B) William Howard Taft

10. A) Harvard

Forms of Address

Chief Justice, U.S. Supreme Court
Form of address: The Chief Justice of the United
States
Salutation: Dear Mr. Chief Justice:

Governor
Form of address: The Honorable John/Jane Doe,
Governor of ———
Salutation: Dear Governor Doe:

President of the United States
Form of address: The President, The White House
Salutation: Dear Mr. President:

United States Senator
Form of address: The Honorable John/Jane Doe,
United States Senate
Salutation: Dear Senator Doe:

U.S. House of Representatives
Form of address: The Honorable John/Jane Doe,
United States House of Representatives
Salutation: Dear Mr./Ms. Doe:

Glossary

In politics, certain phrases and expressions keep reappearing. Rarely will these be defined within the body of the story. Political reporting assumes a basic level of knowledge on the part of the reader.

This glossary defines several of the most common terms and concepts in the realm of politics. Learn these, and you can talk with the pros.

Appropriation: This is a term you will hear again and again, but is rarely defined. An appropriation is an allocation of funds by Congress for a specific government program.

Authorization: Authorization precedes appropriation in the budget process. Authorization establishes a specific program, defines its purpose, and provides an approximate spending amount. In the appropriation process the relevant committee arrives at a specific figure.

Budget authority and outlays: There is a crucial distinction between the two. Budget authority is the spending levels *authorized* by Congress for government agencies; outlays are the amount of funds that are *actually spent* in a given year.

Budget resolution: Here is where every year Congress gets a chance to show fiscal responsibility. The budget resolution—not signed by the president—sets funding limits on all major areas in the budget. Spending cannot exceed the dollar amounts prescribed in the resolution.

Bureaucrat: It's not too much of an exaggeration to say Washington is a city of bureaucrats. The massive agencies in the executive branch— Department of Commerce, Federal Aviation Administration, Pentagon, and so forth—are staffed with bureaucrats. Democrats and Republicans on Capitol Hill often say there are too many bureaucrats in D.C., but rarely have they taken concrete steps to reduce that number. Bureaucrats have a kind of entrenched power that tends to protect them from massive cuts.

Carpetbaggers: Here is a political term that will probably be around forever. Originally, carpetbaggers were Northern politicians and businessmen who moved down South after Reconstruction to take advantage of opportunities. For a long time now, carpetbaggers have been candidates who move into a district solely for the purpose of running for that seat.

Caucus: Caucuses once assumed the role primaries assume today; until 1824, presidential candidates were nominated by caucuses of members of Congress. Still, the Iowa Caucus, which has emerged as the traditional opening of the presidential campaign, holds symbolic importance in determining the early favorite or favorites. Caucuses are informal political meetings, usually staffed by party activists.

Conference committee: Sometimes the House and Senate pass similar versions of the same bill. To resolve the differences, a conference committee is assembled, consisting of selected members from both chambers. When they have reached an agreement, the final bill is put to a vote in the House and Senate. Members of the conference committee are called conferees.

Congressional Black Caucus: Formed with fifteen members in 1971, the Congressional Black Caucus had thirty-nine members in the 105th Congress. The CBC emphasizes issues that mostly reflect the members' inner-city constituents. Their agenda might include more money for education, compassionate welfare reform, and increased federal efforts to eradicate drugs in the inner city.

The CBC was more powerful when Democrats controlled the House of Representatives. Since the members are all Democrats (there were no black Republicans in the 105th Congress), the CBC has little influence with the House GOP leadership.

Congressional Budget Office: You will often hear a reference to the "CBO figures." The Congressional Budget Office (CBO) was established in 1974 to provide independent cost estimates of all legislation and economic forecasts. The CBO figures are traditionally used by budget committees of the House and Senate to determine whether pending legislation is within already determined budgetary limits. On April 1 (no fooling!) the CBO sends its report to the budget committees.

Congressional Hispanic Caucus: The Congressional Hispanic Caucus, which consisted of seventeen members in 1997–98, lobbies on behalf of Hispanic issues and causes. These include immigration rights, welfare, and voter registration.

Though most of its members are Democrats, the CHC has been openly critical of the Clinton administration for not appointing more Latinos to key positions.

Dark-horse candidate: The term actually has two meanings, but only one applies to contemporary politics. It was once the case that the dark-horse candidate represented a compromise between competing factions within a party, but today candidates are selected by popular votes in primaries, and not in smoke-filled rooms.

Now we think of the dark-horse candidate as the one who upsets expectations to emerge at or near the top of the field. An example is Gary Hart, who at the outset of the presidential campaign in 1984 was given no chance of winning the Democratic nomination, yet within a couple of weeks overtook favorite Walter Mondale in the race for delegates.

Democratic Congressional Campaign Committee: Commonly known as the D.C.CC, the Committee raises money for House races. The 1997–98 chair, Texas congressman Martin Frost, is known as a master at raising funds. During the first six months of 1997, the D.C.CC received $6.3 million, which smashed its own record, set in 1995. The D.C.CC raised the money despite the campaign finance scandals that were then enveloping Washington.

The Republicans' equivalent of the D.C.CC, the National Republican Congressional Committee, raised $10.4 million during the first six months of 1997. Both parties also have fund-raising apparatuses for U.S. Senate races. The National Republican Senatorial Committee is led by New York senator Al D'Amato.

The Democratic National Committee (DNC) raises money primarily for presidential races.

Devolution: A theory made popular by Republicans in the 1990s, "devolution" argues that many responsibilities traditionally assumed by the federal government would be better off turned over to local, county, and state governments. The idea was to "devolve" the strong central government in Washington. Number one on the Republican list was welfare; this was accomplished as part of the 1996 welfare-reform bill. The new rules stipulated that states be put in control of the disbursement of aid to welfare recipients.

Discharge petition: Sometimes members of Congress get angry or frustrated when a committee refuses to report a bill to the floor. The House of Representatives allows for a discharge petition, in which a bill may be brought to the floor by majority vote, despite the failure of the relevant committee to report the legislation. The discharge petition can be used no sooner than thirty days after a bill has been referred to committee.

Discretionary spending: At budget time, agency heads hold their breath: will this be the year Congress makes good on its promise to slash our funds? In recent years the Departments of Commerce, Defense, Education, and Energy have all been targeted for reductions, as have programs such as foreign aid and welfare. Their budgets fall under the category of discretionary spending; program-funding levels set annually by the congressional appropriations process. This is opposed to entitlements, such as Social Security and Medicare, which are automatically funded every year.

Divided government: For example, Ronald Reagan and a Democratic Congress; Bill Clinton and a Republican Congress. Divided government occurs when the president is from one party, and Congress is controlled by another. Some believe that divided government is good for America, because no one party should hold all the cards. On the other hand, rabid Democrats like the idea of their party being in charge of the executive *and* legislative branches of government; rabid Republicans say the same.

It's a myth that nothing gets done under a divided government. In 1996, President Clinton and the Republican-led Congress collaborated on several important bills. Compromise is the key.

Earmarking: An "earmark" establishes the spending level for a particular program. It serves as a legal guarantee that the program will receive full funding. You will often hear reference to funds being "earmarked" for a specific purpose.

Executive privilege: The most famous example of executive privilege occurred in the summer of 1974, when President Nixon refused to turn over the White House "Watergate tapes" to Congress. He claimed that as president (or chief executive) he was under no constitutional obligation to surrender the tapes to Congress.

In this case, the Supreme Court ruled that executive privilege did not apply. The president relinquished the recordings. This has not, however, stopped subsequent presidents from asserting the principle.

Fast-track: Emergence of the global economy has made trade issues increasingly important to the United States. There is ongoing debate between those believing in free trade and those who think America should protect some of its most vulnerable industries from foreign competition.

"Fast-track" is a legislative device used to speed up the approval of trade agreements. The Trade Act of 1974 allows Congress to grant the president fast-track authority. This means Congress will consider trade agreements with limited debate, according to a fixed deadline, and *without adding amendments*. Cases in which Congress granted fast-track authority include the United States–Israel Free Trade Implementation Act of 1985 and the North American Free Trade Agreement (NAFTA) in 1993.

Favorite son: The favorite-son candidate is the man from your home state whose name is placed in nomination for president. This is the traditional meaning. But in recent years the term has been expanded by the media to include primary ballots cast for home-state favorites: Ronald Reagan (California), Bob Dole (Kansas), and Jimmy Carter (Georgia).

Franking privilege: Every year your member of Congress sends mail touting his legislative accomplishments, or sharing his plan of action regarding an important local issue. According to the franking privilege, he or she can send these pieces for free by substituting a frank (signature) for postage. The letter must be approved by the Franking Commission, a group within the House that checks to see that the message is not partisan.

You can brag about yourself, but you can't say bad things about the other party; franked mail is not meant to be a campaign piece, though it can have that effect. To minimize the impact on elections, and to prevent the incumbent from too great an advantage, franked mail is prohibited within three months of the primary election and three months of the general election.

Gerrymandering: If you have heard of Massachusetts governor Elbridge Gerry, it's no doubt because of the process that bears his name. "Gerrymandering" means drawing district lines to give maximum advantage to a particular party. By the way, Gerry was governor in the early part of the nineteenth century.

Gridlock: You know what this term means at around five P.M. Friday evening on any major urban freeway. It's much the same for Congress. Whenever legislation is bottled up in committee, you have gridlock on Capitol Hill. The reasons could be political, or simply that Congress doesn't want to vote on a tough issue.

Gridlock is usually a temporary condition. Eventually the electorate insists Congress take some action. If they aren't going to do anything, why send them to Washington?

"The Hill": Shorthand for Capitol Hill. No congressional staffer admits to working on Capitol Hill; it's always the Hill. If you travel to Washington you will see the majestic building in which Congress conducts the nation's business is, in fact, located on a hill, albeit not one that's especially steep.

"Hit the ground running": If memory serves, this expression came in with the Reagan administration in 1981. A phrase associated with paratroopers, "hit the ground running" was appropriated by political people who liked the image of charging into battle. No wait-and-see, no give-and-take, but results, results, results.

The 1996 Libertarian candidate for president, Harry Browne, had four radical proposals that he promised to implement his first day in office. Harry Browne planned to hit the ground running.

Independent counsel: The Watergate scandal of 1972–74 brought the passage of several bills designed to prevent cover-ups and conflicts of interest in the White House; one of these was the independent counsel law (1978). The law took from the president and gave to the attorney general the power to hire and fire an independent counsel to investigate charges of corruption within the executive branch. Congressional Republicans champion the independent counsel law when a Democrat is president; Democrats do the same when the GOP is in power.

Lame duck: November and December are great months for parties, but boring ones for politicians. Especially lame-duck politicians. These are the incumbents who were defeated in the recent election, but are still in their final few weeks in office. (A president at the end of his second term is another example of a lame duck. He is constitutionally prohibited from running again.) Lame ducks usually just bide their time until they are free to do something else, like teach, go into television, or become a lobbyist.

Majority: In politics, majority means 50 percent plus 1. The dominant party in Congress fits the definition, as does the winning candidate in an election, who receives a majority of the vote.

Midterm elections: Every two years the 435 members of the House of Representatives (and many senators) are up for election. Those that occur in the middle of a presidential term are known, logically, as midterm elections. It's an axiom of electoral politics that the party in the White House fares poorly in this round of balloting.

Most-favored nation: Most-favored nation status is not as prestigious as it sounds. It simply refers to those countries with which the United States has non-discriminating trade agreements. Tariffs are applied equally to all MFNs. Most MFNs have long-term agreements with the U.S. An exception is China. During the 1990s Congress considered MFN status for China on an annual basis because of criticism of that country's human-rights record and its export of nuclear technology.

Motion: "Motion"—as in, "Mr. Speaker, I make a motion to . . ."—is probably the word used most in deliberations on Capitol Hill. Its meaning is the same in Congress as in most governmental bodies, or boards of directors around the country. Some of the most common motions in the House and Senate include adding amendments to legislation, calling for a vote, and striking a statement from the Congressional Record.

Office of Management and Budget: The Office of Management and Budget (OMB) functions as the president's watchdog on budgetary matters. OMB prepares the president's annual budget request to Congress, monitors all government programs and policies, and estimates the budgetary costs of all legislation and government programs. That's a lot of numbers to crunch. OMB employees always look very tired during the State of Union speech, which occurs a week before the President formally submits his budget to Congress.

"On message": Today, candidates are provided with a slogan, or a phrase, that defines their contest. The most famous example is probably from the Clinton campaign in 1992: "It's the economy, stupid." Everywhere Clinton appeared, he talked about the poor performance of the American economy under Bush. And every time he did so, he was "on message."

Opposition Research: "Getting the dirt" on your opponent is a tradition in American political campaigns. Today it's up to the opposition-research staff to find the dirt. These are the people who pore over public records, interview old flames or disgruntled ex-employees, and scan the Internet in pursuit of bad or embarrassing information.

Partisanship and bipartisanship: You will regularly encounter the words *partisan* and *bipartisan*. *Partisan* means favoring one party over the other; *bipartisan* means cooperation between the two. When Congress passes a bill that has Democratic and Republican supporters, you have a classic case of bipartisanship. When the two parties are sniping, you have an example of partisanship.

Generally the American public thinks bipartisanship is good and partisanship is bad—unless bipartisanship produces bad policy, or partisanship is required to resist bad policy.

Plurality: These are the votes tallied by the leading candidate, though not necessarily a majority of all votes cast. You will find pluralities when more than two candidates are in a race. Sometimes the rule is that the two top vote-getters in a crowded field will face each other in a run-off election, since neither received a majority of the votes. If the field broke down this way— 1.35 percent, 2.25 percent, 3.22 percent, 4.18 percent—then candidate number one received a plurality.

Pocket Veto: A congressional recess is a great time for members to return to their districts and meet the voters. It's also a great time for a president to exercise a pocket veto, which is more sly than a regular veto. A pocket veto occurs when Congress has adjourned and is unable to override the president's veto.

Pork-barrel legislation: "Pork," for short. "Pork" is money a member of Congress procures for a (non-critical) program specifically benefiting his or her district. Pork is a double-edged sword; it makes the member popular with the recipients of federal money, but unpopular with those who resent members taking care of key constituents in the name of public service. Even representatives who profess to hate government waste and the granting of special favors have been known to steer dollars to their district. Pork and incumbency go hand in hand.

Quorum: The meaning is no different on the floor of the House of Representatives than in your local city council: the number of members who must be present in order to commence official business. In the House that number is 218; in the Senate, 51.

Second: As with most governing bodies, in Congress a "second" is the method of bringing an issue for a vote or formally commencing debate. A couple days of watching C-SPAN and you will get a sense of how parliamentary procedure works in the House and Senate.

Seniority system: The longer a member of Congress stays in office, the better are his or her chances of becoming head of a congressional committee. (No wonder federal lawmakers are reluctant to back term limits.) This is what is known as the seniority system. With few exceptions, the most powerful members of a committee are those who have served the most years in Congress. Committee chairs are always members of the majority party. The top representative on the committee from the other party is called the ranking minority member.

Simple majority: A simple majority is one in which an issue receives more than 50 percent of the votes cast, as opposed to an absolute majority, which is more than 50 percent of all voters in a given election. A proposition, for example, that is approved by a distinct minority of eligible voters would be said to have received a simple majority.

Slate: Various organizations will endorse a slate of candidates, which are communicated to voters on slate mailers. Labor, women's groups, gay groups, and others will put out slates urging support for a slew of candidates on the ballot. Slates are usually mailed in the final week before an election to targeted districts and likely voters.

Sound bite: The goal of every politician or candidate is a positive story on the evening news. This is the best way to get voters' attention. However, in order get on the broadcast, it's necessary to give news directors what they want. Here's where sound bites come in. A sound bite is the most quotable part of a press conference or a media event. If a candidate or politician is "outraged" by something, if he or she "demands" an investigation, it makes for good, dramatic television. Witty or sarcastic sound bites also have a good chance of getting on the air.

Spin: How you tell your story is one of the most important tasks of a political office. The "spin" you put on something can make the difference between favorable and unfavorable press, or the difference between winning and losing the next election. When tax increases are called "revenue enhancement," that's a classic case of spin. You will be alternately amused and appalled watching politicians and their press secretaries try to spin the news their way. Your job is to separate truth from public relations. That's not easy.

Spoiler: Politics uses many expressions associated with war and sports. In sports the spoiler role is played by a poor team whose surprising victory or victories changes the order at the top of the standings. In politics the spoiler is a third candidate who siphons votes from the front-runner, thus enabling the other candidate to cruise to victory. Ross Perot was the spoiler in the 1992 presidential race. Without Perot, Clinton might not have defeated Bush.

"Spoils" system: The "spoils" system traditionally has been a way of rewarding party loyalists with plum government jobs. Education and experience were secondary qualifications. According to historians, the system expanded with the election of Andrew Jackson to the presidency in 1828. While the "spoils" system is not officially in use today, the practice of rewarding highly coveted ambassadorships to big contributors or close political friends is not much different.

Stuffing: "Stuffing" is a catch-all term for a particular form of voter fraud; people voting more than once in a given election. In recent years, the Federal Election Commission's definition of "multiple voting" has been expanded to include the intimidation of voters, which has the effect of making the votes of those who do go the polls count twice. There was a case in California in the late 1980s where guards, hired by a Republican candidate for the State Legislature were posted near precincts in Latino districts, thus scaring away a number of potential Democratic voters. The Republican campaign was ordered to pay a fine.

Supply-side economics: Supply-side economics is the theory that reducing marginal tax rates will create incentives for work, savings, and investment, thereby stimulating the national economy. Supply-side proponents were a huge influence during President Ronald Reagan's first term (1981–85). Reagan's 1981 tax cut was their crowning achievement.

In the 1990s, supply-side economics has seen some tough times. According to supply-siders, President Clinton's 1993 tax increase was supposed to destroy the economy. Instead, America went on to experience an economic boom that surpassed the achievements of the Reagan years.

But, like old soldiers, supply-siders never die. A July 1997 story in the the *New York Times* said the supply-side crowd has renamed itself "pro-growth" while advancing the same argument that tax cuts are the sovereign remedy for economic woes here and abroad.

Ticket ("straight" and "split"): Voting a straight ticket means casting your ballot for all Republicans or all Democrats; a split ticket means you split your vote between candidates from both. The Constitution prohibits voting for a president and vice president from different parties; but in California, for example, it is possible to vote for a Democratic governor and a Republican lieutenant governor, and vice versa. The last time this happened in California was 1994, when Pete Wilson (GOP) was elected Governor and Gray Davis was elected Lieutenant Governor.

War Powers Act: Congress felt burned by the presidency during the war in Vietnam. With good reason. The Constitution grants to Congress the sole power to declare war, and yet several presidents ordered troops and armaments to Vietnam without congressional approval.

In November 1973, after American forces had withdrawn from Vietnam, Congress approved the War Powers Resolution, or War Powers Act. Under the act, the president is expected to consult with Congress before using the military "in every possible instance," and is required to report to Congress within forty-eight hours of introducing troops. Use of the armed forces is to be terminated within sixty days, with a possible thirty-day extension, unless Congress acts during that time to declare war or enact a specific authorization for use of the armed forces.

Since Vietnam, American troops have gone to Grenada, Lebanon, Panama, Kuwait and Saudi Arabia, Somalia, and Bosnia. Has the War Powers Act been faithfully applied in each of these? You might want to ask a constitutional scholar.

Ways and Means: The oldest committee in the House of Representatives, Ways and Means celebrated its two hundredth birthday in 1989. The Ways and Means Committee handles all revenue collection and tax-reform legislation in the House.

Bibliography

The readings listed below cover a range of topics, including the mechanics of politics, life on the campaign trail, Congress, the presidency, American government, and political ideology. Political books can be as fascinating as a good novel or a trashy biography. You might even want to take one on vacation.

Ideology

Barash, David B. *The L Word: An Unapologetic, Thoroughly Biased, Long-Overdue Explication and Celebration of Liberalism.* (New York: William Morrow, 1992).

Browne, Harry. *Why Government Doesn't Work.* (New York: St. Martin's Press, 1995).

Dionne, E. J. *They Only Look Dead: Why Progressives Will Dominate the Next Era in Politics.* (New York: Simon and Schuster, 1996).

Gillespie, Ed, and Schellas, Bob, editors. *Contract with America: The Bold Plan by Rep. Newt Gingrich, Rep. Dick Armey and the House Republicans to Change the Nation.* (New York: Times Books, 1994).

Hodgson, Godfrey. *The World Turned Right Side Up: A History of the Conservative Ascendancy in America.* (New York: Houghton Mifflin, 1996).

Marshall, Will, and Schram, Martin. *Mandate for Change.* (New York: Berkley Books, 1993).

Reed, Ralph. *Active Faith: How Christians Are Changing the Soul of American Politics.* (New York: The Free Press, 1996).

Campaigns

Butler, Stuart M., and Holmes, Kim R., editors. *Issues '96: The Candidate's Briefing Book.* (Washington, DC: The Heritage Foundation, 1996).

Campaign for President: The Managers Look at '96. Edited by the Harvard Institute of Politics. (Hollis, NH: Hollis Publishing Company, 1997).

Kamber, Victor. *Are Negative Campaigns Destroying Democracy?* (New York: Insight Books, 1997).

Lewis, Michael. *Trail Fever: Spin Doctors, Rented Strangers, Thumb Wrestlers, Toe Suckers, Grizzly Bears and Other Creatures on the Road to the White House.* (New York: Knopf, 1997).

Morris, Dick. *Behind the Oval Office.* (Los Angeles, Renaissance, 1998).

Popkin, Samuel L. *The Reasoning Voter: Communication and Persuasion in Presidential Campaigns.* (Chicago: University of Chicago Press, 1991).

Sabato, Larry J. *Feeding Frenzy: How Attack Journalism Has Transformed American Politics.* (New York: The Free Press, 1991).

NOTE: Theodore H. White's series entitled *The Making of the President* is an exceptional look at campaigns past. White's first book in the series was about the Kennedy-Nixon race in 1960; his last examined the Carter-Ford contest in 1976. The political reporters Jack Germond and Jules Witcover have together written interesting accounts of presidential campaigns in the 1970s, 1980s, and 1990s.

Congress

Baker, Ross K. *House and Senate.* (New York: W. W. Norton, 1995).

Christianson, Stephen G. *Facts About the Congress.* (New York: Wilson, 1996).

Davidson, Roger H., and Oleszek, Walter J. *Congress and Its Members.* (Washington, DC: CQ Press, 1996).

Harris, Fred R. *In Defense of Congress.* (New York: St. Martin's Press, 1995).

Loomis, Burdett A. *The Contemporary Congress.* (New York: St. Martin's Press, 1996).

Oleszek, Walter J. *Congressional Procedures and Policy Process.* (Washington, DC: CQ Press, 1996).

Penny, Timothy J. *Common Cents: A Retiring Six-Term Congressman Reveals How Congress Really Works—And What We Must Do to Fix It.* (Boston: Little, Brown, 1995).

Uslaner, Eric M. *The Decline of Comity in Congress.* (Ann Arbor: University of Michigan Press, 1993).

Woods, Patricia Dillon. *The New Dynamics of Congress: A Guide to the People and Process in Lawmaking.* (Washington, DC: Woods Institute, 1995).

American Government

Abshire, David, and Brower, Brock. *Putting America's House in Order: The Nation as a Family.* (Westport, CT: Praeger, 1996).

Cone, Anson H. *Jeffersonian Democracy Now: A Plan to Truly Reinvent American Democracy, Part 1.* (New York: Vantage Press, 1995).

Ehrenhalt, Alan. *The United States of Ambition: Politicians, Power and the Pursuit of Office.* (New York: Times Books/Random House, 1991).

Goodwin, Richard N. *Promises to Keep: A Call for a New American Revolution.* (New York: Times Books, 1992).

Gore, Al. *Common Sense Government Works Better and Costs Less.* (New York: Random House, 1995).

Lasser, William. *American Politics: Institutions and Interconnections.* (Lexington, Mass.: DC Heath, 1996).

Patterson, Thomas E. *The American Democracy.* Third Edition. (New York: McGraw-Hill, 1997).

Peters, Charles. *How Washington Really Works.* Fourth Edition. (Reading, MA: Addison-Wesley, 1992).

Rubin, Barry R. *A Citizen's Guide to Politics in America.* (Armonk, NY: M. E. Sharpe, 1997).

Squire, Peverill, et al. *Dynamics of Democracy.* Second Edition. (Madison, WI: Brown and Benchmark, 1997).

Weisberg, Jacob. *In Defense of Government: The Rise and Fall of Public Institiutions.* (New York: Scribner, 1996).

Winograd, Morley, and Dudley Buffa. *Taking Control: Politics in the Information Age.* (New York: Henry Holt, 1996).

The Presidency

Blakesley, Lance. *Presidential Leadership: From Eisenhower to Clinton.* (Chicago: Nelson-Hall, 1995).

Dickinson, Matthew J. *Bitter Harvest: FDR, Presidential Power, and the Growth of the Presidential Branch.* (New York: Cambridge University Press, 1997).

Edwards, George C. *Presidential Leadership: Politics and Policy Making.* Fourth Edition. (New York: St. Martin's Press, 1997).

Fields, Wayne. *Union of Words: A History of Presidential Eloquence.* (New York: Free Press, 1996).

Genovese, Michael A. *The Presidential Dilemma: Leadership in the American System.* (New York: HarperCollins, 1995).

Langston, Thomas S. *With Reverence and Contempt: How Americans Think About Their President.* (Baltimore, MD: Johns Hopkins University Press, 1995).

Levy, Leonard W., and Fisher, Louis, editors. *Encyclopedia of the American Presidency.* Four volumes. (New York: Simon and Schuster, 1994).

Milkis, Sidney M., and Nelson, Michael. *The American Presidency: Origins and Development, 1776–1993.* (Washington, DC: CQ Press, 1994).

Nelson, Michael, advisory editor. *The Presidency A to Z: A Ready Reference Encyclopedia*. (Washington, DC: Congressional Quarterly, 1994).

Ragsdale, Lyn. *Vital Statistics on the Presidency: Washington to Clinton*. (Washington, DC: Congressional Quarterly, 1996).

Strausbaugh, John. *Alone with the President*. (New York: Blast Books, 1993).

The American Revolution

Bailyn, Bernard. *The Ideological Origins of the American Revolution*. (Cambridge, MA: Harvard University Press, 1967).

Calhoon, Robert McCluer. *Revolutionary America: An Interpretive Overview*. (New York: Harcourt Brace Jovanovich, 1976).

Davis, Burke. *George Washington and the American Revolution*. (New York: Random House, 1975).

Fischer, David H. *Paul Revere's Ride*. (New York: Oxford University Press, 1994).

Gross, Robert. *The Minutemen and Their World*. (New York: Hill and Wang, 1976).

Langguth, A. J. *Patriots: The Men Who Started the American Revolution*. (New York: Simon and Schuster, 1988).

Maier, Pauline. *From Resistance to Revolution: Colonial Radicals and the Development of Opposition to Britain, 1765–1776*. (New York: Random House, 1974).

Marrin, Albert. *The Story of the American Revolution*. (New York: Atheneum, 1988).

Morgan, Edmund S. *The Birth of the Republic: 1763–1789*. (Chicago: University of Chicago Press, 1956).

Wills, Garry. *Inventing America: Jefferson's Declaration of Independence*. (New York: Random House, 1978).

Wood, Gordon. *The Creation of the American Republic, 1776–1787.* (New York: W. W. Norton, 1972).

NOTE: American Revolution bibliography compiled by Peter Sanders, assistant head at the Collegiate Upper School in Richmond, Virginia.

The Civil War

Davis, Kenneth C. *Don't Know Much About the Civil War.* (New York: William Morrow, 1996).

Donald, David Herbert. *Lincoln.* (New York: Touchstone/Simon and Schuster, 1995).

Foote, Shelby. *The Civil War: A Narrative.* (New York: Random House).

————.Volume 1: *Fort Sumter to Perryville* (1958).

————.Volume 2: *Fredericksburg to Meridian* (1963).

————.Volume 3: *Red River to Appomattox* (1974).

McPherson, James M. *The Battle Cry of Freedom: The Civil War Era.* (New York: Ballantine, 1989).

McPherson, James M. *For Cause and Comrades: Why Men Fought the Civil War.* (New York: Oxford University Press, 1997).

Oates, Stephen B. *The Approaching Fury: Voices of the Storm, 1820–1861.* (New York: HarperCollins, 1997).

Thomas, Emory M. *Robert E. Lee: A Biography.* (New York: W. W. Norton, 1995).

Ward, Geoffrey C., with Ric Burns and Ken Burns. *The Civil War: An Illustrated History.* (New York: Knopf, 1990).

Woodward, Vann C., editor. *Mary Chestnut's Civil War.* (New Haven, CT: Yale University Press, 1981).

NOTE: The Civil War bibliography was compiled by Delia M. Rios, volunteer historical interpreter at Arlington House, the Robert E. Lee Memorial, Arlington National Cemetery.

The New Deal

Badger, Anthony J. *The New Deal: The Depression Years, 1933–40.* (New York: Farrar, Strauss & Giroux, 1989).

Burns, James MacGregor. *Roosevelt: The Lion and the Fox.* (New York: Harcourt Brace Jovanovich, 1956).

Conkin, Paul K. *The New Deal.* (Arlington Hts., IL: Harlan, Davidson, 1975).

Goldman, Eric. *Rendezvous With Destiny: A History of Modern American Reform.* (New York: Knopf, 1952).

Lash, Joseph P. *Dealers and Dreamers: New Look at the New Deal.* (New York: Doubleday, 1988).

Leuchtenberg, William E. *Franklin Roosevelt and the New Deal.* (New York: Harper and Row, 1963).

McElvaine, Robert S. *The Great Depression: America 1929–1941.* (New York: New York Times Press, 1984).

McJimsey, George. *Harry Hopkins: Ally of the Poor and Defender of Democracy.* (Cambridge, MA: Harvard University Press, 1987).

Parrish, Michael E. *Anxious Decades: American Prosperity and Depression, 1920–1941.* (New York: W.W. Norton, 1972).

Schlesinger, Arthur M., Jr. *The Crisis of the Old Order, 1919–1933.* (Boston: Houghton, Mifflin, 1957).

———. *The Coming of the New Deal,* (1958).

———. *The Politics of Upheaval,* (1960).

Terkel, Studs. *Hard Times: An Oral History of the Great Depression.* (New York: Random House, 1970).

Warren, Harris Gaylord. *Herbert Hoover and the Great Depression.* (New York: Oxford University Press, 1959).

Watkins, T. H. *The Great Depression: America in the 1930s.* (Boston: Little, Brown, 1993).

NOTE: The New Deal bibliography was compiled by Peter Sanders, assistant head, Collegiate Upper School, Richmond, Virginia.

The Sixties

Dudley, William, editor. *The 1960s: Opposing Viewpoints*. (San Diego: Greenhaven Press, 1997).

Gitlin, Todd. *The Sixties: Years of Hope, Days of Rage*. (New York: Bantam, 1987).

Halberstam, David. *The Best and the Brightest*. (New York: Ballantine, 1992).

Hodgson, Godfrey. *America in Our Time: From World War II to Nixon—What Happened and Why*. (New York: Vintage, 1978).

Howard, Gerald, editor. *The Sixties: The Art, Attitudes, Politics, Media of Our Most Explosive Decade*. (New York: First Marlowe and Company, 1995).

Manchester, William. *The Glory and the Dream*. (New York: Bantam, 1990).

Patterson, James T. *Grand Expectations: The United States, 1945–74*. (New York: Oxford University Press, 1996).

Podhoretz, Norman. *Why We Were in Vietnam*. (New York: Touchstone, 1983).

Shesol, Jeff. *Mutual Contempt: Lyndon Johnson, Robert Kennedy, and the Feud that Defined a Decade*. (New York: W. W. Norton, 1997).

Young, Andrew. *An Easy Burden: The Civil Rights Movement and the Transformation of America* (New York: HarperCollins, 1996).

Comebacks

Andersen, Alfred F. *Challenging Newt Gingrich Chapter by Chapter: An In-Depth Analysis of America's Options at Its Economic, Political and Military Crossroads*. (Eugene, OR: Tom Paine Institute, 1996).
Balz, Dan, and Brownstein, Ronald. *Storming the Gates: Protest Politics and the Republican Revival*. (New York: Little, Brown, 1996).

Blumenthal, Sidney. *The Rise of the Counter-Establishment: From Conservative Ideology to Political Power*. (New York: Times Books, 1986).

Campbell, Colin, and Rockman, Bert A., editors. *The Clinton Presidency: First Appraisals*. (Chatham, NJ: Chatham House, 1996).

Cannon, Lou. *President Reagan: The Role of A Lifetime*. (New York: Touchstone, 1991).

Drew, Elizabeth. *Showdown: The Struggle Between the Gingrich Congress and the Clinton White House*. (New York: Simon and Schuster, 1996).

Gillespie, Ed, and Schellhas, Bob, editors. *Contract with America: the Bold Plan by Rep. Newt Gingrich, Rep. Dick Armey and the House Republicans to Change the Nation*. (New York: Times Books, 1994).

Gingrich, Newt. *To Renew America*. (New York: HarperCollins, 1995).

Morris, Dick. *Behind the Oval Office*. (Los Angeles, Renaissance Books, 1998).

Walker, Martin. *The President We Deserve: Bill Clinton, His Rise, Falls and Comebacks*. (New York: Crown, 1996).

General Reference

Barone, Michael, and Ujifusa, Grant. *The Almanac of American Politics*. 1998 Edition. (Washington, DC: National Journal). [NOTE: *The Almanac* features political biographies of all current members of Congress and Senators. It also discusses voting records and the physical and ideological characteristics of every congressional district. A new edition is published with each new Congress.]

Duncan, Phillip, and Lawrence, Christine. *Politics in America*. (Washington, DC: Congressional Quarterly Press). [NOTE: Like the Almanac, a new edition of this book is published with each new Congress. *Politics in America* includes Web addresses for all House and Senate committees, interest-group ratings, phone numbers for the state party headquarters, and a House and Senate seniority guide. A list of PAC donations follows each profile of a member of Congress.]

Lauria, Angela E., and Wagman, Robert, editors. *The World Almanac of U.S. Politics: 1997–99 Edition*. (Mahwaj, NJ: World Almanac Books).

Maguire, Stephen, and Wren, Bonnie, editors. *Torn by the Issues*. (Santa Barbara, CA: Fithian Press, 1994).

All-Time Bestsellers (Political Books), According to the New York Times

(1) *Advise and Consent* by Allen Drury (1960). A novel about the Senate's investigation of the nominee for Secretary of State. *Advise and Consent* was on the *Times'* list for 102 weeks.

(2) *The Making of the President* by Theodore H. White. (1961). White's account of the Kennedy-Nixon campaign spent 56 weeks on the bestseller list.

(3) *Washington Confidential* by Jack Lait and Lee Mortimer (1950). This non-fiction book is described as "discovering ambition and sex in Washington." Why have there not been subsequent editions? *Washington Confidential* was on the charts for 40 weeks.

(4) *The Best and the Brightest* by David Halberstam (1972). One of the earliest and best books about how and why America got involved in the war in Vietnam. The title of this book has since become a common if ironic expression for people of impeccable educational and family backgrounds who are leaders in politics, business, and media. Stayed on the list for 36 weeks.

(5) *All the President's Men* by Carl Bernstein and Bob Woodward. (1974). You've seen the movie about the *Washington Post*'s investigation of Watergate, now read the book which is even better. Thirty-four weeks on the list.

Index

About the Author

Tom Waldman has written about politics for numerous publications, including the *Los Angeles Times Magazine*, *LA Weekly*, and *California Journal*. In the 1980s he spent five years as a political beat reporter for the *San Gabriel Valley Tribune* in Southern California. For the past seven years he has served as press secretary to a member of the United States Congress. He is also co-author of *Land of a Thousand Dances: Chicano Rock and Roll from Southern California*, published by the University of New Mexico Press in 1998. He lives with his wife and two sons in West Hills, California.